DEFENDING
BRITAIN

DEFENDING BRITAIN

TWENTIETH-CENTURY MILITARY
STRUCTURES IN THE LANDSCAPE

MIKE OSBORNE

TEMPUS

First published 2004

Tempus Publishing Ltd
The Mill, Brimscombe Port
Stroud, Gloucestershire GL5 2QG
www.tempus-publishing.com

British Library Cataloguing in Publication Data.
A catalogue record for this book is available from the British Library.

ISBN 0 7524 3134 X

Typesetting and origination by Tempus Publishing.
Printed and bound in Great Britain.

CONTENTS

ACKNOWLEDGEMENTS

A large number of people have shared information with me over the last ten years. I have tried to remember as many as possible in the following list of those, for whose help I am most grateful:

Adrian Armishaw, Colin Alexander, Trevor Ball, Bill Bartlam, Alec Beanse, Mark Bennet, Guy Bettley-Cooke, Christopher Bird, Michael Bowyer, John Bracey, David Burridge, Graham Cadman, the late Hugh Cave, Greg Child, David Clarke, Peter Cobb, Wayne Cocroft, Stephen Coleman, Nigel Dawe, Geoff Dewing, Colin Dobinson, Jeff Dorman, Jim Earle, William Foot, Paul Francis, John Goodwin, John Guy, the late Jock Hamilton-Baillie, John Harding, Geoffrey Harvey, John Hellis, Richard Hillier, Tim Hudson, Colin Jones, Peter Kent, Alistair Graham Kerr, Bernard Lowry, Martin Mace, Ron Martin, the late Henry Mein, Philip Moody, Fred Nash, Charles Parker, Medwyn Parry, Ron Payne, Simon Purcell, Neil Redfern, Eric Rhodes, Alan Rudd, Ian Sanderson, Mark and Terri Sansom, David and Margaret Sibley, Roy Silverlock, Bridget Smith, Roger Thomas, Ray Towler, William Ward, Mick Wilks, the late Henry Wills, John Worswick.

My thanks and apologies to anyone I have inadvertently missed.

INTRODUCTION

Throughout the twentieth century Britain has been involved in military conflict of some kind, and this has been reflected in the British landscape. A wide spectrum of military activity, ranging from the training of troops or the development of military technology to support Imperial aspirations, through the defence of the homeland against threatened invasion, to the maintenance of intelligence-gathering systems as part of global deterrent mechanisms, have all left their marks on the land. There can be few locations in Britain which cannot provide examples of this. Whether it be the chains of fortifications which girdle much of our coastline; the airfields, which in some parts of Britain are so numerous that they almost touch; the networks of observation and listening posts which, but for a few parts of the far north-west of Scotland, cover the whole of Britain; the civil defence structures, munitions factories, barracks and drill halls which pack our towns and cities; all the camps, depots, formation headquarters, and training facilities which were based on country houses; even the remote caverns in the Welsh mountains which gave sanctuary to our art treasures; and the rugged hills and lochsides of Scotland where the commandos trained. Not only is the range and variety so surprising, but also the sheer numbers. By the end of the First World War, there were around 300 military airfields across Britain. This number shrank to under 30 in the interwar period, but by 1945, had again risen to nearly 750. No-one knows exactly how many pillboxes were built in either world war, but there are informed estimates for the Second World War which top 28,000. Something like 1.5 million Anderson shelters were issued, along with large numbers of other types, and hundreds of communal surface shelters were constructed. Tens of thousands of huts were built in both World Wars: Nissen, brick-built, timber and prefabricated types in the First World War, and temporary-brick, Nissen, Romney, Iris, Laing, BCF, Seco, MoWP, Handcraft, Orlit, curved asbestos, and many more, in the Second World War. There were dozens of radar sites, hundreds of AA batteries, thousands of searchlights, and tens of thousands of obstacles against tanks, gliders and invasion barges. As William Foot has pointed out, by 1944, 20 per cent of Britain's land surface was under some form of military control. In the Cold War period there were 1,500 or so underground Royal Observer Corps posts, and countless bunkers housing civil and military functions ranging from command posts to BBC studios, from missile silos to emergency food stores.

So much of this was perceived as being so familiar, so recent, and even, through the post-Second World War period, so secret, that it was not generally seen as worthy of study by historians or archaeologists. For instance, the relevant volume of the official history of the Second World War barely mentions fortifications, beyond the barest references to strategy. In fact, the map which illustrates this aspect of the defence of Britain even manages to get towns in the wrong places. Most other books on the 1940 invasion scare tended to focus more on the German details of Operation Sealion, than on the British counter-measures. Even histories of the Home Guard units focus on training, organisation and equipment, rather than on fixed defences. The big shift came in the mid–1980s, when Henry Wills, a press photographer for local papers, based in Salisbury, embarked on the enormous task of recording the type and location of pillboxes throughout Britain. He did this by appealing for information, initially in *The Times*, then in over 200 local newspapers, and then sending out postcards to respondents, for them to record details of pillboxes, both extant and demolished. This approach had one or two problems. It is sometimes apparent that not all respondents had as thorough an understanding of the workings of national grid references as might have been expected or desired. There were also multiple reports of the same pillbox but with differing co-ordinates. Basically, Henry was for obvious reasons unable to exercise total quality control over the results of his survey. In the context of the sheer size of the task, however, and of its ground-breaking nature, Henry's achievement was immense. In 1979, he won BBC Television's Chronicle Award, which itself stimulated interest, and in 1985, he published *Pillboxes: A Study of UK Defences 1940*, in whose appendices are listed the 5,000 pillboxes recorded by his survey. Throughout this period a number of groups of enthusiasts, academics and former military professionals continued to study this area and to publish the results of their researches in their journals. These included the Fortress Study Group (FSG), the Airfield Research Group (ARG), the UK Fortifications Club (UKFC), the Kent Defence Research Group (KRDG), and Subterranea Britannica, amongst others. It was a group of FSG members who, at the behest of the Royal Commission for Historical Monuments of England (RCHME), carried out a pilot survey of the Holderness area of east Yorkshire in 1992. Their intention was to determine the population of twentieth-century military remains in a fairly representative area, in order to test the recording methods and systems, the categorisation of sites, and the identification and interpretation of remains, as well as the density and survival of military sites. In all, over 300 sites were found and recorded by the seven-man team, in the four days of the pilot survey. In the light of the coastal erosion in this area, it was recommended that a fuller survey should be carried out, but it was also recognised that such surveys were necessary over the whole of Britain, in order to record a significant but fast-disappearing dimension of Britain's heritage. Parallel surveys by Historic Scotland, and by Roger Thomas for the Pembrokeshire National Park added to both methodology and knowledge.

The time was now ripe for a full survey of the whole of Britain and Northern Ireland, and the Defence of Britain Project (DoB) was born. All the national heritage bodies had combined with the Council for British Archaeology, and were supported by funds from the National Heritage Lottery Fund. Networks of volunteers were supported in recording sites, and contributing them to a central database, using an agreed thesaurus. Over 13,000 sites were recorded during the Project's life, between 1995 and 2002. Much of the material is accessible on the Internet. Despite a long history of contraindications, it was discovered that there was an extensive corpus of supporting documentation. The Monument Protection Programme of English Heritage funded Colin Dobinson to trawl the Public Record Office (now the National Archive) in order to use this documentary evidence to establish the location, lifespan, appearance and numbers of twentieth-century military monuments. This research was collated into volumes of commentaries, appendices, gazetteers and sources under 11 separate subject headings. Neil Redfern tackled a similar task in Wales, Scotland and Northern Ireland, but on a much-reduced scale. All this work was distributed to Sites and Monuments Records (SMR) and Dr Dobinson's synthesis of each of the 11 topics is currently in the process of being commercially published as discrete volumes. The DoB has certainly raised public awareness and contributed to the body of knowledge at a time when the fund of first-hand experience of the First World War has all but gone, and that of the Second World War is fast depleting. Some aspects have a literature of their own. Paul Francis, in particular, has written extensively on the military architecture of airfields, and the ARG journal is indispensable to the historians of airfields and their buildings. As the secrets of the Cold War are revealed, many of the monuments have already been destroyed. *War Plan UK*, Duncan Campbell's book in 1982, was unique in that it talked about organisations and structures which were virtually unknown to the public. The next year, Malcolm Spaven and Scottish CND produced a similar exposé north of the border with *Fortress Scotland*. Since the end of the Cold War, Nicholas McCamley has written extensively on underground factories and nuclear bunkers. Wayne Cocroft has produced definitive works on the monuments of the explosives industry, and, with Roger Thomas, those of the Cold War.

This book seeks to provide a commentary on the military landscape of the twentieth century by combining the essence of documentary research with the fruits of fieldwork. To know merely the plans is not enough for we know that plans are not always implemented, or not always implemented in ways originally envisaged. Neither is the physical evidence on the ground sufficient in itself, for often, without some idea of the wider context, it may be misleading or meaningless. The chosen approach adopted here is one of examining themes chronologically, and illustrating them with examples drawn from across Britain. In this way, the evolution of technologies, policies or ideas can be explored from beginning to end. The first four chapters look at the ways in which defence strategies relate to topography within the constraints of the available technology or of prevailing circumstances. The defences of the coast, of defined inland lines, of a whole range of points selected for their importance and vulnerability in general, and of airfields in particular, are examined in detail. The next two chapters explore the development of buildings which served both the disparate and the shared needs of the armed services: airfields, barracks, drill halls and dockyards. As airpower was not only the newest aspect of warfare in the twentieth century, but also the dominant one, the struggle to find a defence against it merits a chapter on its own. This covers both the active AA defence systems, and, to an albeit lesser extent, the passive systems of civil defence. The final chapter includes all those elements which keep the fighting machine in business: the munitions factories, storage and distribution systems, training and testing facilities, accommodation for headquarters and housing for military personnel and munitions workers, and aspects of the communications and transport infrastructure.

It is obviously impossible to include everything, nor would the reader appreciate an inventory. Attempts have been made throughout to include a range of examples, representative of the whole of Britain. These examples are supplemented by gazetteers for each chapter, again, not exhaustive, but extensive enough to provide local sites across the whole of Britain. It has to be said that sites are disappearing, and so readers must be warned that inclusion of a site in either the text or in the gazetteer is, unfortunately, no guarantee of that site's current survival. However, only those sites inspected by the present writer in the last few years are included. Sadly it has been necessary to remove sites included in previous gazetteers but which have subsequently been demolished. It is easy to become paranoid and to make a connection between the inclusion of a site in such a gazetteer and its sudden and often apparently pointless demise. Somewhat surprisingly, there are still defence sites to be discovered, and local SMR officers should welcome notification of such discoveries.

Finally, a word must be included about safety. Many of the sites recorded in this book are easily and freely accessible. Many of them are perfectly safe. Equally, some are on private land, and some, particularly Cold War and other underground sites, are dangerous. Sites in current military occupation may be particularly sensitive and security-conscious. Many landowners are happy to allow access and even to interpret sites for visitors, if asked. Obviously, the usual caveats apply. Permission must be sought where necessary, and care must always be taken.

1

COAST DEFENCES

Whilst most of Victoria's small wars had been fought a long way from home, the growing acceptance of imminent European war rekindled Britain's traditional fears of invasion. The previous invasion scare, prompted by France's construction of ironclad warships in the 1850s, had resulted in a massive and costly building programme, soon regarded as irrelevant, obsolete and unnecessary in the first place. Within another generation, the inexorable development of naval technology, and the inevitable response of the coast gunners had made a review of coast defence arrangements unwelcome, but nevertheless imperative.

In 1900, Imperial powers such as Britain saw their future in the maintenance of the command of the seas. The Naval Defence Act of 1889 had accelerated the modernisation of the Royal Navy, and it was almost as an afterthought that a small part of the expenditure authorised by the Naval Works Act of 1895 was devoted to defending dockyards and naval ports. The received wisdom of the time was that sufficient warships would always be maintained in home waters to respond to any attack on the ports. The navy felt that nothing short of a continuous wall around the entire coastline could guarantee that no invasion would be possible. Therefore, the argument ran, there was little point in putting resources into coast defences other than around naval bases. Even in the case of the minor ports, it was envisaged that within 48 hours naval relief would arrive. Coast Defence works therefore had two functions. One, generally, was to hold off enemy attack for the requisite time to allow help to arrive. The other, specifically, was to protect fleet anchorages from the new threat of attack by fast torpedo boats, which could operate across the Channel or the southern North Sea. A pre-emptive strike, in the build-up to any formal declaration of war, was especially feared.

The final years of the nineteenth century had seen an across-the-board improvement in the artillery available to coast gunners, driven by Sir George Clarke. Various trials had concluded that it was virtually impossible for moving warships to hit the tiny targets presented by coast defence guns, so the experiment of the disappearing gun, for instance, was discarded. The guns in service by 1905, when a Committee on the Armament of Home Ports favourably assessed the efficiency and

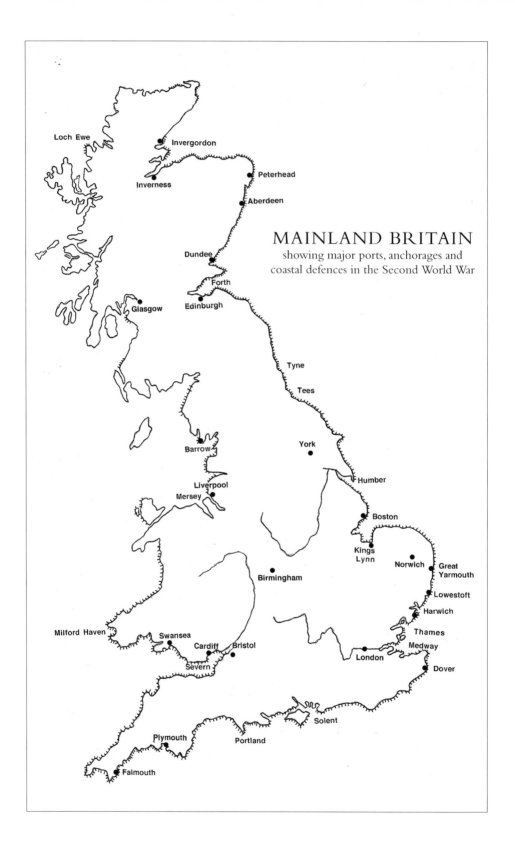

MAINLAND BRITAIN
showing major ports, anchorages and
coastal defences in the Second World War

effectiveness of coast artillery, were largely to remain those in use until the service was shut down in 1956. The report of the Owen Committee in 1905 more or less confirmed that there should be basically three main guns in service – the 9.2in (234mm), for Counter-Bombardment work, and the 6in (150mm) and 4.7in (120mm) for Coast Defence tasks. Added to these, for harbour defence against the fast motor-torpedo boat, was the 12-pounder QF gun. Modern, open, concrete emplacements were provided, as were emplaced searchlights, and the new range-finding equipment. Booms, electrically-controlled minefields and wire-guided Brennan torpedoes completed the armoury of available weaponry.

Given that France continued in her traditional role of country most likely to invade, Britain's coast defences were clustered, for the most part, around the ports of the English Channel and the South East: Plymouth, Portland, Portsmouth, Dover and the estuaries of the Thames and Medway. Of the 35 new permanent coast defence batteries opened between 1900 and 1914, only six lay outside this area, and only three of those were on the East Coast. The bombardment, by German cruisers, of East Coast towns in mid-December 1914, highlighted the vulnerability of unprotected coastal settlements. Although it can be argued that the attacking ships were seen off by the 6in guns of Hartlepool's Heugh Battery, taking hits as they sailed away, the levels of casualties, both military and non-combatant sustained in Hartlepool, Whitby and Scarborough, and also in separate incidents in Gorleston and Great Yarmouth, suggested that the defences needed improvement. Of the 23 new batteries started between 1914 and the end of the war, consequently, 15 of these were located on the East Coast.

Batteries for counter-bombardment or coast defence were sited as high as the terrain would allow, and forward of the targets they were protecting. When guns had only a short range, they had to be close to the areas under their protection. As ranges increased, so the guns could be moved further away. At Hull, for instance, it is possible to track the coast batteries from the Citadel of Henry VlII's time, hard up against the city walls on the River Hull, through the Georgian and Victorian forts and batteries ranged along the banks of the River Humber, until, by the time of the First World War when the 9.2in gun had a maximum range of over 15 miles (24km) the guns are out on Spurn Head, and up the Holderness coast. In order to engage their faster-moving targets, the QF guns were sited at sea level, preferably on a pier or breakwater as at Dover, Plymouth and Portland. Although the components of each battery were the same, the location often demanded differing layouts. The guns were often mounted in linked, twin concrete pits with wide, sloping aprons. They fired *en barbette,* that is over low parapets. Given that they presented only a small target to enemy warships offshore, and that there was, as yet, no perceived threat from the air, no overhead cover was provided. Underneath were magazines from which shells were delivered to the gun via band or ladder lifts. In the 4.7in batteries, hoists were used for the lighter shells. Also underground, were crew shelters. Behind the guns was a Battery Observation Post (BOP), containing range-finding equipment, which was linked

1 Sunk Island, East Yorkshire, TA252178; the Port War Signal Station and Fire Control Post, built 1915

to remote position-finding (PF) cells. The guns were served by an engine room containing a generator to power all their electrically-operated functions. The coast-defence and the QF batteries also had searchlights, called Defence Electric Lights (DELs) until after the First World War, located in appropriate spots to illuminate targets at night. These also had their dedicated engine rooms nearby. The magazines below ground had segregated sections for the sensitive cartridges, usually stored on wooden racking, and the shells themselves often on metal shelves. Although the possibility of fully fledged invasion was officially discounted, batteries often had some form of close defence such as unclimbable fencing, wire, blockhouses and machine-gun posts. The QF guns were worked in conjunction with carefully-placed lights. Some DELs had solid front walls with slits, which allowed lights to be permanently fixed onto particular spots, on which the guns were pre-ranged. The 12-pounder QF gun had a rate of fire of 15 rounds per minute and could react quickly to fast-moving targets. There were also moving lights, played not only low enough to avoid black-spots through which boats might speed, but also high enough to avoid the distortions of wave movement. Again, the guns had only a short time in which to react to brief sightings of potential targets.

Some batteries were also designated Examination Batteries, which meant that in commercial ports in time of war or of particular tension, incoming merchant ships would be required to establish their *bona fides* whilst anchored under the guns of the battery. In such situations, the battery commander would communicate with local naval patrols, the port authorities, other batteries, and the ships themselves, through the Port War Signal Station (PWSS) *(1)*. We should remind ourselves at this point, that much of the activity outlined above was wholly dependent on the visual: finding targets, setting ranges, and receiving messages.

One further element of coast defence batteries was accommodation. Crew shelters near the gun-positions were simply for the use of gun crews on stand-to. The large complement of a gun battery lived in a small village of huts, generally a few hundred yards behind the battery. Living accommodation, canteens and messes, workshops, offices, guardroom, garages, gun stores, all took up a large space. In the newer permanent batteries, all these buildings were solidly built of brick, on concrete bases, but many coast gunners had to live in quarters which had been constructed up to 300 years previously.

Throughout the First World War, the navy's policy of protecting only their bases against enemy bombardment held firm. Thus, counter-bombardment batteries of 9.2in guns are found exclusively around the major ports. At Portsmouth, these were located around the Needles and Spithead approaches either side of the Isle of Wight. Spithead was covered by batteries at Puckpool and Nodes Point with a further pair of heavy guns mounted on Spitbank, one of the old sea forts. The other passage, past the Needles, was covered by the New Needles and Warden Point Batteries. In addition, Sandown Bay was protected by Culver Down Battery, and two more 9.2in guns were mounted on the eastern flank of Southsea Castle. Plymouth was also well protected by heavy artillery, and Penlee Point, Renney, Hawkins and Rame Church Batteries mounted a total of ten 9.2in guns between them. Portland's, East Weare Battery A, and Blacknor and Upton Forts were all equipped with 9.2in guns, as were Langdon and Citadel Batteries at Dover. The Thames and Medway defences with batteries mounting 9.2in guns included Slough and Isle of Grain Forts, Ravelin Battery at Sheerness, and Fletcher Battery *(2)* on the Isle of Sheppey, added in 1918. Tynemouth Castle and Frenchman's Point Battery, each had one 9.2in gun in its armament. The reinforcement of the East Coast, begun in early 1915, included 9.2in guns at Brackenbury Battery to protect Harwich, at Green and Godwin Batteries, covering the Humber Estuary, and Palliser and Pasley Batteries, unusually, single-gun batteries, covering the Tees. These last two only opened for business, however, in 1921. The Firth of Forth was the gateway to the battlecruiser base at Rosyth. Both Kinghorn Battery, and the fort on Inchkeith Island, in the throat of the Firth, mounted 9.2in guns in 1914, as did Braefoot Battery, briefly, in 1918. At Milford Haven, South Hook Fort and East Blockhouse and Chapel Bay Batteries, all remodelled in the late 1890s, mounted 9.2in guns. Probably the most ambitious plan of all was the strengthening of the Tyne defences with two pairs of

2 Fletcher Battery, Isle of Sheppey, Kent, TR003727; Battery Observation Post/ Fire Control of this First World War battery of two 9.2in guns, opened in 1918

12in guns from the obsolete HMS *Illustrious*. These were mounted in their turrets, Roberts Battery at Hartley (*3*), north of Whitley Bay, and Kitchener Battery at Marsden, below South Shields, and were quite unique in British coast defence design. Each whole turret, with its thick, steel armoured face, sat at ground level with four levels of magazine and operating gear sunk beneath it in a 40ft (12.5m) deep pit. They were not completed until after the end of the war, firing their proving rounds in September 1921, and, despite the great expense, were scrapped in the 1920s. It should be noted that these attempts to defend the Tyne represented not a softening of the Admiralty's policy in order to preserve the citizenry of the North East but, rather, a somewhat belated recognition of the danger posed to the shipbuilding industry by a possible landing by enemy troops on the Northumberland coast.

There remain a number of survivals from these heavy batteries, albeit in many cases in a modified state, owing to subsequent use. Most of Portsmouth's heavy gun sites remain if only as featureless open pits. At Culver Down Battery the pits are easily seen, but their conversion to 12-pounder emplacements in the Second World War means that the detail has gone. Plymouth's Hawkins and Renney Batteries largely survive although the BOP at Renney has been demolished. Rame Church and Penlee Point Batteries have been levelled, but probably survive, largely intact, underground. Upton Fort near Portland survives in good condition, but the overhead cover for the gun pits dates from its conversion to a 6in battery in the

Second World War. At Dover, Langdon Battery has the Coastguard Station built into it, and Citadel Battery is derelict, but the gun pits, complete with holdfasts, are visible. Of the Thames and Medway defences, Fletcher Battery is particularly well preserved, with both gun pits, some surface buildings, and its BOP surviving. The site now lies within a caravan park. Ravelin Battery's gun pits survive at Sheerness. On the East Coast, most of Brackenbury Battery has vanished, but the gun pits and associated engine-room at Green Battery on Spurn Head survive. Godwin Battery further north at Kilnsea retains its gun pits and some quite substantial barrack buildings, but, owing to the cliff erosion which has already carried away much of the battery's outworks, they cannot last much longer. Further north almost everything has gone. Of the Tyne Turrets, however, it is possible to see some remains. At Marsden, only the distinctive gateposts remain, hovering above the ever-expanding stone quarry. At Hartley, Fort House represents the fire-control centre for Roberts Battery. It is surrounded by a defensive perimeter wall with two loop-holed blockhouses, one of which must surely be the only fortified latrine in Britain. The contemporary water tower also survives. Behind the Grand Hotel in Tynemouth, stands the six-storey command post for the turrets *(4)*, both of which are visible from here. With help from the National Heritage Lottery Fund, it has recently been refurbished as a home, enjoying wonderful views out to sea. Splendid isolation in the middle of the Firth of Forth has ensured Inchkeith's almost total survival, and the gun pits can be seen at Braefoot Battery. Most of Milford Haven's 9.2in emplacements remain.

3 Hartley, Northumberland, NZ341759; a blockhouse, also serving as a latrine, on the defended perimeter of the northern Tyne Turret, whose fire control post is now Fort House

4 *Left* Tynemouth, North Tyneside, NZ237699, Percy Gardens; the Fire Control Post for the two Tyne Turrets, at Hartley, to the north, and Marsden, to the south; recent refurbishment has been supported by the National Lottery Heritage Fund

5 *Below* Blyth, Northumberland; First World War battery known as Fort Coulson; these gunhouses for the two 6in guns, connected by their magazines, were provided with overhead cover in the Second World War

6 *Opposite* Blyth, Northumberland; two battery observation posts at Fort Coulson, that on the right is from the First World War, and the other one is from the Second World War; they each, in their time directed the fire of the battery's two 6in guns

There were, of course, many more 6in batteries for general coast defence, as these were built to protect all the minor ports, and, to a lesser extent, parts of the coast deemed to be particularly vulnerable to enemy landings, such as river estuaries, or, simply very isolated, like the Scilly Isles. Such batteries were sited on existing fortifications such as the sea forts in the Solent, or Pendennis Castle at Falmouth, in many of the Royal Commission works of the 1860s, particularly around the major ports, but also at sites such as Paull Fort on the Humber, and on greenfield sites such as Stromness in Orkney. Examples of 6in batteries from the early years of the century can be seen in Plymouth, on Drake's Island and at Watch House and Lentney Batteries. At Cliff End Fort on the Isle of Wight, 6in gun emplacements can be seen superimposed on earlier Victorian ones. A similar process has occurred at Beacon Hill Fort, Harwich, where earlier muzzle-loaders were replaced in the early years of the century by 6in breech-loaders. Three 6in positions remain at Paull Fort, one of which is now occupied by a later searchlight position. One of the best surviving examples of a 6in battery from this period is at Blyth (Northumberland) *(5)* built in 1917. Consisting of two, linked gun emplacements with magazines, BOP, engine rooms, two DELs, barracks, and close-defence pillbox, it is virtually complete. The gun pits were given overhead cover in the Second World War, and a second BOP was built *(6)*, but the battery, known as Fort Coulson, largely retains its original appearance. Extant examples are also to be found at Tynemouth, on the Forth, and at Milford Haven, for instance. The Heugh Battery, at Hartlepool, one of only a select few to fire their guns in anger in the First World War, remains, but in the remodelled form which

7 Sheerness, Kent; Centre Bastion Battery, TQ914754 often referred to as Martello Battery; two concrete towers for 4.7in QF guns, built 1915, modelled on Martello towers; originally linked to the Observation/Fire Control tower behind, disguised as a house, by raised walkways; in the Second World War the left-hand tower was converted to an XDO or Minefield Control Tower; the right-hand tower was adapted as a searchlight control tower

followed all the excitement of December 1914, with gun pits for a 9.2in gun and a 6in gun, a magazine in between the two, and a BOP to one side.

The universal open gun pits were suitable for most situations but with a few exceptions. The Humber estuary was unusual in that the navigable channel was some distance from the firm shore line. Also, in many places a high sea-bank was interposed between the guns on dry land and possible targets up to four miles away in the channel. The solution chosen was the use of gun towers. Sunk Island Battery, on the north bank, and Stallingborough Battery, opposite it, were each given a pair of 6in guns on concrete towers with magazines below in the bases of the towers. The guns were mounted on steel platforms, 36ft (11m) above ground level, and supported on steel joists. In this way, the guns were enabled to traverse through 360°. Both batteries were surrounded by fieldworks, with blockhouses at the angles, and temporary buildings within the fortified compound. Fragments of one tower can just be discerned at Stallingborough, along with a DEL and part of a blockhouse, but at Sunk Island, both towers still stand, though masked by trees. Also to be seen here is the combined Fire Control Post and Port War Signal Station of 1915, a concrete box on a lattice-work tower. This was built to enable Sunk Island Battery to function in an Examination role. Only recently demolished was a further pair of towers which held two 12-pounder QF guns at Killingholme, on the south bank of the Humber. The only other instances of such towers remain at Sheerness, where, in 1915, two substantial concrete drum towers, modelled on Martello Towers, were built to carry the 4.7in guns of Centre Bastion Battery *(7)*. Topped by later additions, they stand, linked by raised walkways, to their accompanying BOP, like a group of monster chess pieces on the cliff, overlooking the approaches to the harbour. The 1850 Martello at Grain Spit, on the opposite side of the Medway to Sheerness, was equipped with 12-pounder QF guns, replaced by Twin 6-pounders in the Second World War.

The old nineteenth-century forts of Spithead had retained their usefulness as guardians of the eastern approaches to Portsmouth. In 1915, such sea forts were seen as the solution to the problem of defending the wide estuary of the Humber. Two forts were started, Bull Sand, nearer to Spurn Head, and Haile Sand, off the coast by Cleethorpes, and armed with a selection of weapons: four 6in guns on Bull Sand, and two 4in QF guns on Haile Sand. As well as the guns, each fort mounted several searchlights in sponsons, and range-finding equipment in armoured revolving turrets. Though work had begun in May 1915, the problems of building in such difficult circumstances, and the sheer volume of materials involved, meant that progress was slower than expected. Haile Sand was exposed at low tide and work could proceed more quickly, enabling completion in March 1918. Problems with the scour continually washing away its first foundations delayed the completion of Bull Sand until December 1919.

Another even more ambitious scheme evolved to defend the English Channel. A chain of 16 gun towers, linking minefields, anti-submarine nets and booms, was proposed to seal off the channel. Towers were to be 300ft high, two-thirds under water, to be built in the sheltered waters of Shoreham Harbour, and floated into position, to be sunk on the seabed. Several were under construction at the end of the war. Unfinished towers were broken up but, in 1920, a completed one was towed out and sunk into position as the Nab Tower lighthouse off Bembridge (Isle of Wight), where it remains in service.

One of the dangers anticipated by coast defence planners was unexpected attack by fast torpedo boats, and a third of the batteries opened between 1900 and the end of the First World War were for 12-pounder QF guns. As the war progressed, the ratio of 12-pounder QF guns to heavier weapons gradually shifted, in the major ports, from 1:3 at the beginning of the war to something over 1:2 at the end. Part of this was down to the removal of obsolete heavy guns, still present in some older works in 1914. More pressing, however, was the recognition of the damage which could be achieved by small numbers of torpedo boats running amok, especially at night, in a fleet anchorage. Of the balance of the guns, many were 4in and 4.7in QF weapons. Often these guns were sited to operate in conjunction with other elements of the defence. The two 12-pounder QF batteries established either side of the east end of the Needles Passage in 1914 were sited to cover the anti-submarine net which sealed off the western arm of

8 Bawdsey, Suffolk, TM353394; pillbox; note the irregular loopholes. A hexagonal concrete roof-slab has been added on top of the earlier roof, possibly early in the Second World War

the Solent. These guns in twos and fours, combined with powerful lights, either fixed or searching, which could pick out enemy boats up to a mile away, formed a formidable obstacle. Examples of 12-pounder QF batteries of this period can be seen at Devil's Point, Plymouth, at Tilbury Fort on the Thames, at Tynemouth Castle where it had gone out of use by 1914, and on Orkney at Roan Head (Flotta), and Clestrain (Upper Sower) Batteries, for instance. Others survive on the roofs of Calshot Castle and Hurst Castle in the Solent; at both Pendennis (Nos. 2 and 3 Bastion Batteries) and St Mawes Castles at Falmouth; and in the Firth of Forth. One of Hurst Castle's emplacements was converted for searchlight use during the First World War.

Surprise attacks on the batteries themselves, as a prelude to wider operations, also began to exercise the minds of the planners. Batteries, once again, assumed the character of the fort. We have already noted the defended perimeters of the batteries of Stallingborough and Sunk Island on the Humber, and of those of the Tyne Turrets. Wire obstacles, blockhouses or pillboxes and rifle trenches became essential parts of batteries both new and established. Blockhouses from this era can be seen at Spurn Head, at South Gare at the mouth of the Tees, and at Renney, Lentney and Lord Howard's Batteries at Plymouth. Hawkins Battery at Plymouth has side walls loopholed for musketry, and neighbouring Maker Battery, for instance, has unclimbable fencing.

Whilst the obvious targets enjoyed the protection of coast batteries, the most vulnerable lengths of landing beach were defended by pillboxes and fieldworks. Pillboxes were named for the cylindrical containers with overhanging lids, in which the Edwardians collected their tablets from the pharmacist. Large numbers of such a form, built out of interlocking concrete blocks were built on the East coast. They were generally looped for musketry. There was also a hexagonal design which appeared on the Lincolnshire coast, and in East Anglia, and also squares and rectangles. A number of these remain, some having been reused in the Second World War. Those designs used on the Home Front appear to have been entirely different from those built by the BEF in France and Belgium. Examples of the cylindrical design can be seen in Suffolk, at Bawdsey *(8)*, on Oxley Marshes, and at Alderton. In Norfolk, there are examples at Aylmerton, Weybourne, and Sea Palling. A pair of hexagonal pillboxes with steel doors straddle the A47 approaching Great Yarmouth, and another similar pair at Rushmere have had a third, later pillbox added to the position in the Second World War. At St Olaves in Norfolk, a boatyard office is built on top of a hexagonal pillbox from the First World War. A rectangular pillbox can be seen at Blyth Battery, and a square one on the beach at Bawdsey (Suffolk).

If the lack of any repeat of the 1914 coastal bombardments, and the absence of actual enemy landings, can be seen as valid indicators, then the coast defences of the First World War could be adjudged as effective. This may, in part, account for the lack of activity in this area in the interwar years. Some batteries were dismantled on the grounds that they were obsolete, others, because they were deemed unnecessary. A reluctance to commit to defence spending in a rapidly deteriorating financial climate, coupled with the comforting notion that there would be a ten-year lead-in to the next major conflict, fostered an apparently justifiable complacency. A few heavy guns were emplaced in colonial hot spots, notably 15in (38cm) guns in Singapore, and a new mounting for the 9.2in gun was developed, thereby increasing its range to over 15 miles (25.5km). It had also been recognised that a replacement was needed for the 12-pounder QF gun, whose 15 rounds per minute (rpm) rendered 'quick' a relative term. In 1925, designs for a twin, 6-pounder, anti-motor torpedo boat (AMTB) gun were produced. By 1928 the gun had been proved at Shoeburyess. However, manufacture commenced only in 1933, and installation a year later. With a well-drilled crew, its fire could be maintained for the necessarily brief duration of any action, at 120 rpm. It had an arc of fire of 130°, and 1,500 rounds held in close reserve, so targets were engaged for as long as possible. Despite such upgrades of equipment, few new batteries were built. A QF battery and boom, were added to the Thames defences for instance, at Scars Elbow, and 6in batteries at Canvey Island on the Thames, and at Bouldnor, on the Isle of Wight. Many of the issues of these years related to the inter-Service competition exacerbated by the lack of resources. The fledgling RAF, for instance, argued that, given the capability of torpedo-bombers to destroy any invading fleet, coastal defences had become entirely obsolete.

9 Kings Lynn, Norfolk, TF589241; the Battery Observation Post of the emergency 6in battery; it soon became apparent that the shallow waters of the Wash would prevent the approach of a target worth firing 6in shells at, and the guns were soon removed to Druridge Bay, Northumberland

Thus, apart from those changes outlined above, Britain faced the beginning of the Second World War, with, essentially, the same coast defences with which it had weathered the previous one. The major response to the threat of imminent invasion signalled by the German offensive into France, Holland and Belgium, which led to the Dunkirk evacuation, was the emergency battery programme. In May 1940, the navy decided to make available for coast defence purposes 150 old 6in guns, stripped mainly from First World War cruisers, and stored in naval arsenals for such an emergency. More followed the next month, and subsequently over the next year. As Colin Dobinson observes, deliberations which previously might have taken months were cut short and within days it was decided to establish emergency batteries, each armed with a pair of these Mk.Vll 6in guns, or, in a few cases, 4.7in guns. The first 46 priority locations stretched from Sullom Voe in Shetland, to Worthing in Sussex, with two-thirds of them north of the Thames, essentially to defend the eastern approaches. Over the next year or so, this number was to more than double, as new batteries were added, both to thicken up the existing defences, extending the continuous chain around the coast as far as north Devon, and to add in discrete locations on the English north-west coast, such as Fleetwood (Lancashire).

A typical emergency battery, when completed, consisted of two gunhouses, each having a holdfast for the gun, set in a sunken pit, in front of which was a semi-circular, concrete apron, ready-use ammunition lockers and crew shelter. What distinguished these from earlier emplacements, was that experience had, by now, identified the need for overhead cover against strafing and dive-bombing. Thus, the emergency batteries' guns were enclosed in solid gunhouses with concrete canopies. Behind, or often below, each gunhouse was a magazine, generally with three compartments for fuses, shells and cartridges. Operations were directed from a two- or three-storey Battery Observation Post (BOP), and targets were illuminated by Coast Artillery Searchlights (CASL) mounted in concrete emplacements. Engine rooms housed the generators to power all these elements. The basic complement of such a battery was two officers and 60 men, roughly half of whom were gunners. These were all housed in hutting to the rear of the gun site, along with guardroom, office, workshop and MT garage. Sites were surrounded by barbed wire, rifle trenches, and close-defence pillboxes. Lewis guns provided minimal AA cover. Often, the permanent buildings themselves were loop-holed for close defence. Batteries had varying lifespans. That at Kings Lynn *(9)*, one of the first to be opened, was closed, early in 1941, when it was realised that no target deserving of a 6in shell could get within range in the shallow waters of the Wash. The existing gun-platforms seem not to have reached the stage in the construction programme of receiving overhead cover, although the

10 Minsmere, Suffolk, TM477682; Battery Observation Post of Second World War emergency 6in battery, built onto the end of a row of Coastguard Cottages; very little else remains, and the site is now a nature reserve

11 Left Aldeburgh, Suffolk, TM464561; the battery observation post of an emergency 6in battery at Fort Green; the original Second World War observation slits can be seen beneath the cap of the converted drainage mill; there is one of the gunhouses close by still

12 Below Folkestone, Kent, TR241364, Copt Point; gunhouse for 6in gun, one of two at this Second World War emergency battery; the command post is above, and to the rear

13 Opposite Loch Ewe, Highland, NG815920; battery observation post of a 6in battery built to protect transatlantic convoys as they formed in the loch; the battery is virtually complete

magazines below are loopholed. The guns were moved to Northumberland. Boston (Lincolnshire), one of the few relatively deep-water ports never to have been given a battery before the implementation of the emergency programme in 1940, was designated an Examination Battery, and therefore remained armed and manned for much of the war. Although something over 120 some-time emergency battery locations can be identified, it was, maybe, only during the middle months of 1941, that the majority were simultaneously active.

Built to a necessarily lower specification than so-called permanent batteries, the emergency batteries have not fared well over time. A number, however, do survive in good condition. Boston is a good example. Here most of the components are still present. Two gunhouses, two CASLs, two magazines, an engine house, an office and a battery-charging room stand on, or behind, the old Roman sea-bank. The absence of a BOP may be explained by the presence of a four-storey hotel which stands behind the battery, whose top floor would have provided ample visibility and space. Two close-defence pillboxes are provided with AA mounts. Behind the battery a wartime building may have been a garage or equipment store. Bawdsey (Suffolk) retains both gunhouses linked by a semi-sunken magazine. Its distinctive BOP, two CASLs, engine room, and a number of pillboxes from two world wars also remain. At Minsmere (Suffolk) *(10)*, the BOP is still built onto the end of a terrace of Coastguard cottages, whilst that at Aldeburgh *(11)* was integrated into the windmill at Fort Green. At Dunwich, the battery, a solid block with BOP on top, now a house, mounted two 4.7in guns, one of whose holdfasts now sits in the middle of the living room floor. Other

well-nigh complete examples can be seen at Stranraer, at Soldiers Rock, Milford Haven, at Folkestone (Kent) *(12)*, at Kings Lynn, Winterton and Mundesley (Norfolk). At West Mersea, one of the two gunhouses, for a 4.7in gun, survives as a cafe, along with one of its attendant CASLs, now bearing advertising posters for ice cream. As we have seen in the case of the First World War QF batteries, emergency batteries can be seen superimposed on older fortifications such as Dymchurch Redoubt (Kent), and at Coalhouse Fort (Essex). At Newhaven, the two 6in emplacements, part of the 1902 upgrade, were roofed over, but three new emplacements were constructed on the adjacent Castle Hill to take the 6in guns of the emergency programme. These appear to have lost their overhead cover, but retained their BOP as a Coastguard lookout. Very often, only parts of batteries survive such as CASLs at Berwick, Gibraltar Point (Lincolnshire) and Shoreham (Sussex); gunhouses at Swanage (Dorset) and Brixham (Devon); and BOPs at Pett Level (Sussex), and Hunstanton (Norfolk). One almost complete battery must be mentioned here, although it falls into no convenient programme of construction. Loch Ewe 6in Battery *(13)* was built to protect the anchorage in which many transatlantic convoys gathered, prior to setting off with their escorts. It has many of the construction characteristics and layout typical of the emergency programme, but appears not to have been part of it. BOP, gunhouses, CASLs, and engine rooms remain. Coastal erosion is taking its toll at both Happisburgh and Brancaster (Norfolk), for instance as batteries are disappearing into the sea. Other agents of destruction have been, and, to some extent, still are, those bodies charged with preserving the nation's heritage.

14 Opposite Felixstowe, Suffolk; Twin 6-pounder gun emplacements with their director-towers, at the Second World War Darrell's Battery, Landguard Fort

15 Right Felixstowe, Suffolk, TM282319; searchlight position using fixed beam, below the twin 6-pounder emplacement at Landguard Fort

16 Below Orkney, South Ronaldsay, Balfour Battery, ND403931; almost complete Second World War twin 6-pounder battery, with two director towers, gun pits, magazines and searchlights

Whilst the emergency battery programme was designed to plug the gaps in the coast defences, it remained no less important to maintain the defences of the defended ports, and in some cases, to upgrade them. One of the obvious ways of doing this was to install the new 6-pounder Twin AMTB guns, promised since 1933. This involved more than a straight substitution of the new weapon for the existing 12-pounder QF guns. The 6-pounder Twin was mounted in a revolving turret in a semi-circular emplacement sunk in an aproned pit, 6m in diameter, within a semi-circular gunhouse with overhead cover, itself having a diameter of 10m. Behind, was a three-storey director tower, set in the angle of the rectangular crew-shelter, on one side, and magazine on the other. These structures often came in pairs. Examples can still be seen at Beacon Hill Fort, Harwich, and across the River Orwell at Landguard Fort *(14* and *15)*; in the Orkneys at Balfour *(16)*, Burray, Galtness, Graemsay, Holm, Links, Neb, Scad, and Walls Batteries; in Plymouth, the emplacements remain at Western King and Drakes Island without their director towers; both have gone from Fort Picklecombe, but two remain relatively complete at Bovisand, atop the nineteenth-century casemates. The Solent defences include 6-pounder Twin emplacements on the roof of Hurst Castle, where the eastern one has lost its tower, but that on the western wing is complete; and two on the roof of Fort Albert which, for some reason, retained their guns until 1972. Other examples can be seen in the Forth defences on Inchcolm and Inchmickery Islands. These very effective weapons enjoyed some success, particularly in Malta, where, in one action in July 1941, five Italian fast torpedo boats were sunk inside two minutes.

If the guns remained very much the same as in the previous war, then, the fire-control methods were very different. Just as radar transformed air defence, there was a big part for it to play in the area of coastal artillery. Radar helped in three ways by improving on the visual spotting of targets, by enabling more efficient gun-laying, and by providing feedback on the course of an action against targets at sea, by registering the echo from the fall of shot. These methods were pioneered by the Dover batteries, and in February 1942, began to pay dividends. The 6in battery at Fan Bay used radar to engage E-boats, and the 9.2in guns of South Foreland, scored three direct hits on the battlecruiser *Gneisenau*. Such radars as these made little impact on the landscape, generally needing small buildings and gantries. Chain Home Low (CHL), which developed alongside Coast Defence (CD) radar utilised high masts, that at the low-lying, tri-Service station at Humberston (Lincolnshire), stood 184ft high, but the two systems were combined under RAF control during 1942. It was ironic that just as the coast gunners were acquiring the technology which would improve their effectiveness, the receding threat of invasion resulted in a staged reduction of coast defence provision, in order to free up trained manpower for redeployment in the light of changing priorities. Standing remains of dedicated coast defence radar systems are scarce. At Beacon Hill Fort, Harwich, is a hexagonal, three-storey brick radar tower. A similar structure, but with brick ground floor and a brick second storey supported on a steel skeletal framework, stands on piles on the Thames foreshore, upstream from Coalhouse Fort. It was associated with a minefield in the river. A third structure exists built onto the lower, seaward level of Newhaven Fort (Sussex), below the BOP of the 6in battery. It is a D-shaped brick building with blank walls, containing the plinth for the radar set. Adjacent are the associated offices, crew shelters and plotting rooms, all concealed in a fold of the cliff.

As well as the emergency programme prompted by the overriding need for an urgent response to the danger of invasion, the provision of counter-bombardment (CB) batteries with 9.2in guns, and of close-defence (CD) 6in batteries continued. The term used for their construction, was 'accelerated wartime', in recognition of the fact that urgency, coupled with problems of acquiring building materials and the services of skilled labour, meant that earlier standards of finish or solidity were not always met. Battery buildings were either splinter-proof or bombproof, depending on function, but also on situation. Where possible, buildings were sited so as to benefit from cover provided by natural features. CB batteries could be out of site of their targets, all could be camouflaged, particularly against air attack. South Foreland Battery at Dover was built in 1942, with four 9.2in guns, as a CB battery. The four gun pits can be found along with a magazine, and a position-finding (PF) cell on the cliff-top. Dover was also protected by new CD batteries, Fan Bay (1941) Lydden Spout, Capel and Hougham (1942). Of these, only Lydden Spout's gun pits are discernible. Hougham was buried under Channel Tunnel spoil. At Portsmouth, the major addition to the Second World War defences was the 6in CD battery at Bouldner on the Isle of Wight opened in 1938. It was recently described as significant, and worthy of preservation. Ringborough CD Battery, opened in 1942, with three 6in guns, to defend the Humber, was intact until the 1980s. Since then, all three gunhouses have fallen over the cliff, leaving the BOP and other structures likely to follow quite quickly, as the pace of such erosion on the Holderness coast has accelerated. It was not, however, always necessary to build new batteries in order to improve the established port defences. At Plymouth, for example, Lentney Battery was rearmed with new 6in guns in 1941, and neighbouring Renney Battery's 6in guns received new mountings early in the war, increasing their range to 35,000 yards. Many such batteries, some of which had been in service since the beginning of the century, were similarly upgraded in terms both of weapons, and of fire-control. A number of batteries were rearmed in order to fulfil alternative functions. The two forts in the Humber, for example, were largely rearmed with the new 6-pounder Twin AMTB guns, in order to protect the anchorage inside Spurn Head.

During the 1930s, a 15in CB gun was developed, particularly with Singapore in mind, and, indeed, five were installed there, to protect against invasion from the seaward side. A pair of similar guns were eventually emplaced in Spring 1942, in Wanstone Battery at Dover. These were nicknamed 'Jane' and 'Clem', and were joining a sizeable group of other heavy and super-heavy guns of varying age and

17 Rye Harbour, East Sussex, TQ948181; post for six machine guns mounted on concrete tables; the structure appears very vulnerable, and must have been sandbagged; Appendix I: 5g

effectiveness. Throughout 1940 about a dozen 12in, rail-mounted howitzers, held in store since the First World War, and reconditioned in the railway workshops in Derby, were assembled alongside the 18in gun 'Bochebuster', the two ex-Naval 14in guns 'Winnie' and 'Pooh', and three more 13.5in ex-Naval guns: 'Piecemaker' (sic), 'Sceneshifter' and 'Gladiator'. 'Winnie' and 'Pooh' were mounted on permanent, turntable mountings, accessed by rail, but the rest were all rail-mounted on lines, for the most part, laid, or strengthened, for the purpose. One last experimental, super-heavy gun, 'Bruce', arrived in 1943, aimed at the far-away ranges at Shoeburyness, where its fall of shot might be measured. Very little remains of any of these installations. At Wanstone Battery, one or two ancillary buildings remain in the farm, and the gun pits and magazines can just about be traced. Elsewhere vestiges of railway track may be discerned. Rail-mounted howitzers were used on other sections of the invasion coast. Where possible, these lived in rail tunnels and suchlike. At Trimley Heath, near Ipswich, there still stands a shed which housed a rail gun on its own siding. The roof of the shed ran back on rails to unveil the 12in howitzer's barrel.

The established port defences and emergency batteries were only part of the overall coast defence picture. Once the certainty of invasion after Dunkirk was accepted the only possible strategy open to Ironside was one of linear defence, with the hope that it would be a defence with some depth. Despite the horror of static warfare engendered by the experience of the First World War; despite the

18 Bishopstone, East Sussex; TV469999; railway station with built-in pillboxes, reminiscent of Charles Holden's London underground stations but with the added defensive dimension

perceived recent failure of the Maginot Line; despite the fact that anything other than mobile warfare was regarded as heresy, the circumstances dictated that the British Army would have to stand and fight, and the first place that this would happen would be the invasion beaches. In May 1940, Ironside quickly set about creating what he called the 'Coastal Crust' *(17)*. The British Army had left its tanks, its artillery, and its motor transport along the roads of Belgium and France, and on the beaches and quaysides of the Channel ports. If an invading force came, as it surely would, then it had to be delayed on the beaches, long enough for two things to take place. First, the navy had to sail down from Scotland and interrupt the passage of supplies and reinforcements. Second, the two remaining cohesive formations with tanks, motor transport, and artillery, could be brought into action to throw the invaders back into the sea. In the meantime, the Crust had to hold firm. Ironside was forced to see the possibility of an attack at any point along hundreds of miles of coastline. It was probably unlikely that a full-blown invasion would occur anywhere but at the eastern end of the English Channel, but too much was at stake to gamble on this as a certainty. The very notion of Blitzkrieg seemed to suggest combinations of attack from the air, the landing of troops by parachute, by glider, by transport planes onto captured airfields, by raids to secure ports, by subversion, and by terror. Thus all eventualities had to be anticipated, and appropriate force deployed to deal with them. And the first step was to defend the beaches *(18)*.

19 Above Swanage, Dorset, SZ040786, Peverill Point; gunhouse for small coast defence gun, one of a cluster of three, one of which now serves as a coastguard lookout

20 Below Scremerston, Northumberland, NU032481; gunhouse for 4in naval gun in coast defence role

We have already seen how the ports were defended by a combination of counter-bombardment, coast defence, and anti-motor (torpedo) boat batteries. These covered only limited sections of the coast, and were primarily intended to prevent the enemy seizing port facilities. The emergency batteries protected a further group of minor ports, and plugged some of the other gaps, but many miles of beaches quite suitable for amphibious landings remained vulnerable. Ironside ensured that every available gun would be emplaced on the coast. These ranged from naval 4in and 12-pounder pieces, to 60-pounder howitzers and 13-pounder field guns from the First World War, to 75mm guns from the USA and Canada, or from France via the Norwegian campaign, to 3- and 6-pounder naval Nordenfeldt or Hotchkiss guns which had once graced the decks of early twentieth-century Dreadnoughts, and had already been previously redeployed in First World War tanks. Some of the smaller guns were mounted on field carriages as towed artillery or mounted on the backs of lorries. Many, however, were mounted in permanent emplacements as Beach Defence Batteries *(19)*. Examples of gunhouses for some of these weapons can be seen around the coast. There are 4in gunhouses at Budle Bay and Scremerston (Northumberland) *(20)*. Druridge Bay once had some of the dozen 6-pounder gunhouses built in Northumberland, but only two now remain, at Bamburgh, and at Lynemouth. At least one of these had a dummy emplacement holding a telegraph pole, alongside the genuine gun. These 6-pounder gunhouses can be recognised by the circular plate with nine bolts, mounted on the plinth upon which the gun would have been secured. At Budle Bay and Scremerston the holdfasts for the 4in guns have 20 bolts. On the north-east coast beyond Dundee, are two gunhouses at East Haven and at Carnoustie. On the promontory at whose end is the lighthouse just south of Montrose stand two gunhouses for 18-pounder guns, which could command both a stretch of coastline, and the airfield. They are protected by two Type 25 Armco circular pillboxes, which had been shuttered with corrugated iron sheets. On Portsdown Hill, next to old Fort Purbrook, stand a pair of gunhouses, built for 4in naval guns, and sited to command the approaches to Portsea and Hayling Islands. On the Lincolnshire coast there are several 6-pounder gunhouse, one of which, at Boston Haven, has now been converted into a gazebo. A similar gunhouse stands on Chesil Bank in Dorset. Occasionally, emplacements designed for use in the inland Stop-Lines, are found on the coast. There are Type 28a gunhouses for 2-pounder AT guns at Dymchurch Redoubt (Kent), Heacham (Norfolk), and at Sandend Bay (Grampian), and a Type 28 at Brancaster (Norfolk). At Corton, north of Lowestoft (Suffolk), two quite different emplacements for 6-pounder guns stand. One is an open pit made of concrete sandbags, and the other is a circular gunhouse similar to those on the Taunton Stop Line, and Worcestershire's river lines.

The coast defence landscape consisted of many different elements, most of which have disappeared through postwar eyesore clearance, commercial and housing development, and coastal movement or erosion. It is rare to find traces of

21 Dover Castle, Kent; anti-tank pimples ascending the outer banks of the castle; the medieval wall near the Constable's Tower has an anti-tank gun position built in

22 Holme-next-the-Sea, Norfolk, TF695440; two spigot mortar pedestals for beach defence; an explosives and inflammables store stands nearby to safeguard the weapons

the often ingenious devices for preventing enemy landings. A framework of scaffolding poles stood between the high and low-tide marks. In front of this were concrete slabs with steel stakes slanted seawards to rip the bottoms out of barges before they were able to ground. There were inshore minefields, controlled from Extended Defence (XDO) posts, booms, and flame fougasses which would set the surface of the sea ablaze, and there were AT blocks *(21)* by the thousand. These ran parallel to the water, but also at right-angles, limiting movement across a beach, and funnelling the enemy into killing zones. The beaches themselves were enfiladed from concrete machine-gun posts, supported by pillboxes, rifle-trenches, all surrounded by miles of barbed wire. Sometimes beach batteries would have their own accompanying beach-lights in emplacements. Behind the beach, road-blocks of AT rails, pimples, and other obstacles would obstruct the exits, and further systems of AT ditches would limit the movement of any enemy vehicles attempting to break out. Flat areas offering landing grounds for gliders or powered aircraft, were obstructed with poles and wires, and solid objects such as old vehicles filled with rubble. Very often, nowadays, all that can be seen is the odd pillbox, looking frail, vulnerable and often isolated. It is difficult to visualise the hostile environment into which an enemy landing would have ventured *(22)*.

The Fortifications and Works Department (FWD3) of the War Office provided plans for a range of pillbox types, numbered from 22-28, to some of which reference has already been made. Whilst examples from this range can be found all over Britain, they exist alongside a far greater range of locally-designed pillbox types, many of which, now, have no recorded type-number. We shall examine the FWD3 range in subsequent chapters, but here, we will look at a number of strong-point types not only unique to the coast, but unique to particular stretches. On the coast of Holderness, from Withernsea up to around Scarborough, there are lozenge-shaped pillboxes designed for riflemen with light automatic weapons. They are often accompanied, as on Flamborough Head, for instance, by a hexagonal machine-gun emplacement with a projecting forward-facing entrance at each rear corner, hence its dubbing an 'eared' pillbox by its discoverers. Similar lozenges may be found throughout the north-east of England, but those in Northumbria differ in small ways from those further south. In Suffolk, or more specifically, that part of the Suffolk coastal strip in which pillboxes were constructed by 558 Field Coy. RE, can be found more than 30 examples of a square pillbox with two loopholes in each side. A porch covers the entrance, but the leading edge of this is chamfered in order to increase the arc of fire from the adjacent loophole. They are all shuttered in concrete blocks. William Ward has found instances of one of each pair of loops being blocked, in order, presumably to render the pillbox less vulnerable to intense fire given that, unusually, this type has no internal anti-ricochet wall. A group of four guard a road junction at Knodishall near Leiston, and more can be seen at Sizewell, around Lowestoft, and concentrated at Corton Cliffs. A few examples of a small, irregular hexagonal pillbox is found only at Walberswick. Only found on the Lincolnshire coast, is a variation of the standard FWD3 Type 23, a square, covered chamber with three loopholes, and an integral, rear, open, well with LAA mounting. The Lincolnshire version has two enclosed chambers, with the open well in the middle. A group in the north of the county, around the Theddlethorpes, has the well covered over, and loops either side of the entrance. Some, have loops for heavy machine-guns. Also found mainly in Lincolnshire is a rectangular blockhouse with a door and a loophole in each end wall, and three loopholes in each long side. At each end, some examples have mortar pits and/or LAA mountings. Along the Essex coast there are large numbers of sardine-tin-shaped pillboxes, built astride the sea wall. In effect, they are two irregular hexagonal pillboxes built back-to-back, as there is no access from one to the other. Another local variation in Essex places the lower part of the pillbox into the sea wall with a hexagonal superstructure with six loopholes. On Holyhead Island, Anglesey, are some remarkable circular pillboxes, faced in rock and battlemented. At Barrow-on-Furness (Lancashire) there are a number of hexagonal pillboxes with loops, not only in each face, but in each angle as well. One has to assume that at no time would all 11 loops be manned simultaneously. On the coast north of Liverpool there are square, open pillboxes with concrete canopies supported on corner-posts. They might enjoy good visibility,

23 Balmedie, Aberdeenshire, NJ977176; an unusual type of pillbox, in a group with two others of differing design

but appear to be very vulnerable. The Cornish coast has a D-shaped pillbox, and at Findhorn Bay in Moray, eight small pillboxes in four different variations of the Type 22 can be seen. At Balmedie *(23)*, north of Aberdeen, are three large pillboxes, one a large octagonal section-post with nine loopholes, the other two with semi-cicular, loopholed front walls facing inland, and blank, half-hexagonal walls to the sea. These quite unique designs must have been formulated on site to meet a particular need. It would appear, then, that local RE officers, garrison commanders and builders, all had inputs into the design, siting, and tactical use of fixed defences. As in other contexts, existing buildings were adapted for defensive purposes. A folly tower at Llanfrothen (Gwynedd) was converted into a strong-point, and the Harbour-master's office at Carnarfon has a loopholed position, once one of a pair, built on its roof.

There are a number of places where surviving collections of beach defences can be seen, although AT cubes have, in many places, been shifted around to serve as flood defences. At Tentsmuir in Fife, Polish troops laboured on extensive beach defences which largely survive. Hundreds of AT cubes, concrete blocks with slots to hold RSJs forming roadblocks, pillboxes with wide-open embrasures, probably for beach-lights, and pillboxes astride the lines of AT blocks, still line three or four miles of coastline. A similarly extensive beach defence system can be seen at Fraisthorpe, south of Bridlington, on the East Yorkshire coast. Here pillboxes, including some now thought to date from the First World War, machine-gun emplacements, beach-lights, AT blocks, and lengths of AT wall can be seen. The Moray coast between Lossiemouth and Kingston *(24)* is defended by a continuous line of AT blocks, punctuated by pillboxes, and with the Innes Links emergency 6in battery halfway along. There are concentrations of AT blocks at Fairbourne (Merioneth); on the southern bank of the Firth of Forth around Aberlady and Gullane *(25)*; at Holy Island (Northumberland); Chesil Bank (Dorset); and Grain Beach (Kent). Overshadowed by the medieval defences of Dover Castle, lines of AT pimples block the inland approaches, covered by an emplacement for an AT gun, built into the curtain wall next to the tower NE of the Constable's Gate. Dover Castle, of course, retains many of the structures involved in command and fire-control, the Port War Signal Station, the tunnels in the cliff, now known as 'Hellfire Corner', and several (B)OPs, tasked to observe the fall of shot from some of the heavy guns we met earlier. The XDO post deserves a mention as a distinctive structure. This two/three-storey concrete blockhouse was sited to be able to house extended defence officers, whose task it was to activate electrically-controlled minefields. Its odd silhouette suggests nothing more than a knight's helmet, with irregular facets, pierced by loops and shuttered observation ports. Examples survive at Coalhouse Fort on the Thames, at Harwich (Beacon Hill Fort), Felixstowe (Landguard Fort), Holliwell Point on the Crouch estuary in Essex *(26)*, Paignton (Devon), and elsewhere.

One element present in wartime but now usually vanished is camouflage, as applied to defensive features. In a number of places with rocky beaches, pillboxes have had large pebbles set into concrete rendering. Examples can be seen at Minehead (Somerset), Sennen Cove (Cornwall), Holyhead (Anglesey), Llandwrog (Gwynedd), and between Llantwit Major and St Donats (Glamorgan). At Tentsmuir (Fife) and at West Aberthaw (Glamorgan) *(27)*, attempts have been made to hide pillboxes in the lines of AT blocks. At Tentsmuir, the pillboxes have paving slabs set on their roofs to give the impression of an uninterrupted line of AT blocks from the air. At West Aberthaw, the AT blocks are built into the corners of the pillboxes to achieve the same effect. Sometimes the whole pillbox was built inside an existing structure. At Minsmere (Suffolk) the ruined medieval chapel houses a rectangular blockhouse with loopholes both facing the coast, and enfilading the approaches inland. The upstanding fragment of the thirteenth-century Cluniac Broomholm Priory at Bacton (Norfolk), contains a square blockhouse at ground-floor level. There are embrasures for light machine-guns in three faces, and another pair flanking the entrance in the fourth. Diagonal rifle-loops have been cut in each corner. Also in Norfolk, at Ludham and at Stracey Arms, drainage mills have had loopholes inserted in upper floors. Those at Stracey Arms are now blocked, but at Ludham, there is a spigot mortar pedestal beside the mill.

As the war progressed, so coast defences were gradually reduced. From late 1941, many batteries were put into care and maintenance. Of those retained, many of the emergency batteries were manned by the Home Guard. One new weapon did come into service, though, before the end of the war. In 1942 it was proposed

24 Moray, north-east Scotland; beach defences between Kingston on Spey, and Lossiemouth; lines of anti-tank blocks are interspersed with machine-gun posts which are sited to enfilade the beach; halfway along Spey Bay is Innes Links coast defence emergency battery; Appendix I: 6f

25 Above Gullane, Lothian, NT476814; one half of an anti-tank barrier obstructing a beach exit; three RSJs would have rested in the slots, their other ends in corresponding slots in another block; there are large numbers of such obstacles along this coast

26 Left Holliwell Point, Crouch Estuary, Essex, TR017958; Minefield Control Tower capable of independent defence; it stands just back from the sea bank, on which stand pillboxes

27 West Aberthaw, Glamorgan, beach-defence pillbox at ST010664, built to blend into a line of anti-tank blocks

to develop dual-purpose AA and CD capability using the 5.25in gun. This gun fired an 80lb, (36.4kg) shell to a ceiling of 43,000ft (13,230m), at a rate of fire of ten rounds per minute. Complex mountings were developed for AA, for dual–role AA/CD, and for service afloat. Gun-laying radar formed an integral part of the control system from the start. A number of batteries were identified as potential recipients of this weapon, but when the programme was cancelled in December 1943, only one prototype, at Park Battery, South Shields on Tyneside, had been built. This has long vanished, but the distinctive emplacements of a 5.25in AA battery can be found at Weybourne, on the north Norfolk coast. This was built for the AA practice camp, now a military museum. Four examples of these guns still stand, in their turrets, at Princess Anne's Battery on Gibraltar.

Hitler's unexpected attack on Russia in 1941 made the possibility of an invasion of Britain more remote. However the Chief of Staffs' committee which regularly reviewed the invasion threat, and tried to plan from the enemy's perspective, still felt the need to meet well into 1942. Fortunately, the invasion never came, and the defences were not tested. A number of exercises, simulations and wargames have subsequently speculated with what-if scenarios. Most, unsurprisingly, have been inconclusive. There are always just too many variables and unknowns. Coast defences were maintained until 1956, when missile technology was deemed to have rendered them obsolete, and they were closed down. It must be noted, however, that neutral Sweden still retains radar-controlled coast-defence guns, of modern design, in armoured turrets.

2

INLAND DEFENCE LINES

Whilst the combination of the Royal Navy and strong coast defences around its bases had been traditionally seen as an adequate defence against foreign invasion, the last decades of the nineteenth century, and the early years of the twentieth, saw a shift in military thinking. Strategic planners were beginning to feel a need to acknowledge at least the possibility of enemy troops exploiting a foothold on the coast. Advances in technology and the corresponding acceleration in the obsolescence of military hardware meant that it was not impossible to put a large force ashore across 300 miles of ocean, or North Sea, to be precise. In the 1880s, a system known as the London Defence Positions was constructed to enable a speedy mobilisation of militia and volunteers in case London were to be threatened. The components were defensible mobilisation stores along the North Downs from Guildford to Farningham, and up into Essex pivoting on North Weald. The plan was to link these 13 redoubts by trench-lines, if and when a threat became serious enough to warrant such a massive undertaking. A less-than-generous four days were allowed for this to be effected by labour battalions to be recruited in the Capital. Particular attention was to be paid to the natural gateways through the Downs. Thus the rash of contemporary literature, which both caused, and resulted from the public awakening to an invasion threat, rejoiced in such titles as Chesney's *The Battle of Dorking* (1871). Such works as Erskine Childers's *Riddle of the Sands* developed the genre. Many of these redoubts and depots remain, as their use continued into the next century. There would appear to be some form of reassurance, some form of psychological benefit to be gained from linear defence systems. Maybe the examples from history of the Great Wall of China, the Cherta Lines of Russia's eastern frontiers, Offa's Dyke, or Hadrians Wall, for example, were responsible. Maybe ideas to do with the 'bottom line', or 'they shall not pass' are influences. In spite of the doctrine of mobility, which dominates much of the century's radical military thought, paradoxically, for whatever reason, linear defences still appear to have permeated much of twentieth-century military planning.

In 1914 an invasion across the North Sea was perceived as, at least, possible, and parts of the earlier defensive plan were implemented. An outer line of fieldworks ran from Chelmsford to Maldon in Essex. To the south, a line ran from the redoubt at North Weald, past Ongar, to the Thames near Canvey Island. These works were echoed south of the Thames, where lines were planned linking the River Swale, the Chatham land defences, and the North Downs redoubts. Most of the works were of earth and timber, with mobile artillery in emplacements with log roofs, covered in earth, but some square, concrete pillboxes survive at Newington (Kent), for example. In Norfolk, a line of pillboxes, anchored to the coast at Weybourne in the north, and at Sea Palling in the east, follows the River Ant. These pillboxes were, for the most part, cylindrical, but there remains a D-shaped one near Aylsham. They were made of interlocking concrete blocks, with sliding steel shutters inside their loopholes, and steel doors. Some were built in pairs to cover particularly vulnerable river crossings. In some examples, the loopholes are at different levels. Over 30 pillboxes were constructed in Norfolk, the last, according to grafitti in one box, well into the last year of the war. This might represent the response to the notion that an invasion attempt might be made in order to break the stalemate of the Western Front.

We have seen how the response to the very real invasion threat of Summer 1940 resulted in Ironside's system of defence in depth, whose first layer was the Coastal Crust. Although Ironside realised the importance of delaying an enemy invasion at the point of landing, and was therefore forced to place, as he put it, all his goods in the front window, much effort was invested in the other layers of the system, and it is with these that this chapter is concerned.

The most important component was the General Headquarters (GHQ) Line. This was designed as a major obstacle to enemy progress. In the event of the Coastal Crust being breached, the advance of the invading force was to be held up by a strong and continuous defence line comprising an anti-tank (AT) ditch, supported by concrete blockhouses for AT guns, automatic weapons and small-arms, manned by whatever forces were available. This was, again, envisaged as a secondary delaying mechanism, which would enable the only remaining viable, mobile formations left in existence, the 1st and 2nd Armoured Divisions, to be brought up to the threatened area, in order to defeat the invading force in a set-piece battle, on ground of the defenders' choosing. Forming the next layer in what was essentially a hierarchy of defence lines, were the Command Lines. These were initiated, planned, constructed and manned at a regional or Command level. Depending on its location, and its relationship to the probable invasion points, these lines could be forward of the GHQ Line, as those of Eastern Command inevitably were, or essentially, back lines, built either as extra layers, or to protect a specific geographical area or directional approach. Within the Command areas, there were Corps Lines, enjoying more tactical or local significance, either adding to the over-arching notion of defence in depth, or shielding a particularly sensitive or vulnerable objective. Much of this system, unlike the Coastal Crust, was seen as a multi-layered fall-back position, ready to be manned as and when necessary. The unpredictability of the enemy's invasion intentions have already been noted.

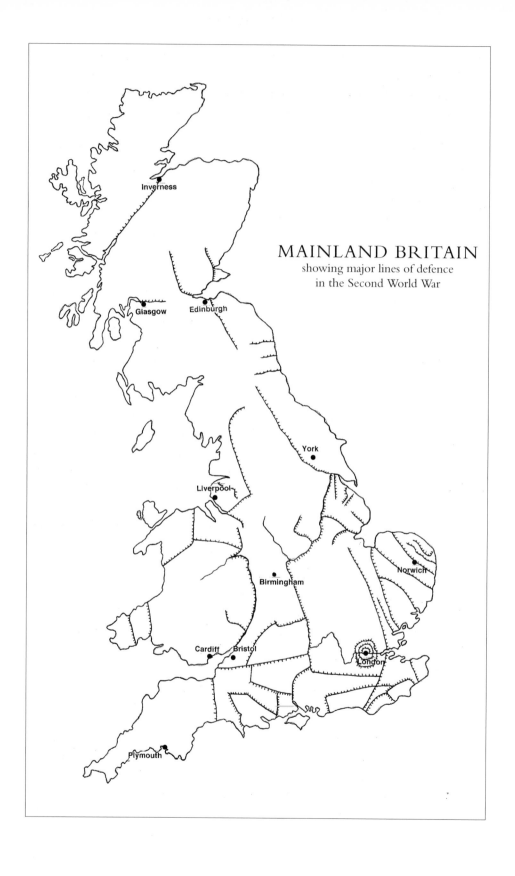

MAINLAND BRITAIN
showing major lines of defence
in the Second World War

One possible response was to think of these defence lines as ways of dividing up the country into boxes into which the advancing enemy might be drawn. To that end, some lines could be fought in both directions, with AT ditches constructed to entrap enemy tanks coming from either direction, and AT gun emplacements built to both enfilade the obstacles, and to engage targets from front and rear. Strings of AT obstacles, minefields and fieldworks could funnel attackers into killing grounds.

The GHQ Line was planned as a series of linear defences based on existing waterways and other natural obstacles, ultimately combining as a continuous and coherent system, protecting the country's capital, and industrial heartlands. The first part, known as the Green Line, runs from the Somerset coast at Highbridge, along the River Brue, over Dinder Heights and along the rivers Wellow, Frome and Avon, the 80 miles (128km) to Great Somerford (Wiltshire). The original intention had been to continue this line through to the Severn, at Upper Framilode below Gloucester to form an Outer Bristol Defence Line, but, of this extension, only a short stretch east of Tetbury and Avening appears to have been built in any strength. The GHQ Line proper, leaves the Green Line at Semington (Wiltshire), to follow the Kennet and Avon Canal, an effective AT obstacle, all the way to Theale, west of Reading (Berkshire). This section is the Blue Line, and is 60 miles (96km) long. Recognising the inherent weakness of a linear defence, the planners built a rear or switch line behind. This Red Line, 68 miles (109km) in length, runs from Great Somerford, north of Swindon, following streams to join the Thames at Cricklade (Wiltshire), which it then follows as far as Pangbourne. It then drops south, down the Sulham Valley, to link up with the Blue Line again. It continues south along minor rivers to Farnham, through the 30 miles (48km) of Aldershot Command, re-entering Southern Command at Shalford (Surrey). From here it runs along the rivers Mole and Eden, entering Eastern Command, and on to the Medway at Penshurst (Kent), an important junction of Lines. This is the pivot of a dog-legged southerly extension running the 30 miles (48km), up from Newhaven (Sussex), which continues on through Kent for about 30 miles (48km). Following the Medway through Tonbridge and Maidstone to Rochester, it then turns north across the Hoo Peninsula to the Thames at Higham Marshes. North of the Thames, the GHQ Line East runs 50 miles (80km) through Essex, up the line of the old A130 road and around Chelmsford. Entering Cambridgeshire at Great Chesterford, it follows the River Cam, then along an artificial AT ditch to the east of Cambridge, and links up with the Eastern Command Line (see below) near Littleport. It then runs along the Forty Foot Drain to Ramsey, where it turns north past Whittlesey and Thorney to reach the River Welland, around 70 miles (112km) in all. The course of the line north of Ely, is often shown, even in the official history, as following the rivers Cam and Great Ouse, terminating at Kings Lynn (Norfolk), but, according to contemporary papers commissioning work from local building contractors, the true course is that detailed above. This part of the GHQ Line, from the Bristol Channel to the

River Welland, including the Newhaven spur, totals nearly 400 miles (640km) and forms a continuous AT barrier. In addition to the existing waterways, rivers and canals, many of which had to be improved by revetting, dredging, deepening and widening, Colin Alexander has identified over 112 miles (180km) of new, purpose-dug, artificial AT ditches.

North of the Welland, in Northern Command, it is more difficult to trace the GHQ Line. Added to the fact that work here had been put on hold in order to maximise scant resources, both labour and materials, by advancing work in those areas seen as most vulnerable, were a number of other reasons. By the end of July 1940, several factors pointed to a change in the overall situation regarding the country's readiness to resist invasion. Ironside had been promoted and replaced by Brooke (later Lord Alanbrooke), who had fought with the BEF in France earlier that year, and now brought a wholly different approach to anti-invasion strategy. The nation's factories had produced large quantities of tanks, lorries and AT guns, to replace losses incurred in France, and to equip new, mobile formations. More and better trained troops had become available, including a Canadian division and two New Zealand brigades. The Local Defence Volunteers (LDV, later the Home Guard) had been recruited in large numbers, enabling regular troops to spend more time training. Brooke's changes to policy were radical. He felt that the fixed, linear defences already constructed in the southern half of the country were unrealistic in terms of the manpower available to man them, and he felt, based on his recent experience in France, that many of the AT obstacles were as much of a hindrance to defending forces as they would be to attackers. He had little sympathy for any defensive strategy characterised by static structures. His solution was to call an immediate halt to much of the construction work on the GHQ Line; convert much of what had been done, from linear defences, to the development of all-round nodal point defence; to place strong, mobile strike forces with tanks and artillery behind the most vulnerable and likely invasion beaches, leaving weaker, static formations on other stretches of coast; to demolish AT obstacles which might hamper the movement of defending forces; and to suspend the construction of fixed defences on parts of the GHQ Line not yet developed. In Northern Command this was quite significant. Very large numbers of concrete pillboxes and gun emplacements, as we shall see, had already been built in Southern and Eastern Commands as part of the GHQ Line defences. Evidence on the ground, suggests that fewer were built on Northern Command's sectors of the GHQ Line.

In June 1940, the Reconnaissance Report for the Forward Defence Line (later GHQ Line) from the River Welland to the River Trent is undecided as to which of two equally unsatisfactory routes to take. Just at that time, such work was suspended anyway, and in July, the order came not to construct any more pillboxes. The Line of the rivers Trent, Ouse, Ure and Swale took the notional Line as far as Richmond (North Yorkshire) and these came to delineate demolition belts. Defences were confined to bridges which easily fitted into the nodal point/defended locality approach. The rivers continued to be regarded as AT barriers, even as boundaries, behind which counter-attacking forces might be deployed, but the notion of a continuous line of fixed, manned strongpoints was gone. Further north, other natural obstacles were able to supplement rivers, and the idea of the GHQ Line became much more flexible. Lateral defence lines across the grain of Northumbria, following the rivers Coquet, Wansbeck and Tyne, employed a combination of fixed defences and of demolition belts. The Line in Scotland was planned to use rivers and railway embankments over the Cheviots and through the Borders to meet the Forth at Musselburgh. The Line would continue up the Forth to Stirling, then north through mountainous country to Killin, at the western end of Loch Tay.

Given the short space of time during which much of the GHQ Line was built, it can, in many ways be seen as a homogenous structure. The defensive principle was simple. Obstacles, principally an AT ditch, would stop armoured vehicles, which would then be destroyed by the fire from emplaced AT weapons. Attacking infantry would be engaged by automatic fire from defending infantry in fieldworks and in concrete emplacements. Crossing points such as canal bridges on the existing waterways, or causeways over the AT ditch, were defended by AT rails or blocks. In some places, a second line of usually smaller pillboxes gives some depth to the defence, and in other places, AT emplacements are positioned forward of the Line, to ensure that, should the ditch be crossed, enemy armour will be hit from behind. Generally, however, the Line is thinly defended. It was a recognition of this vulnerability, and the sheer impossibility of holding lines against a determined attacker able to concentrate force in one place, therefore, that produced Brooke's policy of defended localities. Now, defending forces were to be concentrated in places which could block the enemy's advance. Along the GHQ Line, towns and bridging-points were chosen to be given all-round defences. The enemy could cut the Line as often as he liked, but if he was unable to manoeuvre, was unable to gain access to roads, was faced with strongpoints in his rear which could prevent his reinforcement and resupply, then forward progress was meaningless.

The types of fixed defences which made up the GHQ Line came from quite a narrow repertoire. Contractors were appointed for sectors of the Line, and were responsible for subcontracting work to smaller firms as necessary. They were advised by RE officers who provided plans of standardised defence works, sited individual defences, and ensured the coherence of the system. This left little room for individuality, and, combined with the extremely compacted timescale, explains why the same designs are almost universal along the length of the GHQ Line. The most common pillbox on the GHQ Line is the Type 24 which appears in two versions, the shellproof one with walls 42in (107cm) thick *(28)*, and, in this context, a less common, bulletproof one with a wall thickness of 24in (0.6m) *(29)*. Both versions are hexagonal, with the base longer than each of the other five sides. Each face has an embrasure for a Bren gun, with a pistol-loop either side of the

28 Hanningfield Crossroads, Essex, TL754001; Type FW3/24 shellproof pillbox; NB the attempts at camouflage; this is one of a number of pillboxes clustered around this crossing-point on the GHQ Line; Appendix I: 4a

door, in the base. The roof is of solid concrete, at least 12in (30cm) thick. The sides are made of poured, reinforced concrete, shuttered in wood, for preference, as the same shuttering could be used for up to six pillboxes, but often in brick, which is then left in place. Inside, is a Y-shaped, anti-ricochet wall. Hundreds of these Type 24 pillboxes were built, and many still stand. Inevitably, in such a large operation, there are variations on this central theme. Many concern dimensions, and this can be seen on the Green Line, and on the Newhaven–Hoo Line, where different base lengths produce different angles and affect the lengths of the other sides. Some variations appear to be based on tactical considerations, an example being a reduction in the number of loopholes. Scarcity of materials also accounts for the modification of some Type 24 pillboxes on the Red Line which are otherwise shellproof but for thin back walls. Another reason was the equipment held by troops who were stationed in a particular sector. Some Type 24 pillboxes in Aldershot Command are fitted with a mounting unlike that for the normal Bren gun. They were manned by French cavalry who were equipped with Hotchkiss light machine-guns requiring different fittings. Construction methods were also responsible for design changes. At Shalford (Surrey) *(30)*, Mowlem's engineer decided that curved sheet-steel shuttering would be more effective if the normal angles of the hexagonal Type 24 were rounded out. Unique to that area, therefore, is a group of D-shaped pillboxes with straight rear walls. Their accompanying 6-pounder gun emplacement is completely circular. In the Somerset levels, many of the Type 24 pillboxes have porches. The majority of these modified versions appear to have no design or drawing numbers. However, surviving accounts for work done by Hugh Cave, a building contractor working around Whittlesey and Thorney (Cambridgeshire), have made it possible to identify one local variation of the Type 24, as a Type 350/40 *(31)*, i.e. the 350th drawing produced centrally in 1940. Thus, along the 400 or so miles of the GHQ Line, the overriding imperative is uniformity, but with localised exceptions as and when justified.

Where a back-line was built, as in Essex, it was usually composed of small Type 22 pillboxes. These are regular hexagons, with rifle-loops in five faces, and a door, flanked by, usually, a single pistol-loop. Walls were 12-15in (30-38cm) thick. Another design which can be found extensively on the GHQ Line is a rectangular, shellproof pillbox for three Bren guns *(32)*. The door, in the rear wall, is often protected by a loopholed blast wall. These may represent a modification of another FWD/3 design which is for a single Vickers medium machine-gun, and therefore has one large, stepped embrasure in the front face, a table-type mounting for the gun, and two further loops for brens. Odd examples of the former can be found on the Line in Surrey and Kent, and, in large numbers, in East Anglia, but the latter is confined to small, heavily-defended areas around Aldershot. Dotted along the Line are small numbers of other bulletproof pillboxes: circular, Type 25 (Armco), square Type 26, and, in Hampshire, some square prefabricated pillboxes.

29 Chetwynds Bridge, Staffordshire, SK187138; Type FW3/24 bulletproof pillbox guarding a crossing of the River Tame along the Tamworth to Ashbourne defence line; Appendix I: 2b

30 Chilworth, Surrey, TQ015475; one of the shellproof pillboxes built by Mowlem using the Type FW3/24 layout, but with curved steel sheet as shuttering; there are about a dozen of this style, confined to the area between Shalford and Chilworth; Appendix I: 11a

31 Turningbridge, Whittlesey, Cambridgeshire, TL281975; one of the Type 350/40 shellproof pillboxes built by Hugh Cave, the building contractor responsible for the GHQ Line in the northern Fens; note the brick shuttering, and the prefabricated loopholes; Appendix I: 4d

These pillboxes constructed from in-filled, prefabricated concrete panels occur all over Britain. One, on the Isle of Wight has a table-mounting for a machine-gun, and near Filey (North Yorkshire) there is a double-size version. Mick Wilks, by reference to the detailed War Diary of the local RE unit, has identified an example at Eckington Bridge (Worcestershire) *(33)* as a Stent pillbox, a name, presumably derived from its manufacturer, a company which may, incidentally, still be trading. In the Red Line are a number of shellproof pillboxes which are regular hexagons in shape. At Chiddingstone Causeway, near Penshurst Station, are a pair of most unusual machine-gun emplacements facing north as a precaution against this important position being out-flanked. Each one is hexagonal, shellproof, and has two, large, stepped embrasures, fitted with Turnbull mounts, in the front two faces. The rear door has a blast wall protecting it.

The avowed intent of the GHQ Line was to provide a barrier against armoured vehicles, and the most impressive of the Line's blockhouses reflect this. These are the emplacements for AT guns. The most common is the Type 28a *(34)*, designed to accommodate a single 2-pounder. AT gun firing through a forward-facing embrasure, and three or more Bren guns. The gun was brought in through the back, and pivoted on a fitting in the floor, giving it 70° of traverse, its two forward-facing trail legs fitting into slots in the front wall. Less common is the Type 28, which is a smaller version without the separate Bren gun chamber. Even rarer is a twin version which allows the gun to be fired from either of two embrasures at right-angles to each other *(35)*. In Sulham Valley, near Reading, probably the most heavily-defended sector of the entire Line, getting on for a dozen of these twins, and a similar number of single Type 28a emplacements, often built in pairs, back-to-back survive, along with AT ditch, rails, blocks and cylinders. In the summer of 1940, 2-pounder AT guns were scarce. Many had been left in France, along the roads leading to, and on the beaches of Dunkirk. Although the factories were turning replacements out as quickly as possible, they were needed for tanks' main armament, for the AT regiments attached to armoured divisions, and for the artillery manning beach defences. Not unreasonably in the circumstances, the requirements of static fixed defences came well down the list of priorities, and an alternative had to be found as a stop-gap. In the First World War, old 6-pounder Hotchkiss guns, originally fitted to Dreadnoughts as saluting or anti-boarding weapons, had been rehabilitated for mounting in sponsons on male tanks. These guns were destined to serve, or at least to be available for service, in another conflict, and were issued, on wheeled carriages for beach defence, and, on concrete pedestals, for inland defence lines. The Types 28 and 28a emplacements needed only minimal modification. The embrasure was reduced in width, and a concrete pedestal with a mounting plate with nine fixing bolts was built into the front wall. Since the gun could be introduced through the embrasure, the rear entrance could be better protected. On the Red Line, an even simpler solution was adopted, but in small numbers. Here, an open hexagonal gun pit was constructed, with expense lockers built into the side walls. These pits enjoyed the

32 Hartford End, Essex, TL695167; shellproof pillbox for three light machine-guns; NB the loophole in the blast wall, and the evidence of wood shuttering; this is on a particularly heavily-defended, and well-preserved stretch of the GHQ Line; Appendix I: 5b

33 Eckington Bridge, Worcestershire, SO922424; a square prefabricated pillbox, possibly known as a 'Stent' after its maker; the bridge on the Avon Stop Line, was also defended by spigot mortars; these prefabricated pillboxes appear in most of England; Appendix I: 6t

34 Stanton St Bernard, Wiltshire, SU091620, on the banks of the Kennet and Avon Canal; Type FW3/28a blockhouse for two-pounder anti-tank gun, with separate bren chamber; NB the wide embrasure, and the rear access for the gun; one of dozens along the GHQ Line; Appendix I: *10b*

advantage of 360° traverse. They were probably camouflaged with netting. In at least one case, near Tonbridge, the pedestal stands devoid of any surrounding structure at all. On the Red and Blue Lines, the emplacements are mainly fitted out for the 2-pounder gun, whereas on the Newhaven–Hoo Line and in Kent, the 6-pounder predominates. In East Anglia, there is a mixture of all four types of emplacement.

If the 2-pounder AT gun was scarce, the 6-pounder was obsolete, and attempts were made to find further alternatives. Near Farnham (Surrey) is a group of around a dozen field-gun emplacements. These have large embrasures, loopholes for light automatics, and a rear, walled, and in some cases castellated, enclosure, giving protected access for the gun. These may have accommodated French 75mm guns, or old 13- and 18-pounder guns. Another symptom of the lack of AT guns was the fact that there are a number of examples, all along the Line of Type 28a emplacements being converted into infantry strongpoints. The big embrasure is blocked, often having two Bren gun loopholes substituted, and the doorway is reduced in size. In other places, the concrete raft for the emplacement has been laid, but no further work has proceded. Some of this can be explained by changes in policy, but some may be down to the realities attached to the supply of weapons.

Despite its beginnings as an entirely linear defence, the GHQ Line was adapted to function in ways more acceptable to Brooke. All along the Line, locations were

35 Sulham, Berkshire, SU643742; the twin version of the Type FW3/28a blockhouse for 2-pounder anti-tank gun and Brens; only one of the two embrasures may be used at any one time; these are on the GHQ Line mainly around the west end of Section Red; Appendix I: 10a

identified to be turned into defended localities. Nodal points with all-round defences were established at Semington, Devizes, Hungerford and Newbury, on the Blue Line, and Lewes, Uckfield, Tonbridge and Maidstone further east. In 1941, these eight places and 34 others, were developed as AT Islands. Just as they were on the original Line, many of the defences of these points were fieldworks, but one particular innovation helped to make these defences appear more formidable. This was the Blacker Bombard, or spigot mortar. Rejected by the War Office in 1939 as ineffective, it was, nevertheless in 1941, seen as the answer to the Home Guard's need for sub-artillery. Prepared positions with pedestals and pits were built, and mobile positions were identified. Thousands of these weapons were issued to units manning AT Islands, and new positions were still being added to the Line proper, late in 1941. Home Guard explosives and inflammables stores were used to house the weapon and its ammunition, as were redundant pillboxes. Along the parts of the Line which were too late to receive fixed defences in 1940, such as the River Trent north of Nottingham, these were welcome, if late, additions, and the combination of spigot mortar and explosives store can still be seen at Cromwell Lock, north of Newark.

The GHQ Line is still highly visible along most of its length. The Red Line is most probably the best-preserved stretch with over 150 extant pillboxes, half of which are AT emplacements. Some of the concentrations of defences, guarding the approaches to Aldershot, for example, remain almost complete at Ewshot, Beacon Hill and Hog Hatch. The junctions of separate parts of the Line at Semington, Penshurst, Theale and Littleport/Prickwillow are particularly well-preserved still. Apart from the centres of towns, it is difficult to indicate many stretches which have disappeared. In East Anglia, the best-preserved linear sections are just south of Great Dunmow, and at Hartford End, north of Chelmsford. The sector which runs from Whittlesey (Cambridgeshire) north to the River Welland retains 70 structures. In Northern Command where pillboxes are rare as far as the GHQ Line is concerned, there are, nevertheless interesting survivals. At Aldwark and Naburn Bridges over the Ouse in North Yorkshire, can be seen loopholes, AT blocks and a weapons store. At Torksey (disused) railway bridge over the Trent in Lincolnshire, the slots for AT rails remain.

Command Lines were designed to fit in with, and to complement the GHQ Line. In terms of general approach, of their component parts, both fieldworks and fixed defences, and of policy, they look very much like the GHQ Line, but at a tactical rather than a strategic level. In June 1940, they were starting out as linear defences utilising concrete pillboxes and AT obstacles. By early 1941 they were being described as strings of loosely-linked defensive positions, to conform to Brooke's strictures about the dangers of static, defensive warfare. Given the framework of the Coastal Crust and the GHQ Line, each Command had the task of setting priorities for its own defensive objectives, and this clearly depended on its geographical location.

For Southern Command, the task appears quite straightforward. One, strong defensive position was established running from Seaton (Devon) to Bridgwater (Somerset), generally known as the Taunton Stop Line. This would both protect the south-west from an easterly invasion, specifically denying the enemy access to the ports of Plymouth and Falmouth by the back door, and also protect the industrial Severn Basin from raiders utilising the small ports of north Devon and Somerset. This Line was built with over 350 pillboxes and gun emplacements. Southern Command's second priority was to secure the areas behind the potential Dorset/Solent/Hampshire invasion coast. Two Lines were constructed roughly parallel to the coast, with a southerly spur dividing the area into defensible boxes. The Salisbury West Line runs from Bradford-on-Avon, through Frome, to Salisbury, then down the Avon *(36)* past Fordingbridge and Ringwood to the coast at Christchurch. The Salisbury East Line runs along the railway line to Romsey, along the River Test to Basingstoke, then joins the GHQ Line at Fleet (Hampshire). In effect, this is a southern equivalent of the Red (switch) Line.

In Eastern Command, the main effort, at Command level, was on forming barriers, designed to delay an enemy's advance from the coast to the eastern GHQ Line. The Eastern Command Line runs from Wivenhoe (Essex) to Sutton Bridge, west of Kings Lynn, on the Wash. Using a combination of rivers, the Colne, Stour, Lark, and Nene, and railway lines, it runs through Colchester, Wakes Colne, Bures, Long Melford, Bury-St-Edmunds, Prickwillow, Downham Market and

36 Breamore Mill, Hampshire, SU164173; this pillbox, built into an outbuilding, along with two small Type FW3/26 pillboxes, defends a crossing of the Avon on the Salisbury West Command Line

Guyhirn. A more forward, switch position runs up the rivers Orwell, Gipping, Black Bourn and Little Ouse, to join the main Eastern Command Line north of Lakenheath, prior to entering the complex of defences marking the junction with the GHQ Line. Eastern Command was quick off the mark in designating nodal points and defended localities, and it would appear that many of these actually predate the defence lines which ultimately came to join them up. The River Colne in Colchester for instance, was already prepared as an AT obstacle, prior to its late selection as the optimal route for the Command Line to take.

Northern Command's Lines were more piecemeal. In Lincolnshire, existing AT obstacles based on waterways, strengthened by demolition belts, were utilised to link the coast with the GHQ Line. One runs along the River Witham and the Foss Dyke; the other follows the South Forty Foot Drain. The River Ancholme provides a further obstacle and demolition belt below the Humber. Further north, efforts were made to integrate local defences with the GHQ Line, by establishing demolition belts along the rivers which intersected the Line.

Although Western Command covered an enormous area, it was also the Command least likely to have to deal with full-scale invasion. Three major Lines were given priority in England: one, along the River Avon, past Tewkesbury to Coventry; one, east–west along the rivers Calder and Ribble from Burnley to Preston; and, in Cumbria, a line following the River Eden from Ullswater to Brampton. In Wales, the port of Milford Haven was seen as a likely target, and was protected by two strong lines running north–south and isolating the Pembrokeshire peninsula. The line from Cardigan to Pembrey via Llangeler is particularly pronounced. Another Line along the River Severn, from Tewkesbury to Shrewsbury made use of that formidable AT obstacle. In North Wales, two lines crossed Snowdonia diagonally.

In Scottish Command, the priority was very obvious. The GHQ Line, as we have seen, slanted north-west from Edinburgh. The Scottish Command Line, as plotted by Neil Redfern, runs from Loch Tummel, past Dunkeld and Perth, along the Tay to Kinfauns, crossing the Fife peninsula from Newburgh to Dysart on the Forth. This placed an additional barrier between the coast defences and the GHQ Line, and gave further protection both to industrial areas, and to lines of communication.

The third tier in the hierarchy of defence lines was the much more locally-based Corps Line. Whilst these were very much the initiative of individual commanders and their RE advisers, they were fully integrated into the overall scheme of things, which had been developed initially in an ad hoc fashion, then cemented by Ironside, and later modified by Brooke. Seeing itself in the immediate firing line after Dunkirk, Eastern Command's local commanders at Corps and at Division levels, quickly applied themselves to developing a coherent defence system, in Kent and East Sussex especially. Two Corps Lines, one running from Dover to Canterbury, and thence to the coast at Whitstable, and the other following the Royal Military Canal and the River Rother to meet the GHQ Line at Uckfield, began a process of chopping up the threatened area into a grid of defended boxes. A whole network of shorter lines completed the exercise. Many of these lines faced both ways so that attack from different directions might be resisted effectively. In East Anglia, the Corps Lines contributed to the planned defence in depth by interposing demolition belts, and further lines defended by pillboxes and AT obstacles, between the GHQ Line, the Eastern Command Line, and the Coastal Crust. An enemy, unfortunate enough to select the coast of north-east Norfolk as a landing beach, and intending to make a bee-line for London, would have come up against no less than nine discrete defence lines, before he even reached the Capital's own outer defences. We have already seen the strategy underlying Southern Command Lines, and, once again, the Corps Lines supplement the skeleton provided by HQ. The line Weymouth–Dorchester–Blandford–Christchurch adds a further box to those formed by Command Lines. Further east this pattern is continued by Corps Lines down the River Test from Romsey, in the Meon Valley, and on the Chichester–Midhurst–Petersfield axis covering the rear approaches to Portsmouth. Northern, Western and Scottish Commands echo this approach to filling in the gaps, adding depth to the defence, and exploiting any natural advantage the landscape might provide. Ultimately, as the emphasis shifted away from linear to point defence, almost all the places, seen as waymarks along the defence lines, were developed into defended localities in their own right, with all-round defences. The demands of such a defence scheme can be illustrated by the Forth and Clyde Canal which runs from west of Glasgow to Grangemouth. Along its 35-mile (56km) length were 40 locks, 32 railway bridges, and six steel railway swing-bridges. All the bridges were prepared for demolition, machine-gun positions were constructed to cover all 78 crossings, and a combination of road-blocks, various types of flame-trap, OPs, and bombing-posts were integrated into the developing network of DLs which defended the approaches to Glasgow, and the industrial centres to the east of the city.

Across Britain, a remarkable amount survives of these tertiary defence systems. The most complete is probably the Taunton Stop Line. The Line, which begins north of Bridgwater, very close to the western end of the GHQ Green Line, was made up of road and railblocks, demolitions and concrete pillboxes. Quite a narrow range of designs was used. Unusually plentiful, over 60 being provided here, are rectangular, shellproof pillboxes for Vickers machine-guns *(37)*, often deployed in pairs. One example, at Cogload Junction, has two embrasures, one in each of two adjacent faces. There are many shellproof Type 24 pillboxes, but just one, solitary, bulletproof Type 22. There are ten examples of a local design, the TL55 *(38)*, which was adopted to house the 6-pounder Hotchkiss gun. This gunhouse is circular or D-shaped, with a wide-open front, presumably to give the maximum angle of traverse, but rendering itself very vulnerable to gunfire, or grenade attack. The embrasure is so wide that, in one of the circular versions, a substantial pillar is required to support the roof canopy directly in front of the gun. A cast-iron pedestal with integral fixing ring, is provided to mount the gun. Apart from these, the only known examples of the circular type are on the Avon Line in Worcestershire (Holt Fleet and Pershore Bridge), and a single example on the Suffolk coast at Corton. Although there are clearly two different designs here on the Taunton Line, they share a common design number. There is a more normal Type 28a 6-pounder gun emplacement at Ilton. Other unusual items are two double-decker pillboxes at Bridgwater and a third at Ilton. Several of the shellproof pillboxes have standard Bren gun loops in four faces, and then a larger, stepped embrasure in the fifth face. It has been suggested that this was for a Boys 0.55in (14mm) AT rifle, a weapon that was certainly around at the time of construction, and could be effective against soft-skinned vehicles.

On the Scottish Command Line, in Fife, a different set of pillbox types is found. At least two examples of a rectangular, shellproof emplacement with two, forward-facing embrasures backed by a long shelf, possibly for two Vickers machine-guns, remain near Markinch. They are not dissimilar to that built by British REs in France in 1939 on the Franco-Belgian frontier. Here, in Fife, are also at least three examples of the ubiquitous shellproof Type 24 pillbox *(39)*. Two of them have rectangular concrete slabs for a roof, presumably to disguise the

37 Axminster, Devon, SY290975; shellproof Type TL62, emplacement for a Vickers machine-gun, on the Taunton Stop Line; this was the development of a design of 1936; Appendix I: 10d

38 Wrantage, Somerset, ST308224; numbered 'M A/T 602', this gunhouse is designed for the 6-pounder QF Hotchkiss gun; under the canopy is a steel pedestal with a nine-bolt holdfast for the gun; there are about a dozen of these, of different designs on the Line; Appendix I: 5a

tell-tale outline of a hexagonal pillbox. This treatment is seen elsewhere, on the Eastern Command Line, for instance. The Ladybank Depot is defended by three sunken, hexagonal gun-posts with overhanging slab roofs supported on brick piers at the angles, thus providing generous visibility and fields of fire, whilst sacrificing some security. At Kingskettle, a pillbox is built into a stone garden wall, and at Markinch, the cemetery wall is loopholed. One feature of this Line is the profusion of AT features which have survived: whole fields of pimples, AT walls protecting railway arches, and roadblocks.

The Command Line running from Cardigan to Pembrey in South Wales has yet another range of features. Here again are imposing AT obstacles. In one place, near Pembrey, a long row of diagonally-set AT blocks have been cast *in situ*, connected to each other by lengths of railway-line. They are covered by a Type 22 pillbox, and a line of vertical AT rails *(40)*. Nearby are two Type 23 pillboxes with local modifications. Further north are more AT blocks, shellproof Type 24 pillboxes, and, in the village of Cynwyl Elded, two buildings, the cobbler's shop and the milking parlour, have had loopholes inserted to command the road through the village.

The Eastern Command Line appears to share its pillbox designs with the GHQ Line. There are several gunhouses for 6-pounder guns, but, not only have some of them been converted to infantry blockhouses by the insertion of extra loops and the blocking of the main embrasure, but others have been relegated to the status of weapons store for adjacent spigot mortar positions. There are shellproof regular hexagon-shaped pillboxes, in two different sizes, with open platforms in the

39 Markinch, Fife, NO294032; the local version of the Type FW3/24 shellproof pillbox, which includes a squared-off roof, to disguise the otherwise distinctive shape; Appendix I: 4axi

40 Kidwelly, Carmarthenshire, SN410050; the southern end of the Western Command Line running from Cardigan to Pembrey; here two lines of anti-tank rails converge on a pillbox; a parallel line consists of anti-tank blocks joined together by continuous lengths of horizontal rail; nearby are Type FW3/23 pillboxes of the airfield defences

middle with LAA mounts *(41)*. There are two further hexagonal pillboxes, one shellproof and the other bulletproof, and neither having the central, open LAA platform. Colin Dobinson has discovered three drawing numbers for pillboxes designed by the CRE at Colchester. No firm identification has been possible yet, but matching specifications and descriptions with surviving pillbox types on the ground would suggest that the 6-pounder emplacement with Bren gun chamber, very similar to the Type 28a will be the Colchester 1116; the hexagonal shellproof pillbox sited along the AT ditch, may well be the Colchester 1113; and the smaller, bulletproof pillbox, designed to protect the rear of the Line, could be the Colchester 1094. All these three designs are found in large numbers along the Line up as far as Mildenhall. From this point, northwards, it would appear that FWD/3 designs take over: shellproof Type 24, Types 28 and 28a, and Type 22. One, particularly unusual construction, near Lavenham, must be mentioned here. It is a trilobed section post comprising a shellproof, hexagonal pillbox with an open central platform, with a rectangular extension with three loopholes built on to alternate faces.

At the heart of the defence lines covering the south-east corner of the country was London, with its own defences. These consisted of three concentric rings. The innermost had the Thames as its base, and took in the cities of London and Westminster. It evolved as a matter of extreme urgency in May 1940, and was

41 Bures, River Stour, Essex, TL904346; bulletproof pillbox with central open well for light anti-aircraft machine-gun; along the river bank, here forming the Eastern Command Line, are examples of the shellproof version as well; NB how the brick shuttering has become integrated into the structure; Appendix I: 1f

42 Nazeing, Essex, TL404051; a crossing-point of the anti-tank ditch of the Outer London Line is marked by these anti-tank blocks; in an attack, the passage would have been obstructed by rails inserted into sockets in the ground

43 Moor Park, Hertfordshire, TQ076940; Type FW3/27 shellproof pillbox, octagonal, with central, open platform; it overlooks the River Colne, which here represents the Outer London Defence Line; this design is only found on this line; Appendix I: 9a

geared to resisting an airborne attack through the existing airfields such as Hendon or Croydon. As the situation stabilised, this Inner Line developed into a network of defended areas based on government buildings and natural obstacles. A middle line took shape roughly outside the circuit of North/South Circular Road. This was based around fixed, manned roadblocks on all major roads into London, with mobile units with lorry-mounted artillery, stationed at regular intervals, ready to respond to attacks. An outer line, more or less corresponding to today's London Orbital Motorway, and 120 miles long, was reconnoitred in July 1940, and took shape as a much more substantial obstacle. It was developed as a continuous AT barrier, using natural waterways such as the rivers Colne, Lea and Cray, with artificial AT ditches where necessary, and AT blocks and rails at road and rail crossings *(42)*. It was supported by concrete blockhouses along its entire length. The most noticeable of these defences are on the north and east sides, where pillboxes and AT obstacles remain in large numbers. Many of the pillboxes are Type 27, large, shellproof, octagonal section-posts, with loops in each face, a loopholed porch, and an open, central platform for an LAA position *(43)*. Around thirty of these still stand between Rickmansworth and Loughton, along with large numbers of bulletproof Type 22 and Type 24 pillboxes. Parts of the Middle Line are still visible, especially by the River Roding, and, a little further north, where it follows the Underground Railway. Large numbers of AT blocks at Barkingside, Newbury

Park, Hainault and Fairlop stations, for instance, signify the co-incidence of the Middle Line with other, more local targets, such as the underground factory at Newbury Park, and the airfield at Fairlop. These three lines were supplemented by other positions such as the Thames bridges at Kew, Putney *(44)* etc., which were defended by lozenge-shaped pillboxes, and spigot mortars. One interesting feature is at Iver (Buckinghamshire), where the Grand Union Canal crosses the River Colne on an aqueduct. Both levels are protected by pillboxes to prevent attackers from disrupting the flow of water in channels which here represent the front line defences.

Other defence lines throughout Britain were defended by pillboxes of differing designs. The River Coquet Line in Northumberland, one of the lateral ribs of the GHQ Line, employed two local designs. One was a lozenge shape, similar to that seen on the north-east coast *(45)*. This had a combination of loopholes for rifles and automatic weapons, often distributed with reference to the opportunities of the specific location. The other was a small, hexagonal pillbox with loopholes in only the long base, and the three forward faces, the two blank faces being shorter than the others. The line from Tamworth to Ashbourne has mainly Type 23, and bullet-proof Type 24 pillboxes but these are supplemented, at intervals, by a local design which is rectangular, with a sloping roof, and comes in two different sizes. Its most northerly pillbox, at Mayfield (Derbyshire), is a unique design, built into the flood-bank. Nearby, at Ellastone, is a gunhouse for a field gun, which is disguised as a farm-building by the addition of a gabled roof supported on concrete posts. The Oxford Canal formed part of a line linking the GHQ Line Red, with the defences of the industrial Midlands *(46)*. At its southern end are bulletproof Type 24 pillboxes, but further north, around Southam and Rugby, square, prefabricated pillboxes are found. Unique to Sussex, and found particularly on the lines following the rivers Arun and Adur are 20 examples of an open-backed, half-hexagonal gunhouse, reportedly for 25-pounder guns, but, more likely, originally built for older field guns. The other substantial Corps Line in Sussex, following the River Rother as far as Uckfield, and then continuing westward along the Ouse, and south of Horsham, joining the Arun, uses the same designs as the Newhaven-Hoo GHQ line, but with some minor local modifications made to the Type 28a emplacements for 6-pounder guns. Another group of unusual gunhouses can be seen in Lancashire. One, near Inskip, is intended for a 2-pounder AT-gun, but has a profile more like a coast artillery emplacement *(47)*. Built into its rear face is an open platform with the mounting for a LAA machine-gun. Nearby are AT-ditches and AT-rails, so it, most likely, covered a roadblock. Farther north alongside the Lancaster Canal, above Garstang, is an open-fronted, loopholed emplacement into which a field gun could be reversed *(48)*. On the Avon Line in Wiltshire, the main reliance appears to be on the strength of the river as an AT obstacle. There are, however a number of strong-points. At Fordingbridge, the town was ringed by a number of hexagonal pillboxes, and of L-shaped section posts. These latter, like others in Norfolk for instance, consisted of two corridors, each with five loopholes, and at right-angles to each other.

44 Putney Bridge Station, London, TQ245758; this is one of the local design of lozenge-shaped pillbox, but its position, on the end of the railway platform has necessitated the removal of two short sides, and the substitution of an end-wall with two loopholes; the other end of this pillbox has the normal point; at the other end of the platform is a defensible signal box; this pillbox overlooks the Thames which here delineates the Inner London Defence Line; Appendix I: 2eiii

45 Old Bewick, Northumberland, NU074215; this pillbox, a typical lozenge-shaped local design, and its mirror image, 100 yards away, occupy the summit of this Iron-Age hillfort; the hill is situated inside the defensive position formed by the local defence lines which follow the valleys of the Aln and its tributaries, or cross the high ground from Belford, to converge on Wooler; Appendix I: 2e

46 Napton-on-the-Hill, Warwickshire, SP457604; around this part of the Oxford Canal defence line, the defences consist of pre fabricated pillboxes, and this type of anti-tank block which can be rolled into position using a length of scaffolding pole

47 Inskip, Lancashire, SD477378; unique blockhouse for two-pounder anti-tank gun; behind is an open, raised platform with a mounting for an anti-aircraft light machine-gun; nearby are anti-tank blocks and rails, forming part of a defence line based on the River Wyre and the Lancaster Canal; Appendix I: 10h

48 Garstang, Lancashire, SD485475; open-fronted gunhouse for a field gun; to make the structure tenable, it must have been sandbagged around the gun's shield; on the Lancaster Canal, here forming a defence line; Appendix I: 10j

49 Burscough, Lancashire, SD432124; this converted stable block is one of several similar strongpoints, improvised along the Trent and Mersey Canal; NB loopholes at two levels

The protected entrance was in the re-entrant angle. At nearby Breamore there is a pillbox built into the watermill which is further protected by two Type 26 pillboxes. The Leeds–Liverpool Canal, which runs around Ormskirk, and across the top of Burscough airfield is defended by several pillboxes, but mainly by the fortification of existing buildings. There are barns, houses, stables and public houses *(49)*. At least one of the barns has had platforms built inside to give access to prefabricated loopholes inserted high up in the walls. It also has a low-level strongpoint to cover the ground-level approach. Other buildings, mainly covering crossing-points have had windows blocked and loopholes inserted. There is at least one double-decker pillbox, and another similar structure built into the end wall of a house, now a public house. Waterways clearly made instant AT-ditches and were made more formidable in a variety of ways. Possibly the simplest approach was adopted in the fen country, west of the Great Ouse. Here can be seen half-a-dozen instances where spigot mortars have been sited to command crossing points. Some of these positions are provided with explosives stores, in order to keep the weapons dry until the time they might be needed. As we descend the heirarchy of defence lines, the constructions appear to become more and more *ad hoc*, and less and less governed by central direction. The policy might have been determined at national level, but the practice appears to have been very much a matter of local enterprise and initiative.

3

THE DEFENCE OF
VULNERABLE POINTS

Throughout the medieval and early modern periods, Britain was fortunate to be spared the almost continuous state of warfare to which much of Europe was subjected. The Wars of the Roses were characterised by occasional, momentous set-piece battles, and Henry Vll actively discouraged his subjects from fortifying their houses. State-sponsored fortifications from the time of Henry Vlll onwards were confined to the coasts. While the nature of the English Civil Wars forced an emphasis on the winning and retention of territory, evident in the large number of sieges, and the high incidence of garrisoned strongpoints, most towns had found their defences long-abandoned or neglected. Similarly the gentry on both sides found it difficult to put their houses on a war footing. Those fortifications erected against the threat of Napoleonic invasion mirrored the earlier Tudor examples, and covered merely the likely invasion coasts. The massive fortifications built by the Royal Commission of 1859, and dubbed in hindsight Palmerston's Follies, were likewise, largely designed to protect naval bases and their approaches. As we have seen in earlier chapters, fixed defences during the First World War were almost exclusively confined to ports and invasion beaches. Thus, there was an element of culture shock in 1940, when a nation, not used to external threats, felt it necessary to defend its very homes against attack from both sea and air.

We have already seen how the coasts, the likely invasion routes and the airfields were to be defended in the Second World War, but these left a whole range of other targets potentially defenceless. The expressive term designated for these was 'Vulnerable Points', and these included everything from towns and villages, identified as Nodal Points, through munitions factories and stores, to isolated searchlight sites.

From late in 1940, the essentially linear defences hurriedly thrown up throughout the summer, were gradually transformed into Defended Localities (DLs), based on locations identified as Nodal Points. The defining element of the DL, present whether it was a rural crossroads, or a city the size of Worcester, was an all-round defence capability. By 1941, formal Defence Plans were drawn up to define the objectives of the defending forces; the resources available in terms of troops and weaponry; systems of command, communications and control; and the protocols governing the plans' operation. The perimeter of a DL often defined itself given the existence of dominant geographical features, the extent of built-up areas, or specific targets to be included. In exceptional cases, this was impossible. The layout of the Medway towns, for instance, necessitated a network of discrete, but inter-related DLs, governed by a common Defence Plan, but capable of acting in isolation. Similarly, the sheer size of Leeds, meant that at least three Home Guard battalions were involved, totalling some 30 companies. Again, a web of DLs was created, working independently but coordinated by Headquarters 8 West Riding Battalion Home Guard based in the Leeds United football ground at Elland Road. On the other hand, although extensive enough to warrant a north–south boundary between its two Home Guard battalions, Derby, nevertheless had a very clearly-defined perimeter. By 1941, the responsibility for implementing such Defence Plans in the event of enemy invasion, lay almost exclusively with Home Guard units. The resident cadre of the depot of the Northamptonshire Regiment, for example, handed over responsibility for the defence of Northampton to Northamptonshire Home Guard's 12 Battalion. in August 1941. By 1943, Glasgow was defended by twelve battalions of Home Guards, with their headquarters at Park Circus Place. Long lists of DLs, roadblocks and flame-traps testify to the thoroughness of their preparations. Where there were also regular units present, separate areas of responsibility were clearly demarcated. Gainsborough, for instance, appears to have been defended by regular troops, but the stretches of the River Trent either side, were the responsibility of the home guardsmen of the Trent River Patrol. Cambridge's circumstances were different again. Its best-equipped Home Guard battalion was composed of undergraduate members of the OTC, training to be commissioned into the regular forces, and, therefore provided with a tank, an armoured car, a lorry, a field gun, and one of each type of mortar, machine-gun etc., a sort of taster pack. The problem came during the vacations, when the cadets went down. The rest of the defence clearly continued to operate as usual, but without benefit of its mobile column. The mobile column was, in fact, a key factor in the effectiveness of such defences, for its deployment enabled individual DLs to be supported without compromising the entire defence by weakening other, neighbouring DLs. In Leeds, the mobile reserve consisted of elements of four companies. Even at platoon level, as the Wellingborough Plan instructs, a third of the strength was always to be held as a mobile reserve for immediate counter-attack in threatened locations.

The major element in the fixed defences as described in all these Defence Plans, appears to have been the roadblock or road-stop as it is sometimes called, and, to a lesser extent, the railblock. In fact, certainly in the cases of Northampton, and of Derby, the roadblocks of the original 1940 defences went on to become the heart of each of the 1941 DLs. Roadblocks consisted of concrete AT blocks, both the massive 6ft by 4ft by 4ft blocks (1.8 x 1.2 x 1.2m), and the smaller, pyramidal pimples. These blocks were placed permanently to funnel traffic into a

50 Nazeing, Essex, TL382053; a typical combination of bent rail, or 'hairpin', and anti-tank block, sealing off a lane

narrowed carriageway, enabling checkpoints to operate when necessary. Often, blocks were fitted with large iron staples, through which thick steel hawsers were threaded, tying the blocks together, and making it impossible for tanks to push their way through. Bridges were sometimes protected by a cats-cradle of steel cables, threaded backwards and forwards through eye-bolts, across the whole length of the bridge. This method was used on ten bridges in Leeds. There were two common methods of preparing the remaining gap for closure. One was the installation of sockets in the ground, into which would be inserted vertical lengths of bent railway line known as hairpins *(50)*. The other was to flank the gap with large, slotted blocks into which could be inserted three or four RSJs horizontally. When the order to close the roadblock was received, it was a matter of honour that the roadblock should not be sealed before as many defending troops, vehicles and supplies had been allowed time to pass through. The corollary, was of course, that neither should closure be cut too fine. To add to the difficulty, there was a stated requirement that closure should not be so permanent as to hinder the movement of counter-attacking forces. It was reckoned that ten minutes was a reasonable time allowance for closing or reopening roadblocks. A whole range of tests was carried out to find the most effective obstacles, their comparative resilience, and the most effective configuration, or, in the case of the cube AT blocks, orientation. It was noted that railway wheels made very effective AT obstacles, and were virtually impervious to enemy fire. Railblocks were similar obstructions of railway lines, and both suffered from the problem of sockets filling with earth or, in the case of rail-blocks, ballast. Covers were provided, as were special tools to remove them.

Much of this policy and practice was based on experience gained in Spain's civil war by members of the International Brigade, in France and the Low Countries by regulars serving with the BEF, and by locals taking part in exercises. In Peterborough, for instance, the defending regular troops were outflanked and humiliated by attacking home guardsmen advancing along the railway track. However loud the regulars' cries of 'Foul!', the lesson was there to be learned, and rail-blocks were henceforth built and manned. The street fighting in Spanish cities threw up all sorts of tricks for defenders to play on enemy tanks, ranging from hanging blankets across the streets on wires, to strewing the road with upturned soup-plates which might or might not be mines. The object was to halt tanks by presenting their drivers with ambiguities and unknowns. Once a tank was halted, then the defenders could put their Molotov cocktails, and sticky bombs, to good effect. The first attempt at training home guardsmen in these techniques was made by ex-International Brigade officers such as Hugh Slater and Tom Wintringham, until Churchill decided that their communist politics disqualified them from having influence over the defenders of their country. The lessons of the Blitzkrieg of May 1940 were of most relevance to tank tacticians, but it was important that everyone understood that tanks, in themselves, were vulnerable to planned defence. Another element of the fixed AT defences was the use of mines, particularly on the approaches to roadblocks. The intention was always to force the tank into paths chosen by the defender, killing-fields where AT weapons, mines, improvised bombs and other fearsome devices might be used. The Chatham garrison, in 1941, was issued with 8,000 mines, many of which were given specified locations, but a significant proportion of whose disposal was left to the defenders' initiative.Flame fougasses were not a particularly modern invention. The eighteenth-century defences of Malta, for instance employed pits filled with stones and scrap metal which could be exploded to shower an attacker with lethal shrapnel. One 1940 version developed this idea with the 'hedge-hopper', a barrel of highly-inflammable liquid propelled into the air where it was exploded to shower the tank with burning petrol or suchlike. Another consisted of perforated pipes along the sides of a road, preferably in a cutting or running between high banks, through which petrol would be forced, spraying the sides of the tank, to be ignited by a defender firing a Verey pistol. All these ideas, and many others were employed, and their refinement encouraged, by the Home Guard and their mentors.

As well as the AT blocks, mines, barbed-wire entanglements, and fougasses, which were designed to halt the enemy's advance, roadblocks were also intended to contribute to the enemy's destruction. Pillboxes, rifle-trenches, spigot mortar pits, and bomb-throwing positions were all, therefore, integral elements of the roadblock. In towns especially, buildings overlooking roadblocks were adapted to

51 Markinch, Fife, NO303011; a loophole in the cemetery wall overlooks a roadblock on the Fife Defence Line

act as strongpoints, by the insertion of loopholes *(51)*, the strengthening of walls, and the construction of sand-bagged firing or observation positions on flat roofs. Many of the weapons used by the Home Guard were far from robust, so they, with their munitions were stored in, often purpose-built, explosives and inflammables stores.

Roadblocks were employed in large numbers. The Chatham Garrison Defence Plan provided for 625, each detailed with location, method used etc. Many of them consisted of two or three AT cylinders blocking off access roads between houses, in order to preserve the integrity of continuous lines of AT obstructions. Leeds had 36 roadblocks, classified into four groups by priority. Derby's 12 major roadblocks each subsequently became the nucleus of a DL. Northampton had two concentric rings of roadblocks, with ten in the outer ring, and 18 in the inner. Peterborough had nine road- or rail-blocks, Aylesbury had six, while Cambridge had 28 road- and 12 rail-blocks. The geography of Lincoln is such that there are open areas on the edge of the city which, if left un-obstructed, would compromise the whole defence system. Here, then, as well as roadblocks, AT walls were constructed to seal off these entry points. Large numbers of small, portable AT cylinders were also stockpiled for use in an emergency. Little, of course, remains to remind us of these immense civil engineering works. Northampton's 750 AT blocks were cleared away as soon as the war ended. The need to restore traffic flow meant that the AT blocks and cylinders on the bridges of York, Nottingham, Maidstone and Edinburgh, for example, disappeared before the end of the war. Only in a very few places, can remnants of these widespread defence works be seen. In Kings Lynn (Norfolk) can be seen up to 20 sockets for hairpin AT rails, astride Broad Walk in front of the town's reconstructed East Gate. Several similar sockets can be seen in Lincoln's Nettleham Road. Also in Lincoln is a stretch of AT wall at the back of the Militia Barracks, now the Museum of Lincolnshire Life. Ipswich retains two concentrations of AT blocks at Henley Road (9 blocks) and Rushmere Heath (40 blocks). Norwich has a line of AT rails at Hellesdon.

Pillboxes and other strongpoints in towns and cities have fared little better in terms of preservation. In the first enthusiasm, or panic, whichever way you look at it, a number of pillboxes were built in prominent locations. That outside St Giles Cathedral in Edinburgh disguised as a florist's, and one, disguised as a council store, in the middle of the approach to London's Chelsea Bridge, for instance, must have

52 Ipswich, Suffolk, TM195402; these two tiny machine-gun posts on the foreshore of the River Orwell form part of the Ipswich defences; each contains a mounting for the gun, consisting of a steel pin embedded in a concrete corbel projecting from the wall

been motivated as much by the need to raise public morale as genuine considerations of defence. Many towns and cities were given perimeter defences which included pillboxes. Leaving aside those on the coast and those on Defence Lines, few retain these structures. Ipswich still has elements of its defences: four Type FW3/22 pillboxes, plus three more on the airfield perimeter; a Type FW3/28a AT blockhouse; and two small, square machine-gun posts on the foreshore of the River Orwell *(52)*. At Northampton, two circular, open pillboxes, apparently adaptations of the Norcon, sewer-pipe type, stand on the bank of the Nene, alongside the old power station. Whereas Chelmsford appears to have been protected only by the GHQ Line skirting its eastern edge, Cambridge was given all-round defences. At least eight pillboxes survive here, including examples of all of the four main types commonly found on the GHQ Line in Eastern Command. Cambridge's AT ditch, which left the River Cam at Shelford and rejoined it north of the A14, can be seen at several places around the city, both to the east and to the west. At other places, such as Norwich, Luton, and Carlisle, only odd, isolated pillboxes may still be seen.

Private houses, converted into strongpoints, are even harder to find on the ground. Examples have been recorded in Ashford (Kent), where two houses commanding a railway bridge were requisitioned and turned into strongpoints. Another house in Finchley (north London), was converted into a strongpoint by the addition of a 9in (23cm) wall on two sides, with embrasures in each, again, covering railway lines. In the Chatham Garrison Defence Plan more than a dozen private houses are listed as being earmarked for conversion into firing positions, by the strengthening of walls and the insertion of loopholes. It would appear that this was quite a common occurrence, but survivals in built-up areas, as opposed to more open countryside, are rare.

One other defensive feature related to the above is the loophole. Here firing positions are usually inserted into brick or stone walls. The only known built features of the Leeds defences are two raised platforms built behind the red-brick walls of Kirkstall Forge *(53)*, and loopholed for riflemen. Each has four loopholes, two facing forward and one in each flanking wall. There are examples of loopholes surviving in built-up areas at Northampton, Cirencester (Gloucestershire), Witney, Islip, Kidlington, Charlbury and Bicester (all in Oxfordshire).

If many of the fieldwork defences were reminiscent of medieval siegeworks, then the terminology used reinforced this. The hub of the defence was 'The Keep', from which the defenders were directed, and where the final stand would be made. Each Defence Plan identified a building or complex of buildings to be so designated. In Cambridge it was the Shire Hall/Castle complex; in Peterborough, the Power Station; in Northampton, the Drill Hall, Police Station and Gibraltar Barracks each fulfilling a number of functions, served as complementary Keeps; in London, whole blocks were designated, one containing the Tower of London and Royal Mint, another embracing much of Whitehall, based on the Admiralty Citadel, and a third in Maida Vale, enfolding the BBC studios.

53 Leeds, West Yorkshire, SE248368; strongpoint at Kirkstall Forge; an open-backed platform has loopholes on three sides

In Derby it was the Becket Street Drill Hall, and in Aylesbury, the Council Offices, with reserves held in the Drill Hall on Oxford Road. Edinburgh's defence was based on three concentric circles of fortifications, its innermost one, still a large area containing the New Town and the Royal Mile, but specifying particular official or industrial locations within that, as strongpoints with dedicated garrisons such as the Railway companies of the Home Guard, centred on Waverley Station. In the larger cities buildings were often loopholed at high level. Pillboxes were built on roof-tops and street corners, roadblocks sealed off access, and doors were sandbagged and provided with loopholed sentry posts. In London, the under-ground railway tunnels were utilised as shelters, secure barracks, and, if it came to it, safe ways of moving troops around to threatened areas. The Admiralty Citadel *(54)*, a massive concrete block still standing on the north side of Horseguards Parade retains its machine-gun embrasures and platforms for AA guns. Other government offices, notably the Cabinet War Rooms were buried underground beneath 3ft (0.8m) of concrete over a steel frame. In the event of London becoming too dangerous for Government to continue operating, three emergency citadels were prepared for the dispersal of government departments to the suburbs. They were at Cricklewood, Wealdstone and Dollis Hill, each built in the grounds of existing government establishments and designed to withstand direct hits by bombs up to 500lbs. (230kgs). Several Underground stations used by the military, such as Eisenhower's COSSAC headquarters in Goodge Street, were rendered defensible by fortifying the entrance, or creating firing positions on the roof.

In all these DLs, the Home Guard relied very much for its firepower on sub-artillery such as the Blacker Bombard/spigot mortar, and the Smith Gun. Spigot mortars were produced from 1941 on in very large numbers. Cambridge's defenders were equipped with 92 of them, the Chatham garrison had 111. The normal deployment of a spigot mortar was in a brick-lined pit with ready-use bomb lockers built into the sides. In the centre stood the concrete cylinder, about 4ft (1.2m) high, and 2ft (0.6m) in diameter, with the characteristic stainless steel pintle, on its framework of steel bars, the spider, embedded in the domed top of the pedestal. In parts of Suffolk the pedestal was often hexagonal, and square ones have been recorded in Dover and at Pershore Bridge (Worcestershire). There are some very makeshift pedestals in Snowdonia, at least one of which has a timber pintle. Fred Nash excavated a pit in St Albans and found it to be hexagonal, apparently similar to the emplacements, open to the air, built on the GHQ Line (Red) in Oxfordshire, for 6-pounder Hotchkiss QF guns. The spigot mortar pit was for

54 London, Horseguards Parade; The Blues and Royals on their way to change the guard, passing the Admiralty Citadel with its concrete towers, gun positions and loopholes

the protection of the crew, and, in several places along the Eastern Command Line near Thetford and Brandon, because the water table is so high, and there is a permanent risk of flooding, the pedestal is enclosed by above-ground walls. Some pedestals were free-standing, as under the railway viaduct at Wakes Colne (Essex), or on the beach at Holme-next-the-Sea (Norfolk). Former Home Guards at Ramsey (Huntingdonshire), tell the story of the training day they attended, when not one hit was recorded, until the very last man to fire, having spent all day killing time in the pub, blasted the target to bits with his first shot. The ensuing congratulations left him completely bewildered, as he had not been aware that there was a target. It may, therefore, be more than coincidence that a number of spigot mortars were actually located outside public houses, as at Saffron Walden (Essex) and Long Melford (Suffolk). Another spigot mortar pit, with two lockers, has been excavated by Robert Alsos, in his front garden at Wendens Ambo (Essex) *(55)*. As well as the prepared position, two of which were required for each mortar, there was a field mounting which made the weapon more portable. Most of the Chatham spigot mortars were provided with fixed mountings, but, although there are dozens of such pedestals throughout the eastern counties, not one has ever been recorded within the area of the Cambridge Defended Place, where a large number of them might be expected. Chatham Garrison also had 38 Smith Guns, two 12-pounders, 17 of various types of 6-pounder and three 3-pounders. At

55 Wendens Ambo, Essex, TL515365; a beautifully excavated spigot mortar position, this one with two lockers; it commanded the approaches to the railway station, quite close behind the rearmost positions of the GHQ Line; Appendix I: 15biii

56 Guiseley, West Yorkshire; behind the Drill Hall in Victoria Road are a pair of Explosives and Inflammables stores, built to accommodate Home Guard weapons such as the spigot mortar, and ammunition including the ingredients for Molotov cocktails; some were adapted to house Smith guns

Leeds and at Wellingborough the sub-artillery available was limited mainly to Northover Projectors which fired petrol bombs or phosphorus grenades.

The Home Guard was required to keep all but personal weapons, and other munitions in specially-built stores. Ideally, two, brick stores were built side-by-side, one for explosives and the other for inflammables. However, often the reality was different, and the Instruction (No. 1419, 1941) allows alternative arrangements, providing the two categories are separated by a 9in (23cm) brick wall, or by a sandbag wall at least 1ft (30cm) thick. Thus brick-built stores may be found divided internally into several compartments, as can Nissen huts divided by a central cross-wall. In many areas, but particularly in the eastern counties a building very similar to the standard ARP Wardens' Post was used. Pairs of these structures can be seen behind the Drill Halls at Oundle (Northants), Loddon (Norfolk), Luton, Guiseley (West Yorkshire) *(56)*, and at Norwich railway station. Dozens of individual examples remain, many on Defence Lines adjacent to spigot mortar positions. In other areas there exist other standard local designs. Lincolnshire retains half-a-dozen examples of a store with a low, gabled roof. Nottinghamshire has a different design again. A number of examples on the GHQ Line in the Fens are internally divided into up to eight separate compartments. At Drayton (Norfolk) the Home Guard kept their Smith Gun in the store, and it has been suggested that one of the stores behind Oundle Drill Hall has been adapted, by the addition of a wider steel door, to accommodate a Smith Gun.

Many villages also had Defence Plans put together no less conscientiously if on a smaller scale. The Home Guard Defence Plans of a group of villages around Newark (Nottinghamshire) have survived to demonstrate the level of planning. Maps show exactly where roadblocks, rifle trenches, bomb-posts were located. The directions and fields of fire of Lewis Guns and Northover Projectors are marked, as are the numbers of riflemen manning each position. Garrisons were small, ranging from 65 men at Coddington and 75 at Kelham and Caunton, to 24 at Upper Broughton, and just 20 men at Colston Bassett. The headquarters and Stores is often in the pub: the Turks Head at Balderton, or the White Post Inn at Farnsfield. At Hickling, the tower, rebuilt in 1873, of the fourteenth-century St Mary's church housed an observation post. Only at Winthorpe is a pillbox included, and that was actually part of the perimeter defences of the neighbouring RAF airfield. Thus, everything was improvised, making little impact on the landscape, and, once the threat was past, it all returned to normal.

Defended Localities were not confined to built up areas, as many rural cross-roads qualified for defences. A typical example survives at Stradsett (Norfolk). Here, two Type FW3/22 pillboxes stand in two quadrants of the crossing, whilst a spigot mortar pedestal occupies a third. There were originally four spigot mortars here, and a second survives in the form of the unmounted spider, free of any pedestal. The foundations of what appears to be a Nissen hut with a brick cross-wall, also remains, which would be in keeping with the need for a secure and weather-proof store to hold the mortars and their ammunition.

Most rural road junctions received a much lower level of attention. Sometimes a single, unsupported pillbox is seen as sufficient, as at a number of sites around Keith, Dufftown and Tarland (Aberdeenshire). At a crossroads in Hexton, near Hitchin (Hertfordshire), things are very basic. A brick has been removed from a wall to create a rudimentary loophole, and a concrete box is provided as a weapons store. Opposite the T-junction in Newton Blossomville (Buckinghamshire), a stone wall has been raised in order to insert a loophole, clearly drawing attention to itself. Loopholes in a wall at Lyminster (West Sussex) are at two levels for riflemen either standing or prone. A (blocked) loophole in a low wall in the fork of the road at Britwell Salome (Oxfordshire) can have given very little cover to the home guardsman manning it. Where the terrain limits the number of roads and confines them to narrow passes, nature aids the defence process. Two sites in Snowdonia illustrate this particularly effectively. South of Dolgellau, beneath the eastern slopes of Cader Idris, the A487 road is straddled by a line of AT blocks, built of the local rock and hardly perceptible against the backdrop of the mountainside. Farther north, where the roads from Beddgelert and Llanberis meet on their way to Capel Curig, the junction is defended by four pillboxes. Each has been faced in local stone, so as to blend into the hillside. Two are entered by dog-legged passages. At least one is a conventionally-built hexagonal pillbox with brick anti-ricochet wall, concrete prefabricated loopholes, and poured concrete walls, but it is entirely transformed by its outer skin of rock.

57 Duxford, Cambridgeshire; restored Allan-Williams turret at Imperial War Museum; other related exhibits include a Smith gun, a 6-pounder Hotchkiss QF gun, and a spigot mortar; Appendix I: 12c

In the desperate days of autumn 1940, when invasion was expected daily, such establishments as army headquarters, particularly those controlling the defence of stretches of vulnerable coastline, were seen as the likely target of paratroops. In Norfolk, all the unit headquarters, many of them in country houses, were given Allan-Williams turrets *(57)*. This was a steel rotating dome, mounted over a pit, and entered by a short tunnel, manned by two men. Opening or sliding shutters in front and roof enabled a light machine-gun to be mounted as either a LAA weapon, or against an attack at ground-level. Also deployed in this situation was the Norcon pillbox, a loopholed concrete pipe *(58)*. At Brackenborough Hall, near Louth (Lincolnshire) the perimeter of the site was defended by weapons pits, but at the centre, possibly representing a command post, are three rectangular loopholed blockhouses. Two are linked under a common roof, whilst the third stands separately. At Kirkleatham, near Redcar on Tees-side the eighteenth-century Turners Hospital was the headquarters of a battalion of Green Howards. In addition to an outer line of conventional pillboxes, the churchyard wall, and the wings of the almshouses themselves are furnished with gothic bastions, and these, too, have been converted into strongpoints with loopholes.

Early in the Second World War, searchlight sites were permanent structures and as such were felt to merit fixed defences. In June and July 1940, Operational

58 Witney, Oxfordshire, SP362097; Norcon pillbox, one of two defending the approach into town; by Earley's blanket factory on Mill Street at SP355103, are loopholes cut in a side wall; Appendix I: 11g

59 North Luffenham, Rutland, SK941055; Type FW3/22 pillbox on the airfield perimeter, but clearly built to protect one of a string of searchlight sites; Appendix I: 1a

Orders issued by 40 and 41 AA Brigades, stationed across East Anglia, included instructions to construct a pillbox, of brick or concrete, depending on whatever building materials were available, on every searchlight site. Each site was then to be surrounded by Dannert wire, rifle trenches etc. and, liaising with the (then) LDV, and the regular Field Force, integrated into the general scheme of anti-invasion defences. Pillboxes were almost invariably the simple Type FW3/22. This procedure explains the isolated positions of many pillboxes, and goes some way toward exploding one of the myths, that they were plonked down anywhere, regardless of defensive viability. Many such existing sites can now be explained, lists of former searchlight sites can be used to trace hitherto unrecorded pillboxes, and patterns of pillbox sites, once regarded as lacking a rationale, can now be used to infer searchlight deployment *(59)*. Several strings of sites, usually at three mile (5km) intervals across the East Midlands, defending the Corby steelworks and the concentrated industrial centres of Nottingham, Derby and Leicester, have been plotted in this way. Since the pillbox was the only permanent building on the site, that is all that remains, apart, maybe, from some circles on the ground, only discernible through aerial photography, and often misinterpreted as barrows. Although this requirement only obtained for the second half of 1940, there are dozens of sites, the length of Britain, where solitary pillboxes explain the previous existence of searchlight sites.

Factories, public utilities and transport networks could receive protection at two levels. Most major employers encouraged the formation of Home Guard companies recruited from their workforce, and committed to defending their workplace whether it be factory, warehouse, railway depot, or waterworks. Owing to the importance of their output, or the reliance placed on them by the community for the continuance of normal life, many of these locations would have been classified as Vulnerable or Vital Points, in any case. It made sense for those who knew their workings, weak points and layouts best, to be responsible for guarding them against sabotage, or full-scale attack. Eventually these independent companies were integrated into the mainstream Home Guard battalions, often tasked with guarding those same targets, but giving commanders more flexibility of organisation and deployment.

Some factories, however, warranted permanent fixed defences. Royal Ordnance Factories, in particular, were defended by pillboxes. At Glascoed (Gwent), Enfield Lock (Greater London) and Norton Fitzwarren (Somerset) are examples of a version of the Type FW3/24 (thin-walled) built on a thick, concrete plinth, thus raising the exterior wall-height up to 12ft (3.6m). At Steeton (West Yorkshire) is a two-storey pillbox with seven loopholes only at the upper level. Much more common is a square design with four wide letter-box loopholes, and a low entrance behind a half-height blast wall *(60)*. These can be seen at Rotherwas (Herefordshire), Willaston (Wirral), Creekmoor (Dorset), Steventon (Oxfordshire), Purfleet (Essex) and Puriton (Somerset). They are also present at an evacuated government office site in Droitwich (Worcestershire), and at the RAE

60 Steeton, West Yorkshire, SE033447; standard guard post for a Royal Ordnance Factory; nearby is a hexagonal pillbox of two storeys; Appendix I: 6y

Farnborough (Hampshire). Willaston retains one of its related, loopholed gate-houses. A further development of this type with an open, upper level reached by external ladder, and most probably mounting a LAA gun, is found at Norton Fitzwarren (Somerset) *(61)*, and a very slightly different version at Summerfield (Worcestershire). Rectangular pillboxes with porches, and in some instances, pairs joined together as doubles, remain at Wrexham *(62)*, and at Puriton (Somerset). At Wrexham can also be seen hexagonal pillboxes with open rear annexes, and other loopholed buildings. At Swynnerton (Staffordshire) are guardposts with half-hexagonal fronts, and protected entrances. The ordnance depot at Priddy's Hard (Hampshire), and the mines depot at Milford Haven (Pembrokeshire) have the small L-shaped guardposts, and T-shaped pillbox/LAA emplacements, found at many other naval establishments. Both Summerfield (Worcestershire) and Elstow (Bedfordshire) have elevated watch-posts, octagonal at Summerfield, and square at Elstow, both standing at second storey level. At Pontrilas (Herefordshire) there are loopholed walls and other one-off defensive structures. It would appear that in this area of factory defence as in others, we find a widely-used, small range of standard designs, with adaptations, modifications, and improvisations, adopted for partic-ular circumstances or functions. The Chattenden RE armaments depot in Kent, retains two most unusual 11-sided, domed, concrete pillboxes, little more than 10ft (3m) in diameter, with a low, hinged, concrete door in one face, and loopholes in

61 Norton Fitzwarren, Somerset, ST201258; guardposts at this army camp turned REME depot, have loopholes at ground level, and an open deck above for light anti-aircraft machine-guns; the upper level is reached by an external fixed ladder; Appendix I: 6yiii

62 Wrexham, Denbighshire, SJ381483; a double blockhouse seen at several Royal Ordnance Factories; each chamber is loopholed, and a covered porch connects the two; Appendix I: 6r

five other faces *(63)*. It was not only ROFs which were fortified. An example of a'civilian' plant having built-in fortifications, is Fort Dunlop (Birmingham), where the massive, seven-storey block, now converted to residential apartments, had pillboxes and LAA gun positions added to its roof. Many other such factories had small, square, brick cabins built on their roofs, serving the dual purposes of fire-watching post and close-defence pillbox. There are examples in Derby, Northampton and, reportedly, in east London. In Birmingham there is a cylindrical tower on the corner of industrial premises (probably a small engineering works) between Bournville and Kings Norton, alongside the Worcester and Birmingham Canal. It is shaped like a factory chimney, but with loopholes cut in the lowest section, to command the canal and the road bridge carrying the Redditch road into Birmingham. At Bridgend (Glamorgan), probably connected with the defences of the two ordnance factories here, is a very unusual pillbox. At first glance it appears to be a standard hexagonal pillbox raised up on a platform. In fact it is a three-decker construction with loopholes at three levels. There are doors on each of the higher levels, which must have been reached by ladder. It consists, therefore, of three pillboxes piled on top of each other.

Had all these defences failed in their aim of containing the invader prior to his speedy expulsion, then the last phase of the nation's defence plan would have been implemented. The Auxiliary Units were composed of small groups of home guardsmen, training undercover, and in isolation as units. Their task would have been to disrupt an enemy occupation by sabotage, assassination, and other acts of clandestine and guerrilla warfare. They were armed to the teeth with weapons and explosives, and based in Operational Bases (OB) or hides, literally hidden in the woods and entered through counter-balanced treestumps, concealed trapdoors and the like. These OBs consisted of a sunken chamber, akin to a buried Nissen hut with a main entrance down a shaft, and a further bolt-hole, usually emerging some way in the opposite direction from the entrance. End walls were of brick. Auxiliary units were usually based within 50 miles (80km) of the coast, but there were units around the Worcestershire area as well. They tended to be rural, although at least one OB is known in a town. Inside each OB were bunks, food and water storage, weapons racks, and storage for ammunition and explosives, in a separate compartment. Lucky auxiliaries, also had a separate compartment for their chemical toilet and washing facilities. The width of the main compartment was about 10ft (3m), and there was 8ft (2.4m) headroom. Length depended on how many sections of corrugated iron panels were used, but the average OB was probably around 20ft (6m) long. Ventilation was through a pipe in the roof, through the earth covering and capped with a chicken-wire filter, and camouflaged. The escape tunnel was about 20ft (6m) long and made of 2ft (60cm) diameter sewer pipe. Auxiliary units or patrols usually consisted of five to eight men. There were also hidden radios, known as Zero Stations for communicating between the patrols and headquarters. The actual existence of the organisation, let alone membership was a closely guarded secret, so family members were not even

63 Chattenden, Kent, TQ757728; guard post for the Royal Engineers' depot, but almost on the GHQ Line which crosses the Hoo Peninsula at this point; domed, 11-sided, and with thick concrete door; it has a First World War look about it

aware that their husbands, sons, uncles or brothers were members. Only recently has much of this emerged, along with the locations of OBs and Zero Stations. Many of these remain, but in sad states of decomposition. A practice OB in the grounds of Coleshill House (Berkshire), the Auxiliary Units' training centre, survives in good condition. Although the house has gone, the outbuildings still stand, and include stores for arms and explosives.

4

THE DEFENCE OF AIRFIELDS

The evolving military airfield of the First World War met needs as they arose. The whole notion of flight itself, let alone flight as a way of waging war, was so new that there was no orthodoxy. Improvisation was the rule. Neither camouflage, nor active airfield defence figured in the official priorities. In fact, flyers welcomed the bright liveries of their requisitioned commercial support vehicles, which enabled them to recognise their landing grounds, on their return from sorties over the Western Front. At home, guards were mounted to prevent sabotage or espionage attempts, but fixed defences were not deemed necessary. Only on the East Coast, might airfields such as Aldeburgh (Suffolk) or Bircham Newton (Norfolk), be protected incidentally by the anti-invasion defences close by.

The development of the RAF and its new bases in the interwar years were geared to providing security for the Bomber force which represented a deterrent against enemy aggression. The only perceived danger was the pre-emptive strike, and a policy of dispersal was adopted. Neither aircraft, materiel nor personnel would be allowed to become concentrated together. Aircraft storage, bomb dumps and living quarters were spread over large areas. Whole units could be moved to satellite airfields such as Alconbury, serving Wyton (Cambridgeshire). The most active step for the defence of airfields was the suggested provision of AA guns, but shortages, and competing priorities, meant that at the outbreak of war in 1939, very few guns had been emplaced. Hardly a third of the HAA guns deemed the minimum number necessary for the defence of Britain, were in service. The regimental diaries of AA units throughout the summer of 1940 reveal a constant juggling of scarce resources to defend East Anglia's bomber bases. In January 1940, two pairs of old 3in, 20 cwt guns were diverted from Derby, to defend Duxford and Marham, thus supplementing the few modern 3.7in guns scattered amongst Watton, Feltwell and Debden as well. Only a very few 40mm Bofors LAA guns were available, and a heavy reliance was consequently placed on a miscellany of mainly obsolete light machine-guns. The lack of conventional AA guns meant that alternative weapons had to be extemporised. In the famous attack on Kenley (Surrey), on 18 August 1940, a rocket-driven Parachute-and-Cable barrage brought down at least one of the attacking Dorniers.

In early summer 1940, two compelling probabilities came together to convince the RAF that much needed doing in a very short space of time, in order to safeguard the security of airfields. It had been observed how effective an element of *Blitzkrieg* the airborne dimension was. In Norway and in Holland, aerial bombardment had preceded parachute drops and the air-landing of assault troops with light armour and artillery. In many cases, airfields were the specific targets. Not only were the defending aircraft destroyed, but a ready-made platform for reinforcements was secured. A glider-borne force which landed on the flat and grassy roof of Fort Eben Emael had enabled the defences of Belgium to be uncoupled overnight. None of these shattering events had been foreseen by the planners of the Expansion Period airfields, but England could now expect a similar attack. The second probability became almost a certainty after the disaster at Dunkirk. The expectation of an imminent German invasion of mainland Britain was unavoidable. All RAF Station Commanders were instructed to organise the defence of their airfields using any available means, and Major General Taylor, Inspector General of Fortifications at the War Office was charged with preparing a grand plan for airfield defence.

In the meantime, improvisation continued. Construction centred mainly around fieldworks, trenches for riflemen, and sandbagged positions for Lewis guns which would take on aircraft and ground targets. The few heavier AA guns were also sited to double in the AT role. Flat-bed lorries had double-skinned, wooden boxes, open to the sky, built on them. The cavities were filled with shingle, and Lewis guns on AA mountings fitted. These improvised armoured cars, known as Armadilloes, and, crewed by whoever had nothing else pressing to do at the time, were used to patrol the perimeter track. One possibly useful design came from a Kent construction company seeking government contracts. This was the disappearing pillbox, later, the Pickett-Hamilton fort, specifically designed to engage enemy aircraft seeking to land on RAF airfields. In order to avoid impeding everyday operations, its roof lay flush with the ground. When needed to engage the enemy, the inner of two concentric concrete cylinders, loopholed for firing a light machine-gun, was raised to a height of 2ft 6in (75cm) above ground level, by a pneumatic system using compressed air in bottles. Its crew of two could now fire on the enemy. The New Kent Construction Company of Ashford produced two prototypes for installation at Langley (Hertfordshire), and was duly given a contract to produce 300. Eventually, nearly 350 of these forts were installed, usually three to an airfield. They were allocated to those airfields identified as Class 1 priority in Taylor's report, which appeared in September 1940. They also enjoyed the afterglow of Prime Minister Churchill's approval, and this may have tipped the balance, as it was evident that there were distinct drawbacks to their use. Mechanical rams or jacks, whether hydraulic or pneumatic, were subject to unpredictable failure. It may be significant that Paul Francis has recently discovered a modified version at Middle Wallop (Hampshire), where a manual lifting mechanism not only raised the inner cylinder about 10in (25cm) above ground level, but could also rotate it. The loopholes in the Pickett-Hamilton were replaced by an observation slit, and a possible weapon-mounting operated through a larger hatch. No doubt the surprise element of the disappearing pillbox may have given it an initial advantage, but the inherent operational difficulties might well have proved unsurmountable. A number of examples still exist, and claims have been made that those uncovered in the 1970s at Usworth (Tyne and Wear), and Silloth (Cumbria), remained in full working order. Disembodied inner sleeves can be seen at Llandow (Glamorgan), North Weald (Essex), Tangmere (West Sussex), and Sutton Bridge (Lincolnshire). At Thorpe Abbots (Norfolk) the apron and entrance-hatch are visible, and a static, raised example from Portsmouth (Hampshire), has been reset in front of the city's D-Day Museum.

The Taylor Report laid out a plan for the defence of airfields based on location rather than function. The only exception to this was the inclusion of all Aircraft Storage Units (ASUs) regardless of location. Otherwise, the level of priority given to an airfield was determined by where it was, not what it did. The first criterion for inclusion in Class l was the airfield's proximity (i.e. within 20 miles/32km) to one of 93 specified ports, Thurso to Teignmouth, and Lowestoft to Lytham. If an airfield was considered important in the counter-attack role but was not near one of these ports, then it came into Class IIa. Next, came airfields 5 miles (8km) from Vulnerable Points (VPs) inland, Class llb; then the ASUs, Class llc; with the rest as Class lll. The basic strategy would appear to be one of denying the enemy the airfields on which troops might be landed, in order to sieze ports where stores, heavy weapons and reinforcements might be disembarked. The vulnerability of the ASUs as the last step in the manufacture and supply of replacement aircraft was a separate issue. Whilst there were inevitable anomalies, this scheme offered an immediate solution to the problem of allocating scant resources.

Taylor prescribed the numbers of defence works needed for each class of airfield. The tactical understanding at the time was that any attack would begin with bombing and strafing of the perimeter defences, followed by parachute drops outside the perimeter to capture the flying field intact, for the landing of transport aircraft carrying reinforcements, heavy equipment and stores. Defences needed, therefore, to face both outwards to repel ground attack, and inwards to prevent enemy aircraft landing. Dual-purpose AA and ground defence weapons were to be integrated into this scheme. Class l airfields, it was proposed, dependent on the length of perimeter, should be given 12-18 pillboxes for outward defence, 8-14 for inward, 3 Pickett-Hamilton forts, and a melange of dummy positions, Armadillos, rifle pits, and wire obstructions. Classes ll and lll had similar types of provision but in proportionately fewer numbers. Dedicated garrisons ranged in numbers from 300 men on a Class l airfield, to 200 men on a Class lll one. It was always assumed that ground-crew and other station personnel would man rifle pits around the station buildings in an emergency.

This, then, was the theory, but the lack of personnel with relevant experience created a problem. Superannuated army officers or meteorological clerks surplus to requirement did not necessarily produce effective station defence officers, even after a whole fortnight's training. Many defence works were badly sited, or lacked a tactical framework. The shortage of machine-guns also reduced the effect of these defences. From the evidence on the ground, it would appear that all sorts of compromises were adopted, in order to implement at least, the spirit of the scheme.

Weston-super-Mare (Somerset) was a Class 1 airfield, combining aircraft production with elementary flying training, and the provision of some flying services for the adjacent School of Technical Training at Locking. The airfield still retains ten pillboxes in pairs and trios around its perimeter. Three designs of pillbox are represented, mixed up in the groups. These designs are similar to those used in the anti-invasion Stop-Lines, but with local modifications. One design is almost identical to the thin-walled FW3 Type 24. Two of the three examples here face into the landing field, whilst the other faces out. Another design is similar to the FW3 Type 22, but has a tunnel entry which allows a sixth LMG loop, thus giving 360° capability. It is also slightly larger with 9ft (2.7m) walls. Cantilevered anti-ricochet walls give increased floor space. Unlike many Air Ministry (AM) designs, the walls are only bulletproof, but a roof of greater than normal thickness may go some way toward compensating for this. The third design may be derived from the rectangular Vickers machine-gun emplacement to be found in significant numbers on the Taunton Stop Line. This includes a concrete table under the main embrasure, a vent to allow fumes to escape, a doorway protected by a blast wall, and additional loopholes for rifles. All three examples here face inwards. In addition, there are a couple of shelters which may have doubled as defence posts. At least one further pillbox is known to have been demolished, as has a three-storey tower which carried a Bofors 40mm LAA gun. This site appears well-defended, but the numbers of structures still falls well short of Taylor's prescription. The grouping of pillboxes is an interesting concept. Later in the war, this was to become normal, but Taylor was worried about lucky bomb strikes taking out numbers of defence works in one go. Wellingore (Lincolnshire), a Class lla fighter satellite airfield, appears to have a more conventional defence plan. Here, the perimeter is ringed by a combination of Type 22 pillboxes with Scarff mountings for Lewis guns, and fighter dispersal shelters, loopholed for riflemen. The whole was later to be controlled from a Battle headquarters (BHQ) built to a design of 1941. A number of Class lll airfields, High Post, Old Sarum, and Yatesbury (Wiltshire), Barkston Heath (Lincolnshire) and Sibson (Cambridgeshire) retain one or two Type 22 pillboxes, which may represent their original defences. Several Class lll airfields, Cardington, Cranfield, and Henlow (Bedfordshire), for instance, have a quite distinctly different model of pillbox, which could suggest a re-fortification later in the war, or a more individualistic, and local approach to pillbox design. Here, the familiar hexagonal pillbox has been given an open, square annexe containing the mounting for a LAA gun.

It was necessary to co-ordinate the defence of any airfield under ground attack from a dedicated BHQ. In 1941 the Air Ministry issued a standard design,

64 Merston, West Sussex, SU891027; standard pattern Type 11008/41 airfield Battle Headquarters; Appendix I: 13b

11008/41 for use on any class of airfield *(64)*. This consisted of a domed, concrete observation cupola with underground office, PBX, and minimal accommodation. It had an entrance at one end with stairs down, and a hatch with vertical ladder next to the cupola at the other end. Dozens of these standard structures remain, on sites closely overlooking their landing fields, for example Cark (Lancashire), and Fraserburgh (Grampian). There also remain a number with local modifications. At Ibsley (Hampshire) there are two cupolas; at Goxhill (Lincolnshire) the cupola was raised when the USAAF took over the airfield; at Little Staughton (Cambridgeshire) an extra floor is inserted in the cupola. At Bottisham (Cambridgeshire), a standard BHQ was, according to the Air Ministry plan, disguised as an E-shaped dispersal pen on the airfield perimeter. It does seem odd, though, to disguise one target as another. Perhaps a derelict agricultural building would have provided more protection. There are also a number of entirely non-standard BHQs. Luton (Bedfordshire) has a small hexagonal cupola on the corner of an L-shaped shelter-like structure *(65)*; Waterbeach (Cambridgeshire) has a similar cupola, but on a Stanton shelter; Bicester (Oxfordshire), Windrush (Gloucestershire) Montrose (Tayside) and Lichfield (Staffordshire) all have pillboxes for this purpose, in the first two cases, adjacent to the Watch Office; Redhill (Surrey) has an underground shelter with a hexagonal pillbox on top. So long as it did the job, it would appear not to have mattered too much what it looked like. An L-shaped run of Stanton shelters at Chipping Warden (Northamptonshire) has been put forward by Adrian Armishaw as a candidate

65 Luton, Bedfordshire, TL126222; one-off BHQ; NB small, hexagonal observation cupola on the angle nearest to the flying area; Appendix I: 13d

for BHQ. It has been suggested by Graham Buchan Innes, that another design of surface BHQ, 3329/41, was replaced by the 11008/41, and often, subsequently, converted to a PBX. Examples of both these buildings can still be seen at Kingscliffe (Northamptonshire) and Peterhead (Grampian). One of Taylor's recommendations was that the outer ring of defences might make use of existing structures by converting them into strongpoints. At Sywell (Northamptonshire) a field barn, only recently (2002) demolished, had been converted into the BHQ by loopholing the gables, and by inserting a bombproof cabin at ground-floor level. One of the design criteria for BHQs was the balance between achieving good visibility over the flying field for the defenders, and the need to remain undetected by the attackers. This makes the BHQ, to drawing TG/1, at Hucknall (Nottinghamshire) particularly unusual in its form as a slender, four-storey tower. One other anomaly must be mentioned here. At Goxhill as well as the modified BHQ, or Emergency Control Bunker to the USAAF, there are two surviving examples of a related structure. Here, the cupola of a standard BHQ has been tacked onto the end of a Stanton shelter and labelled as 'observation post' on the Air Ministry site plan. Something very similar was done at Penrhos (Gwynedd). It would appear that at least one other standard BHQ existed, for, according to their official site plans, both Docking and Horsham St Faith (Norfolk) were given 11747/41 models. Unfortunately, both have been destroyed, and no drawing survives at Hendon. The class of BHQ illustrates well, the situation where an orthodox, standard design, or designs, existed, but within a system which did not preclude local initiative or eccentricity. Many surviving BHQs are flooded and dangerous, but that at Wellesbourne Mountford (Warwickshire) has been opened up to house the airfield museum.

The formation of the RAF Regiment in 1942, specifically charged with the defence of airfields, marked a move forward in the theory and practice in this field. Whilst the threat of a general invasion was now more remote, this was not yet recognised. The capture of Crete, largely achieved by the assault on Allied airfields by German paratroops, had reinforced fears regarding the vulnerability of home airfields to such an attack. Again, it could not be known that the unacceptable level of casualties, sustained by the parachute troops of the Luftwaffe had prompted the German High Command to forbid any such future operations. New orders, issued in January 1942, reflecting earlier shifts in emphasis in the Home Army, particularly evident in cities' Defence Plans, moved tactics away from static, fixed defences, to mobile strike-forces. Thus the perimeter defences of the Taylor era, were replaced by a web of defended localities (DLs) manned by troops, trained and equipped to counter-attack the enemy. Station personnel would continue to man some static defences, but the new specialists of the RAF Regiment would operate as first-line infantry, led by officers and NCOs trained at the Infantry Depots by veterans of the Guards.

It is worth noting here that, quite late in the war, airfield defence was still of great concern to military planners. In 1940, a group of railway designers, including the LNER's Sir Nigel Gresley, designer of the *Mallard*, had been brought together at King's Cross Station, to explore the possibility of building a fleet of armoured trains to operate as part of the East Coast anti-invasion defences. Ultimately, around a dozen of these trains were put together and regularly patrolled, on beats between East Anglia and north-east Scotland. Each was armed with two 6-pounder Hotchkiss guns, and carried a platoon of infantry with automatic weapons in armoured trucks. In January 1943, the C-in-C Scotland, pointing out the proximity of a number of airfields to the railway lines which ran along the Moray coast, recommended the use of the three Scottish trains as another layer of airfield defence. He clearly saw the combination of mobility and flexibility of these units as a useful supplement to the permanent defence forces of, specifically, Lossiemouth, Kinloss, Milltown, Elgin, Dallachy and Forres. Further groups of airfields around Inverness in the west, and Fraserburgh in the east, could also receive regular cover from these patrols, or immediate reinforcement in an emergency.

Prior to the move toward DLs, came new instructions from the Air Ministry regarding the building of new pillboxes, the modification of existing ones, and the termination of some established construction contracts. New pillboxes were to have walls 42in (1.1m) in thickness, and fewer loopholes. Existing pillboxes should, where possible be brought up to this standard. No more Pickett-Hamilton forts were to be installed, as Bomber Command had stressed their uselessness. Good examples of the new standard can be seen on the ground on many airfields. The most common design was a regular hexagon, with walls 11-12ft (3.3-3.6m) in length, a tunnel entry, and six gaping stepped loopholes. Such can be seen at Debden *(66)*, North Weald and Great Sampford (Essex), Cranage (Cheshire), and

66 Debden, Essex, TL561355; shellproof hexagonal pillbox with six loopholes, and tunnel entrance; NB vestiges of the brick shuttering; Appendix I: 3aii

67 Crail, Fife, NO622080; hexagonal pillbox with added layer of concrete, creating extremely wide embrasures; the additional thickness extends only to the three sides actually facing seawards, the anticipated direction of attack; Appendix I: 3aii

Shawbury (Shropshire). Alec Beanse has suggested that some of the North Weald examples have been thickened, and that the extreme width of the external splay is one of the effects of this. At Snailwell (Cambridgeshire), three of the more substantial pillboxes have been thickened up to loophole height with skirts, and given tunnel entries. Something similar has been done to several of the pillboxes ringing Bawdsey Radar Station (Suffolk). At Crail (Fife) *(67)*, the process of thickening is immediately apparent. Here, the added external wall stops short of roof-level, and, in some cases, the additions have separated, and begun to fall away. Also visible are blocked loopholes, meeting the second requirement of the Directive. A pillbox at Middle Wallop (Hampshire), surveyed by Paul Francis prior to its demolition, seems to have been thickened during construction. A tunnel entry had been contrived in order to increase the number of loopholes to five, with one blank, redundant face fronting an adjacent wall. The loops were provided with Turnbull mounts *(68)* and protected by half-inch (1.25cm) steel plate. Pillbox construction clearly carried on well into 1941 as there are many thick-walled and loophole-limited examples to be seen on a range of airfields, such as Stapleton Tawney (Essex), Sywell (Northamptonshire), and Hunsdon and Sawbridgeworth (Hertfordshire). At least four of the original ten pillboxes of this type still stand at Sawbridgeworth, two having three loopholes each, with two in each of the others. Most airfield defence pillboxes of this time were given Turnbull mounts, many in armoured ports, for holding machine-guns, and this must have mitigated, to some extent, the excessive width of some embrasures.

Another design to appear in 1941 was the FC Construction pillbox *(69)*. This is often referred to, on official Air Ministry airfield plans, as the Oakington pillbox, drawings are variously numbered 9882/41 at Twinwood Farm (Bedfordshire), T5291, at Warboys (Cambridgeshire), and TG/14 at Kingscliffe (Northamptonshire) where the four examples are called 'Mushroom' pillboxes on the site plan. 'Mushroom' is as good a name as any. It has also been referred to as the Fairlop pillbox, and there is, indeed, one built into the embankment of the Central Line railway, which here forms the perimeter of the airfield. Ironically, the official site plan of Oakington (Cambridgeshire), where there are seven examples remaining, neglects to ascribe a drawing number. The pillbox consists of a circular concrete pit, under a domed, cantilevered canopy, supported on a four-leafed, cruciform, anti-ricochet wall. A tubular, metal ring runs around the inside of the wall, to which are clamped two machine-guns in cradles *(70)*. Having examined the evidence, Bernard Lowry has suggested that the belt-fed water-cooled Vickers 0.303in machine-gun was used. The key things about this design were the ease of camouflage, and the all-round vision. One of these pillboxes at Oakington has had the all-round capability reduced to two loopholes by a process of bricking up. At Peterhead (Grampian) *(71)* there are five standing examples, to drawing 303/41, where the process has been taken all the way. The walls running into the roof are solid, broken only by two, conventional stepped loopholes with Turnbull mounts. There is also a protected entrance with side walls. If this is a response to the

68 Turnbull Mount; the mounting for a machine-gun most commonly found in airfield defence pillboxes; it allows the water-cooled Vickers machine-gun to pivot from the muzzle, thus providing maximum traverse, for minimum exposure; it developed from a First World War design which was still being used by the BEF in France in 1939; they appear in airfield pillboxes, and also in seagull trenches

Directive to reduce loophole numbers, then surely, babies and bathwater come to mind. This design seems to have come on the scene at a particularly schizophrenic time for airfield defence officers. At Burnaston (Derbyshire), a ring of 11 FC Construction pillboxes clearly defended the airfield's perimeter. This may, incidentally, have represented the model's debut, as the blueprint document is labelled 'Burnaston'. Whilst two mushroom pillboxes are slipped in to bolster the perimeter defences of North Weald, at Oakington, there seems to be evidence of a defence system in transition. Two-thirds of the original complement of 21-plus pillboxes remain, a mixture of thick hexagonal, FW3 Type 22s, and Mushrooms. There is a clear line of perimeter defences, which includes all types, but then two clusters beefing up a spot on the east overlooking the flying field, and one in the south around the (now vanished) BHQ, have been inserted. This could represent the switch to DLs. Of the 40-plus existing Mushroom pillboxes, it is remarkable how many are in clusters, sometimes accompanied by Seagull Trenches, and especially associated with BHQs. The trio at Oakington appear to have linking communications trenches, and a similar trio near the BHQ at Long Marston (Warwickshire) most definitely do. Postwar aerial photographs of Honeybourne (Worcestershire) reveal similar patterns with triangles of mushrooms joined by zig-zag trenches. The conjunction of BHQs, mushrooms and Seagull Trenches located

69 Above Rochford, Essex, TQ865895; FC Construction pillbox, one of a pair defending the western perimeter of what is now Southend Airport; Appendix I: 11n

70 Right Machine-gun mount used in FC Construction pillboxes; the RAF probably mounted their air-cooled, belt-fed Vickers machine-gun, which had been used in First World War fighters; the gun was fixed to the continuous tubular ring which ran around the wall of the pillbox just below the embrasure; each pillbox had two such mountings, which could be moved around the ring independently, and clamped in place; there was also the capability for clamping the guns to provide fixed fields of fire

71 *Below* Peterhead, Aberdeenshire, NK073473; this appears to be a development of the FC Construction pillbox in 4.6; it has lost its capability for all-round fire, but the defenders may therefore, be less vulnerable to enemy fire; Appendix I: 11nii

72 Kingscliffe, Northamptonshire, TL034975; loopholed fighter-dispersal pen; the airfield is ringed with a dozen such structures, plus FC Construction pillboxes, BHQ, and LAA posts

in dominant positions, and enjoying all-round defence capability also occurs at Bicester (Oxfordshire), Croughton, Hinton-in-the-Hedges, and Kingscliffe (Northamptonshire) *(72)*, Atcham (Shropshire), and Rochford (Essex). Certainly at Bicester and at Rochford, this DL is superimposed onto a perimeter defence system based on hexagonal pillboxes. A second DL at Bicester, on the opposite side of the flying field to the station buildings, and consisting of a BHQ in a square of four pillboxes, has been lost to quarrying.

Although the form of the DL is particularly noticeable in the groupings of structures described above, there are plenty of instances of more conventional pillboxes forming the key components of such strongpoints. At East Wretham (Norfolk) *(73)* two pentagonal machine-gun posts, each with two large embrasures with concrete tables, occupy two corners of a square with sides of roughly 50 yards. The two other corners have FW3 Type 22 pillboxes, and there is a weapons store/magazine within the defended area. At Feltwell (Norfolk), the BHQ is flanked by two square pillboxes of a type found only here and at neighbouring Methwold. The north end of Marham (Norfolk) is guarded by a trio of hexagonal pillboxes of different designs, suggesting, perhaps, a number of building periods. Carew Cheriton (Dyfedd), Catfoss (East Yorkshire), and Ouston (Northumberland) all appear to retain some of the characteristics of a DL added to a perimeter defence. Rednal (Shropshire) has a very clear example of a DL. At Haughton Farm, three rectangular pillboxes are absorbed into the farm buildings, in order to dominate both the southern side of the airfield, and the approaches through

73 East Wretham, Norfolk, TL911894; double machine-gun post, pentagonal in shape; two such posts occupy two corners of a squareish enclosure, with hexagonal pillboxes at the other two corners, and a semi-sunken magazine or shelter inside the enclosed area, all forming a strongpoint; Appendix I: 8b

Haughton village. Each pillbox has loopholes in three faces, the fourth adjoining a farm building constructed of similar brick. At Bramcote (Warwickshire) the 1945 plan marks a ring of nine pillboxes around the airfield perimeter, and a line of four more fronting the hangar arc. A number of pillboxes survive to an unusual rectangular plan, with loopholes at the corners as well as in the middle of each side. The AM plan notes this as a local design. Many, by 1945, had accompanying gun pits alongside, and there were also gun posts for 40mm Bofors LAA guns. In the south-east corner, independent of the pillbox line, is the BHQ, surrounded by four Stanton shelters, a square of four chevron-shaped rifle fire trenches, and two gun pits, each with two Scarf (sic) mountings. This would appear to be a DL, and maybe, the pillboxes were relegated to being dummy ones by then. A 1941 defence plan for Hornchurch (Essex) records 'dummy pillboxes' which are, even now, indistinguishable from real ones. Could it be perhaps, that many of Taylor's 'dummy pillboxes' were, simply real ones built earlier in the war, but now disused and regarded as useful decoys?

One strongpoint which is quite unlike anything else surviving can be seen at Hethel (Norfolk). The corner of a plantation on the north side of the airfield, has been marked out by ditches as a square with sides of roughly 50 yards, and wet ditches on two sides. This area contains six 7ft (2.1m) square, open, brick-lined pits, each with a solid, 3ft (1m) square, brick platform in one corner, about 1ft (30cm) lower than the top of the revetment. Three of these pits are at the larger square's corners, with the platforms pointing outwards. One of the other three pits is set diagonally, midway in the north side, its platform pointing outwards. Another, on the east side is oriented to the south. As well as the six square pits, there are five rectangular, similarly brick-lined trenches, and a roofed, sunken brick building in the centre of the area. One possible interpretation is that the square pits are to hold machine-guns standing on the corner platforms; the rectangular pits are rifle trenches; the central building is a magazine or, perhaps, a command post. At Martlesham Heath (Suffolk), there are brick-revetted rifle pits associated with a FW3 Type 22 pillbox, an adjacent FW3 Type 23 pillbox, and a sunken, loopholed shelter or magazine, at the south end of the airfield.

We have already encountered Seagull Trenches above. These were elaborate, brick-lined, sunken trenches with integral overhead cover, bays for machine-guns, and straight lengths of parapet for riflemen. Lockers let into the wall held extra ammunition, and equipment. There was, usually, an entrance down steps at each end. The name comes from the profile as seen from the air. Although there are fully-fledged examples such as that at Dinas Dinlle, built into the Iron-Age fort overlooking the airfield at Llandwrog (Gwynedd) *(74)*, the majority of surviving examples appear to be much simpler, either V-shaped or short straight lengths. Kemble (Gloucestershire) has a collection which includes five V-shaped and two straight. Tactically, Seagull Trenches clearly have both advantages and disadvantages as compared to pillboxes. The increased visibility has a downside of increased vulnerability. Any isolated strongpoint has the potential to become a deathtrap, and

74 Dinas Dinlle, Llandwrog, Gwynedd, SH437565; W-shaped seagull trench, consisting of four straight lengths with fire-bays; Appendix I: 14n

it is significant that those fixed defences which continued in use beyond 1941, or were constructed after that date, tended to be included in groups of mutually-supportive works, which were, themselves, part of an integrated defence scheme.

Even if the Pickett–Hamilton fort had its one shot at surprise, and sunken pillboxes and Seagull Trenches kept a low profile, there was still a very real need for camouflage *(75)*. Attempts were made to hide airfields themselves by painting dummy hedges across runways, by dazzle-painting hangars, and by disguising smaller buildings as houses. Some of these techniques were applied to pillboxes. At High Ercall (Shropshire) at least two rectangular pillboxes have been given pitched roofs and painted-on window frames. At Evanton (Highland) an octagonal pillbox with an open, central well for a LAA mounting has a pitched roof of corrugated iron. This could be original camouflage, or it could well be later weather-proofing for other reasons. It was quite normal to encourage turf to grow on the roofs of pillboxes and examples are widespread across Britain.

We have already seen a few of the wide range of pillbox types used for airfield defence. Many seem to have been straight adoptions of the War Office FW3 types. The Type 22, Type 23, and thin-walled Type 24, were all used on airfields. Since an all-round fire capability was usually important, and the threat was as much from bombing as from ground fire, the airfield variations on the Type 22 are widely centred around lowering the entrance in order to gain the sixth loophole, and thickening the roof. Lichfield (Staffordshire), and Hampstead Norreys (Berkshire) both have good examples of these modifications. Another type taken on from the War Office was the Type 27. This octagonal pillbox had a hollow centre in which was a platform carrying a LAA mounting, open to the sky. It seems to have been employed particularly in Scotland on both airfields, such as Drem and Macmerry (Lothian), Evanton (Highland), Montrose (Tayside), Kinloss and Lossiemouth (Moray), and CH Radar sites such as Drone Hill (Borders), where there are at least

75 Angle, Pembrokeshire, SM867019; windmill stump converted to strongpoint; NB loopholes reached by internal timber galleries; this is located near to the BHQ

seven surviving. A slightly smaller version of the octagonal version can be seen at Windrush (Gloucestershire) where it served as BHQ, and there was a large, six-sided version of the design, with walls of 15ft (4.5m) used at Detling (Kent). There are other different variations of the octagonal Type 27 at Oulton Street and Horsham St Faith (Norfolk).

As well as universal types, from whatever source, there were very local designs. One such was confined to Newton and Tollerton (Nottinghamshire). This is a square pillbox with chamfered corners, giving eight faces large enough to take embrasures. However, there is a limited number of actual loopholes in each of the four examples at Newton, four in each, and in the nine surviving examples at Tollerton, each having between two and five loops *(76)*. All of these pillboxes are sited individually to face either inwards or outwards. At both airfields, a variety of other pillbox types are used in a perimeter defence system. At Tollerton, the MAP hangar has an internal pillbox built into an end wall, much like one at Ringway (Greater Manchester). One must assume that it once had external loops as well. If these octagons in Nottinghamshire are really squares with the corners cut off, then two different octagonal pillboxes at Debden (Essex), and Lichfield (Staffordshire) are really rectangles minus their corners. Here, however, they each have the maximum eight loopholes. It has been suggested that the Lichfield one served as the BHQ, but the one at Debden can be nothing more than a perimeter defence as it enjoyed no view of the landing area.

We have already encountered the disappearing pillbox, and a number of the other small turret designs, previously described, were employed on airfields. Two Tett Turrets can be seen at Hornchurch (Essex) *(77)*, an Allan–Williams turret at Spittlegate (Lincolnshire), and two local variations of the latter at Crail (Fife).

The Norcon pillbox, basically a loopholed sewer-pipe, was also used on airfields. One version was given a roof and can be seen at Southrop (Gloucestershire) and Harwell (Oxfordshire). At Southrop, two have been joined together as the front corners of a larger rectangular pillbox, to quite bizarre effect.

Acklington (Northumberland), and Thornaby-on-Tees (Durham) have otherwise fairly standard hexagonal pillboxes built up with side walls to provide open LAA positions. At Thornaby this is reached by a fixed ladder, but at Acklington, a 10-step concrete staircase, integral to a porch, is used. Middleton St George (Durham) has a true, double-decker pillbox with loopholes at two levels. Here, the staircase is contained within the body of the pillbox, forming an annexe on one side, much like that on some domestic maisonnettes.

By 1941, the Air Ministry was commissioning its own designs for pillboxes. Dated August 1941, Drawing number 390 details four alternative layouts for a rectangular, shellproof pillbox with two loopholes provided with Turnbull mounts, two or three compartments, low steel doors, and, in one version, tiered bunks.

76 Tollerton, Nottinghamshire, SK623356; the loophole of a pillbox built to defend the airfield and aircraft factory; NB the Turnbull mount, and, also, that in the opposite loophole; pillbox designers were advised to avoid placing loopholes directly opposite one another for obvious reasons; Appendix I: 9d

77 Hornchurch, Essex, TQ535847; one of a pair of Tett Turrets, on the eastern perimeter of the airfield; they appear not to figure in an airfield defence plan of autumn 1941, unless they provided a base for two of the machine-gun sections which are shown on the plan; given that they only appeared during the summer of 1941, it is strange that they receive no prominence; however, they do appear to be two extremely rare survivors of this model; Appendix I: 12b

Another design, Number 2843 (undated), is a square, bulletproof post with four loopholes in two compartments. Fieldwork appears not to have discovered any extant examples of any of these. One other design, Number 391 dated August 1941, was a shellproof, pentagonal pillbox with with two loopholes fitted with Turnbull mounts, in two alternative layouts. There appears to be an example of this design standing at Catfoss (Yorkshire) adjacent to the BHQ, but built with two extra loopholes. There are very few pentagonal pillboxes anywhere, Alton Barnes (Wiltshire) having three of one unique design, and Lichfield (Staffordshire) having two of another.

Radar sites were also often given fixed defences. Some of the pillbox designs used were drawn from the usual repertoire, like the FW3 Type 27 at Drone Hill (Borders), or the ten FW3 Type 22, and shellproof hexagonal pillboxes at Ottercops Moss (Northumberland), but others were local designs. Wartling (East Sussex) has square pillboxes with attached, open circular pits for LAA guns. School Hill (Grampian) *(78)* has at least six tall, rectangular pillboxes with two loopholes in each face, and a two-thirds height blast wall covering the entrance. At High Street (Suffolk), there is an L-shaped pillbox, centred in each side of the square, inner enclosure, and two more on the administrative site. The inner four have LAA mountings on the roof built up with hinged panels of bulletproof steel plate. At Stenigot (Lincolnshire) two examples remain of a hexagonal pillbox design which is really a triangle with the corners cut off. Another very similar example stands at Ventnor (Isle of Wight). West Beckham (Norfolk) has FW3 Type 22 pillboxes on the perimeter but square, loopholed structures standing high up on the Transmitter/Receiver Blocks. Stoke Holy Cross has its own style of hexagonal pillbox with LAA mounts on the roof. Bempton (Yorkshire) retains two examples of an unusual type of square pillbox with loopholes in three corners, and the centres of all four sides. One corner is left blank to allow for a hatch-type entrance, and a fixed ladder to the brick LAA post on the roof.

What comes across from this brief overview of fixed defences on both airfields and Radar sites is the diverse provision. Within the parameters laid down by Taylor, or the War Office and Air Ministry works departments, there was enormous variety and variation. That may have been no bad thing given the circumstances of urgency and lack of experience. But there was also inconsistency, and it is impossible to know whether this was due to positive or negative motives. It seems unlikely that, on a number of otherwise complete sites, the fixed defences should have been the only targets for demolition programmes. The fact remains that, given the extent of the survival of many other classes of structure, including many which were not designed with longevity in mind, it is surprising that more defence works have not survived. It would seem that the inescapable conclusion must be that fewer were built than at one time were deemed necessary. The variety

78 Schoolhill, Aberdeenshire, NO907983; pillbox with framework for its disguise as a house; this radar site was defended by at least seven of these pillboxes; Appendix 6mii

element is puzzling as well. It is sometimes possible to detect a pattern where different designs of pillbox have been chosen for particular tactical reasons. It is also possible to detect cases where earlier defence systems have been seen as needing strengthening with later, more effective models. What is more difficult to understand is the perimeter defence system which consists of a range of different pillbox styles in ones and twos, such as Lichfield (Staffordshire), with eight surviving pillboxes of six different designs, Honington (Suffolk) with five and five, Oakington (Cambridgeshire) with 16 and four, or Crail (Fife) with 18 and six.

In the second half of the century, a number of factors have necessitated the continued provision of fixed defences on airfields and radar sites. These factors have included both military threats from the Special Forces of Cold War enemies or terrorist groups from home or away, and the more pacific, if no less disruptive, attentions of disarmers. Apart from the deployment of Rapier AA missiles, fixed defences have differed little from those utilised in the Second World War. Wire, infantry fire positions and lights were supplemented by small pillboxes. Some USAF bases, such as Mildenhall and Lakenheath (Suffolk) use a small, square pillbox with four loopholes and a sunken entrance as perimeter defence. At Bentwaters (Suffolk), and Alconbury (Cambridgeshire), an elevated, loopholed pillbox was mounted over the entrance to bomb stores. At Woodbridge (Suffolk), Dave Wood found a small, buried, cylindrical gun post, with a hatch in the roof, firing positions in the side between brick piers, and an escape tunnel. This would appear to offer some of the advantages of the Pickett-Hamilton fort without the problems of fallible machinery and no way out. Royal Air Force airfields went for less permanent strongpoints, using sandbagged positions, some, as at Coltishall (Norfolk), being associated with earlier pillboxes. Where fixed defences have been used, they have tended to be conspicuously visible. A square, loopholed pillbox was used at Fulbeck (Lincolnshire), and Oakington (Cambridgeshire), where can also be seen a double-decker from the 1980s, next to a Type 22 from the 1940s, for instance, as well as many other sites used by other services. Also, of course, the ubiquitous Yarnold Sangar was widely employed on airfields. The Permanent Ammunition Depots (PADs) such as Faldingworth (Lincolnshire) and Barnham (Norfolk), had high watchtowers as part of the protective measures surrounding the storage of nuclear weapons. One tower still remains at each site, and towers remain a feature of a number of other sensitive sites such as Molesworth (Cambridgeshire), the one-time home of Cruise missiles.

One recent (as yet) hypothetical scenario for a Third World War begins with the neutralisation of the RAF/USAF tanker fleet on the ground at their bases in southern Britain. It would appear that the need to guard against ground attack, however unlikely, is going to remain a priority for some time to come.

5

AIRFIELDS AND
THEIR BUILDINGS

Britain's first military airfield was at Larkhill (Wiltshire). Here, during 1908-10, a number of experimental aircraft were being flown and were stored in unremarkable sheds alongside informal grass flying fields. The forerunner of the Bristol Aeroplane Company had loaned a number of their Boxkites to the military for use in military manoeuvres, and, in 1910, they established a factory and flying school at Larkhill. The Royal Engineers had maintained a Balloon section since the 1880s. A factory had been built in the heart of the Army's Aldershot HQ in 1905, and, in 1911, there was an expansion into an Air Battalion, with balloons still based at Farnborough, and Boxkite biplanes operating out of Larkhill. All this interest in the potential of military flying prompted a rationalisation, and, in 1912, the Royal Flying Corps was formed. A Central Flying School was established at Upavon (Wiltshire), and No.3 Squadron RFC, soon to be joined by No.4 Squadron, moved into a new aerodrome at Netheravon (Wiltshire). Meanwhile, a naval wing was established at Eastchurch (Kent) along with Short's aircraft factory, which had moved from nearby Leysdown in 1910. Leysdown had been provided with side-opening sheds, built by Harbrow's of St Mary Cray (Kent). These buildings may well have been re-erected at Eastchurch, as contemporary photographs show similar constructions in use in 1911. In July, 1914, the Royal Naval Air Service (RNAS) was inaugurated, based at Eastchurch. Other RFC squadrons were based at Gosport's Fort Grange (Hampshire), at Farnborough, and at Montrose (Forfar). At some of these airfields, purpose-built side-opening sheds were constructed for storing aircraft. At others, a range of tents and marquees were provided. Many of the permanent buildings were geared to the needs of motor transport, owing to the perceived need to make units mobile. A number of important buildings survive on these pre-First World War sites: Officers' Messes at Farnborough, Netheravon and Upavon; MT sheds and offices at Netheravon; the crescent of four coupled aircraft sheds at Montrose, c.1912; and the earliest aviation buildings of all, the five aircraft storage sheds, built c.1910, at Larkhill. The building at Farnborough (Trenchard House, G1) which housed the Balloon School from 1911-12 and the headquarters of the RFC from 1912-15, has now

79 Cardington, Bedfordshire; Hangar No.1; built in 1924 as part of the programme to construct the R100 and 101 airships; the second hangar at Cardington was brought from Pulham [Norfolk] in 1927

opened as a museum. Eastchurch is now a prison, Netheravon, Larkhill and Upavon are used by the Army, Gosport belongs to the Royal Navy, Montrose is an industrial estate, and Farnborough is currently being redeveloped.

In May, 1914, No.1 Squadron became the RNAS Airship Detachment prior to its move to Kingsnorth (Kent) the following March. Airships were now the responsibility of the RNAS and a network of airship stations was established to counter the threat of marauding Zeppelins. Airship hangars were vast, that at RNAS Cranwell (Lincolnshire) measured 700ft (210m) long, 150ft (45m) wide, and 100ft (30m) high. In addition, many had screens at each end to counter cross-winds as the airship was entering or leaving, and these were each the same length as the hangar, and 70ft (21m) high. Most of these airship hangars have long disappeared, but one of the original ones at Cardington (Bedfordshire) *(79)*, first Short Brothers airship works alongside the RNAS airship station, and, after the end of the First World War, the Royal Airship Works still stands. In its extended form it measures 806ft (248m) long, 273ft (84m) wide, and 178ft (55m) high. Alongside stands a second hangar of similar size, built by the Admiralty at Pulham (Norfolk) in 1917, and removed here in 1927. It is now the Laboratory of the Building

Research Establishment housing an eight-storey building used as a test bed for construction reasearch. Also surviving at Cardington is Shortstown, housing built for workers at the factory, the main Offices dated 1917, and a power house from that era, which housed the machinery for pumping water into airships as ballast. At Howden (East Yorkshire) *(80)* the water tower, so necessary for the firefighters in such a volatile situation, now stands, totally solitary, surrounded by fields of cows. At Pulham, the SILICOL building, where hydrogen was produced by a chemical process which involved introducing ferrosilicate to hot caustic soda, still stands. The resultant pure hydrogen gas was then stored in tanks which stood next to another surviving building. Other RNAS airship bases were at Luce Bay (Galloway), Capel (Kent), Mullion (Cornwall), Wormwood Scrubbs (London), Barrow-in-Furness (Lancashire), Llangefni (Anglesey), Inchinnan (Glasgow), Longside (Aberdeen), Pembroke, Polegate (Eastbourne), and as many again sub-stations. Virtually all traces of most of these have disappeared. At Polegate, for instance, only a concrete slab with a mooring-ring survives.

Almost the entire operational strength of the RFC moved over to France and Belgium with the BEF in September 1914, leaving only training units behind. In some cases, aerodromes were virtually deserted. The defence of the UK was left in the hands of the RNAS airships. At the start of the war, RNAS Kingsnorth faced the expected onslaught of the Zeppelins with one airship, armed with four grenades. By early 1916 the raids by Zeppelins and Gotha bombers forced the development of the Home Defence Scheme. Home Defence fighter squadrons were formed to intercept enemy bombing raids. These squadrons were based down the east side of Britain, and (mainly) new aerodromes were required. These ranged from large stations for whole squadrons, such as Suttons Farm (Essex), to smaller stations such as Buckminster (Leicestershire) for a flight of aircraft, down to unmanned emergency landing grounds such as Cairncross (Berwick). Landing grounds were classified for day or night operation, and by the ease of approach. Some, such as Tydd St Mary (Lincolnshire), were upgraded to aerodrome status, and given more substantial buildinds: a hangar, armoury, flight office etc. in Tydd's case. At Sutton's Farm, a fully-developed aerodrome, initially for a flight, but, subsequently, for a squadron, the buildings were clustered around the old farm-house. These included two large timber hangars, probably not dissimilar to the Larkhill sheds, additional examples of which may still stand at Filton (Bristol), Manston (Kent) and at Beverley Racecourse (East Yorkshire), officers' mess and regimental institute, vehicle sheds and workshops, and lots of, mainly hutted, accommodation, office, and stores buildings. All this was swept away by 1921, but three years later it was decided that an airfield was needed here after all, and Hornchurch was developed on a closely adjacent site. Many aerodromes, at this time, were equipped only with canvas Bessoneau hangars, often in quite large numbers, as the fragile aeroplanes of the day needed protection from all weathers. By 1916, it was realised that more substantial aircraft storage was needed, and the bow-strung truss, end-opening General Service (GS) hangars appeared. One still

80 Howden, East Yorkshire, SE747330; the water tower of the First World War airship station, virtually all that remains

81 Harling Road, Norfolk; First World War Aircraft Repair Shed built around 1917 on this Home Defence squadron base, later to become a Training Depot Station

stands at Tadcaster (North Yorkshire), as does an early example at Calshot (Hampshire). The adoption of Belfast trusses made it possible to link these hangars into twos and threes. Whilst many of the Home Defence stations were given up to six single span GS hangars, the new Training Depot Stations (TDS), built from 1917 on, were given three coupled GS hangars, and a separate, slightly smaller, Aircraft Repair Section (ARS) *(81)*. This layout can still be seen at Old Sarum (Wiltshire). Another type of establishment was the Aircraft Acceptance Park (AAP), built close to aircraft factories, in order to receive newly built planes prior to their issue to operational units. These were equipped with triple-span GS hangars, and an ARS. These survive at Hooton Park (Wirral), Hendon (London), and Filton (Bristol) for instance, and an ARS and an open Running Shed at Bracebridge Heath (Lincolnshire). Regional Aircraft Repair Depots were built at Farnborough, for the southern region, for instance, and at Henlow (Bedfordshire) for the eastern. Here, different types of coupled GS hangars are combined to carry out a number of specific functions. Henlow retains four coupled GS hangars, and a coupled, RAF GS shed with distinctive gabled roof *(82)*. The enormous, five-bay storage shed for the Handley Page 0/400 bomber with its 100ft (30m) wingspan, built at Henlow, has been demolished, but one is reputed to remain at Netheravon.

Examples of other aerodrome buildings from the First World War survive in small numbers. The flight offices remain at Duxford (Cambridgeshire) *(83)* and at Tydd St Mary (Lincolnshire); standard Air Ministry concrete barrack blocks (481/18) at Duxford and Orfordness (Suffolk); a large number of hutted

82 Henlow, Bedfordshire; coupled aircraft sheds, built in 1918

83 Duxford, Cambridgeshire; Watch Office built in 1918

84 Calshot, Hampshire; triple Type F Seaplane sheds built from 1916; along with a double Type F shed, and a 1914 GS shed, these form a well-preserved group of three First World War hangars

workshops and training rooms at Duxford; an MT shed at Orfordness, and a different pattern, designed for airship stations at East Fortune (Lothian); a water tower and pumphouse at Tadcaster; aircraft sheds at Netheravon (Wiltshire) and at Andover (Hampshire). At Hendon two officers' messes remain, one built in 1916 for the RFC, and another, originally built in 1917 as the London Aerodrome Hotel. The grandstand at Lincoln housed the officers' mess for the West Common AAP. The Balloon School at Rollestone (Wiltshire), built in 1917 with two different styles of hangar, still stands, and is used by the Army for storage. Airfields retaining other First World War buildings include East Fortune, Andover, Hucknall (Nottinghamshire), Hendon, Filton, Henlow, Bircham Newton (Norfolk), and Biggin Hill (Kent).

As well as their airships, the RNAS operated seaplanes, from bases in the Orkneys and Shetlands, the Scillies, the Isle of Wight, down the east coast, and from naval bases in the Solent, the Medway, Plymouth Sound and the Humber estuary. In 1916 the RNAS adopted the Type F side-opening seaplane shed. The Type G was a smaller version. A number of these remain *in situ* at Mount Batten (Plymouth) where there are two Type F sheds; at Calshot (Hampshire) with a triple Type F *(84)*, and a Type G shed; and at Cranwell. After the end of the war, many F sheds were taken down and re-erected on Armament Training Stations, and examples may still be seen at Evanton (Highland), Sutton Bridge

85 Farnborough, Hampshire; building F41, Wroath Hall, has had a number of uses over the years, but appears to have begun life in 1921 as part of the Empire Test-Pilots' School

(Lincolnshire), and Pembrey and Stormy Down (South Wales). There remain other odd relics of some of these stations. At Hornsea Mere (East Yorkshire), for instance, the powerhouse and a workshop, now a cafe, both completed in 1918, can be seen on Kirkholme Point.

The amalgamation of the RFC and the RNAS into the Royal Air Force (RAF) on 1 April 1918, should have heralded a celebration of the recognition of air power as an independent force, but the cutbacks in defence spending at the end of the 'war to end all wars' hit the new service particularly hard. From a peak of nearly 400 locations involved in military aviation in November 1918, there was a gradual reduction to just 27 active military airfields by the early 1920s. Although Trenchard was able to introduce measures which would both modernise and professionalise the RAF, he had only scant resources available for these developments *(85)*. It was only ten years later that the renewed threat to European peace appearing in Germany would prompt a real acceleration in Britain's rearmament programme. In the meantime, under the terms of the Romer Plan of 1923, increasing the Home Defence air force to 52 squadrons, Trenchard was able to modernise a number of existing airfields, including Filton, Tangmere, Biggin Hill, Catterick, Bicester (Oxfordshire), and Bircham Newton. A further plan, introduced in 1925, organised the Home air force into a fighter area in a crescent, east and south of London, and three bomber areas, west of the capital. There was also provision for the formation of the Royal Auxiliary Air Force. These developments made the design of new buildings an urgent priority. The larger aircraft coming into service needed larger hangars, new techniques of ground control required purpose-built watch offices, and the reorganisation of aircraft maintenance made it important to combine the workshops which hitherto had operated in dispersed premises. Attempts to both centralise and rationalise the supply of stores of all types meant that a single, and central location would aid these processes. Permanent stations needed proper accommodation for officers, other ranks, and their families. New technology meant that training would now require more specialist facilities. It was also now realised that the large numbers of young servicemen and women who spent their lives on these airfields would benefit from the provision of sports facilities, and educational and recreational opportunities. The peacetime RAF station would be a very different place from one in time of war.

It is tempting to think that there was real uniformity in the airfields which emerged from these plans of the early to mid-1920s, but it would be wrong. Let us take two examples which demonstrate this. Bircham Newton was a TDS in 1918, with the characteristic three pairs of coupled GS hangars and an ARS. Modernised in the 1923 programme, it received some new buildings, including a new guardhouse, power house, reservoir, booster-house and some married quarters. It retained its original hangars, one of which had a rudimentary 'control top' on the door gantry. Upper Heyford (Oxfordshire), along with neighbouring Bicester, one of the new bomber stations of the 1923-4 programme, had been disposed of after the end of the war, and, by 1921, was back under the plough. Building commenced in 1924, and here, everything was from scratch on what was effectively a greenfield site. Six Type A hangars (19a/24, and 420/25), a purpose-built watch office of the bay-windowed bungalow style (2072/26), barrack blocks Types A and C (640/22 and 641/22, 104/23 and 230/27), workshop (1788/25), guardhouse (166/23), and so on. Many of these same buildings were going up at Bicester, Filton (Glos), North Weald (Essex), Tangmere (W. Sussex) etc. at the same time. To further confuse the situation, all of these stations, modernised, in what was to become a continuous process through the 1920s, would undergo varying degrees of additional transformation as part of the RAF's major expansion programme of the next decade. Many of these buildings to 1920's designs survive. The Type A hangar is end-opening, 250ft (75m) long and 120ft (36m) wide, and has a ridged roof. A larger version, the Type B was also designed but only a handful were built. One, at Martlesham Heath, known as the 'Goliath' has been demolished, but two still stand at Pembroke Dock, a Second World War flying-boat base *(86)*. The six Type A hangars can still be seen at Upper Heyford, and other examples at Abingdon and Bicester (Oxfordshire), Catfoss (East Yorkshire), Mildenhall and Martlesham Heath (Suffolk) *(87)*, and North Weald. Bircham Newton, Filton and Bicester share the same guardhouse as Upper Heyford, but that at Hucknall (1621/27) is different. Duxford's Operations Block (1161/24 and 757/27) is replicated at Bicester, whose Station headquarters (1443/24) is a smaller version of that at Sealand (Cheshire) to 1610-1/26. Hucknall retains its Main

86 Pembroke Dock, South Wales; a rare B-Type hangar at Pembroke Dock, seen from the Georgian guard house of the old dockyard and barracks

87 Martlesham Heath, Suffolk; Type A Aeroplane Shed, dating from around 1926; the rare Type B shed which formerly stood nearby, has been demolished

Stores (808/27). The 2072/26 watch offices survive at Upavon and at Netheravon. However, whilst many buildings can be identified as originating in a particular improvement programme, it must be remembered that drawings stayed in use until superseded by something better, and could sometimes still be used well past their sell-by date. The need for a new hangar design, particularly for use overseas, resulted in the Hinaidi (1136/27), a gabled, end-opening shed, based on the parts and dimensions of the old Type F seaplane shed. For some reason Hinaidis were erected at Chivenor (Devon) and at Madley (Herefordshire), where two still stand, now used for storage.

By 1932, the abolition of the Ten Year Rule represented a tacit acceptance that a new European conflict, probably with Germany, was virtually inevitable. The armed forces in general would be rearmed, and the RAF, in particular, would undergo a radical reorganisation and expansion programme. As the new airfields of the previous programmes came on stream, Upper Heyford, having been started in 1924, had only become operational in 1928, they immediately became eligible for upgrading, and new sites were added. The organisational structure was modified so that four independent Commands were created: Fighter, Bomber, Coastal and Training. The Fleet Air Arm returned to the Royal Navy in 1937. Civilian elementary flying training schools (EFTS) were established to feed trained pilots into the system as and when necessary. The aircraft industry was encouraged to open shadow factories, often within the automobile industry, in order to reach the levels of production needed to expand the number of aircraft available to the RAF, and Aircraft Storage Units (ASU) were set up to stockpile military aircraft for issue to new units, or to replenish losses in existing ones. Centralised supply depots with effective rail-links were located in places which could meet the ever-expanding needs of the new RAF.

Although until 1938 all airfields were grassed, their arrival in the landscape still made an enormous impact. Hitherto, the urgency of the wartime imperative, or in the 1920s, the extreme shortage of funds, had made the aesthetics of airfield design, either irrelevant or an unjustifiable luxury. The creation of fifty or so brand-new airfields during the 1930s, and the expansion of dozens more, excited the attention of bodies such as the Council for the Preservation of Rural England (CPRE). The Air Ministry was pressured into taking such opinion into account, and so consulted architects such as Edwin Lutyens when adopting the standard designs for the new buildings. These were then submitted to the Royal Fine Art Commission for its approval. The result was a range of handsome neo-Georgian buildings, both functional and attractive. Such airfields as Hullavington (Wiltshire), where even the water tower was faced in Bath stone, were hailed as examples of institutional development at its best. Still occupied, now by the Army, Hullavington has recently been designated a Conservation Area by the local authority. Although such a high level of finish was neither possible nor appropriate everywhere, efforts were made to use high-quality materials which would blend with the ambient style. Only after the start of the Second World War, were there

88 Newton, Nottinghamshire; Villa-type watch office of around 1939, with fire-tender sheds alongside, and C-type hangars behind

compromises made, when cheaper and less materials-intensive designs were substituted to complete the final stations in this programme. Thus hangar design would be modified, and buildings finished in concrete rather than in hand-made bricks.

The defining features of the Expansion Period airfield of the 1930s are the Type C hangar, the brick-clad water tower, the officers' mess with the entrance loggia, and the villa type control tower *(88)*. These can be found all over Britain from Wick, in the far north of Scotland, to Middle Wallop, in the south-west. The C Type hangar, of which over 150 were built on nearly 80 airfields between 1935 and 1939, can be seen in several versions. The original design, built early on in the programme, with extant examples at Cranfield (Bedfordshire), Turnhouse (Edinburgh), and Tern Hill (Shropshire), has a massive gable at each end, and is finished in brick. By 1936, a cheaper modified version, identical but for its concrete finish, was being put up at, for example, Cottesmore (Rutland), and Finningley (South Yorkshire). Next, the end gables were seen as unnecessarily expensive in materials and labour, and a lower version with exposed, hipped rafters, gravel-filled doors, and reinforced concrete wall panels, were built, known as 'protected'. Five such hangars stand at Newton (Nottinghamshire), and at Binbrook (Lincolnshire) *(89)*, built in 1939. A fourth, 'unprotected' design, with asbestos sheet wall panels, can be seen at Wick (Caithness). At North Coates (Lincolnshire) stands a unique hangar-type with side-opening doors, and double pitched roof, described as C Type, which may represent a prototype which was never further developed. Several airfields including Little Rissington (Gloucestershire) and Brize Norton (Oxfordshire), received Aircraft Repair Sheds, in the same style as C Type hangars but shorter in length. There is a whole series of drawing numbers attached to these C Type hangars, and many probably refer to the layout of annexes along the side, rather than the basic design. Many of these hangars are still in use by the RAF, whilst others, such as Manby (Lincolnshire), are used by government agricultural agencies for grain storage. In a token acknowledgement of the vulnerability of these hangars to air attack, they were commonly grouped in arcs rather than in straight lines, in order to make it slightly harder for enemy bombers to hit them with a single stick of bombs.

Two types of control tower are commonly found on airfields of the mid-1930s. One, popularly known as the 'Fort' (1959-60/34 and 207/36) *(90)* comes in an earlier, brick, finish, and a later, concrete one. A square lower storey is surmounted by a square, two-storey tower. Examples survive at Bircham Newton, Bicester and Cosford (Shropshire). At Hemswell (Lincolnshire), Bassingbourn (Cambridgeshire) and West Raynham (Norfolk) examples can be seen where modifications have been made to the original building, extending its useful life. At many airfields, such as Mildenhall (Suffolk), the Fort was replaced with a wartime model. The other control tower, of this period is often referred to as the 'Villa' type. This is a much larger building of two full storeys, in International Modern style, with wrap-around windows, balcony, and matereological cabin on the roof. There were

89 Binbrook, Lincolnshire; C-type hangar [protected]

90 Bicester, Oxfordshire; Fort-type watch office of *c.*1926; note the Second World War pillbox in front, and the C-type hangars behind

three versions built in different materials. Examples remain at Middleton-St-George (Durham) and Swinderby (Lincolnshire) in brick (5845/39); at Wyton (Cambridgeshire) and Newton in concrete (2328/39); and at Wick, in timber (2423/39). At Waddington (Lincolnshire) the Fort was replaced by a Villa within a few years of construction. A third control tower of this time is found in only a few former training stations. The Chief Flying Instructor's Block (5740/36) was designed as a three-storey tower flanked by single-storey wings. Standing examples such as those at Hullavington and Little Rissington, both have an extra storey. Paul Francis argues, from the evidence of other survivors as well, that this second storey was a later modification in all cases.

Many of those 80-odd airfields which received C-Type hangars were given the whole range of Expansion Period buildings, from new designs which covered everything from armoury to gymnasium, institute to parachute store, sergeants' mess to workshop. Many of these stations are still in military use, and only on their Open Days are Mildenhall or Waddington accessible to the general public. Others serve as industrial estates, office or retail parks, so Manby and Hemswell, Horsham St Faith (Norfolk), enjoy a degree of accessibility. Duxford is a museum, Cranfield a university campus, Bircham Newton the Construction Industry Training Centre, and Binbrook and Little Rissington are new residential settlements. Between them, these sites contain a wide cross-section of all the types of buildings put up during the 1930s Expansion Period. Distinctive specialist technical buildings such as workshops, stores, armoury/photographic blocks, sick bays with and without decontamination centres etc. were matched by two- and three-storey barrack blocks *(91)*, officers'*(92)* and Sergeants' Messes with one, two, and three storeys, and institutes and dining rooms for the other ranks.

Many of the new and improved airfields of the Expansion Period were standard bomber or fighter stations. Certain specialist stations were equipped with buildings more appropriate for their functions. Aircraft Storage Units (ASU) were given two D Type 2312/36) hangars with curved roofs on reinforced concrete walls, for the storage of complete aircraft. Dispersed around the site in two's and three's were low, curved storage sheds for partially-dismantled aircraft. Their design, with the roof reaching the ground on each side enabling turf to be laid over the top, made them virtually invisible from the air. Tarmac approach roads were camouflaged with coloured chippings. There were three types: E (7305/37), L (5163-5/39), and Lamella (6953/36). The Lamella was based on a design by the Junkers firm, which had been used at civil airports and factories since the late 1920s. Kemble (Gloucestershire) has examples of all four of these designs. Various combinations of the four designs can be seen at many ASUs including Wroughton (Wiltshire); Little Rissington; St Athan and Llandow (South Wales); and Kirkbride and Silloth (Cumbria). St Athan's total of 34 hangars probably constitutes a record. Although the majority of the buildings on these ASUs were the conventional 1930s designs, some were quite different. Wroughton and Kirkbride, for instance, have quite unique watch offices. Kirkbride, in addition to its later Seco tower

91 Duxford, Cambridgeshire; barrack-block type B of 1932

92 Bircham Newton, Norfolk; Officers' Mess of about 1934

(WA15/213/53), has a bungalow which was the control building for the Air Transport Auxiliary, whose civilian pilots ferried new aircraft in from factories as far away as the other side of the Atlantic, initially to be stored in the ASUs. Instead of having conventional guardrooms at every exit, ASUs were given Wardens' Offices. Several of these can be seen at Wroughton, Dumfries, Silloth, and Lichfield.

Other ancillary buildings of this time exhibit the same attention to detail and the same architectural style as operational flying stations. The medical blocks of Ely Hospital (Cambridgeshire) for instance, are built in an international modern style, the water tower is brick clad with Romanesque detailing (compare Cranfield), and the ambulance garages are standard vehicle sheds, as they are at Brampton.

At the start of the Second World War, the rush to complete the Expansion Programme made it necessary to adopt more utilitarian designs for key buildings. The 518/40 control tower *(93)*, a less substantial temporary brick version of the 'Villa', was constructed on a number of airfields, and two, new hangar designs, the J and K Types were introduced. These were curved roof sheds on steel columns and were intended to provide something less permanent than the C Type. One J Type was provided as a maintenance or repair hangar on operational airfields as can still be seen at Holme upon Spalding Moor (East Yorkshire), Wellesbourne Mountford (Warwickshire), and Polebrook (Northamptonshire). Some ASUs such as High Ercall (Shropshire), and Dumfries were given several K-Type hangars.

Lichfield ASU retains four Type K and three Type J hangars along with eight Type L, and some later hangars. The 518/40 control tower survives at many of those airfields completed around 1940, such as Wymeswold and Bottesford (Leicestershire), Rednal (Shropshire) and Barrow-in-Furness (Cumbria). The coincidence of a J Type hangar, and a 518/40 control tower can still be seen at Honeybourne and Pershore (Worcestershire) and Goxhill (Lincolnshire).

During the period of accelerating expansion immediately prior to the outbreak of the Second World War, a pressing need for a transportable hangar became more and more apparent. The initial answer came with the Bellman (8349/37), 400 of which were erected 1938-40, and the Callender Hamilton (6633/37), of which a few appeared, mainly on RNAS stations. Both came in two heights. At Booker (Buckinghamshire) Bellman hangars of both heights still stand, and at Baginton (Coventry) two pairs of the 25ft (7.5m) version survive. The lower, 17ft (4.2m) high Callender-Hamiltons can be seen at East Fortune, and Barrow-in-Furness. Castle Kennedy (Wigtown), and Burscough (Lancashire), a RNAS station, have examples of the higher, 25ft (7.5m) version.

Part of the preparation for war had involved the private sector in training pilots, at private airfields. A national enthusiasm for civil flying had resulted in local aerodromes becoming symbols of civic pride. As well as the highly-professional metropolitan aerodromes such as London's Croydon and Hendon, or Manchester's Barton

93 Barrow-in-Furness, Cumbria; a view of the airfield on Walney Island; in the foreground is the Battle Headquarters, then the Type 518/40 Watch Office, and on the right, one of two surviving Callendar-Hamilton hangars

and Ringway, there was, therefore, an extensive network of small, civil airfields, many of which already enjoyed a solid reputation for producing well-trained pilots, through the Civil Air Guard scheme, the University Air Squadrons, the RAF Volunteer Reserve, and civilian flying clubs. Airfields such as Liverpool's Speke, Shoreham (Sussex), Cambridge, Sywell (Northamptonshire), Gatwick, Brooklands (Surrey), Elmdon (Birmingham), and Perth, all with their strikingly individually-designed club-houses, control towers or terminals, were pressed into military service. At many, the necessary buildings to house the RAF personnel and their technical activities were added. At Ringway, the three-storey Officers' Mess survives.

Once it was realised that the war was going to go on for a while, the need for more airfields was accepted. It also became obvious partly through bitter experience, that these new airfields would need to be very different from those opened in the prewar period. There would be three major differences of conception, apart from all those of scale, of operation and of detail. Firstly, the new aircraft were too heavy to use grass strips. Secondly, airfield structures were too concentrated and had to be dispersed to avoid maximum destruction from minimum bombs dropped. Thirdly, earlier construction was too costly in terms of time, labour, and materials. The new airfields would need to be built, simply, cheaply, uniformly, and, above all, quickly. After the entry of the United States into the war, the presence of two US Army Air Forces, the Eighth and Ninth (8USAAF and 9USAAF), required over 100 airfields, new and existing. The expansion of all RAF Commands demanded even more. Specialist functions, hitherto unimagined, such as support for Special Operations Executive activities, or the training of the Glider Pilots Regiment, made their own demands. At the height of airfield construction, in 1942, a new airfield opened every three days. The Air Ministry's contractors employed 32 per cent of the entire labour pool of available construction workers. It took five to seven months from the first building work beginning, to the first take-off by an aircraft, and the entire infrastructure of roads, drains and power cables, as well as accommodation, technical site, and training buildings were completed within 18 months of the start. Every new bomber airfield required 20 miles (32km) of drains, six miles (9.6km) of water-main, four miles (6.4km) of sewers, ten miles (16km) of conduit, and another ten miles (16km) of road. 4.5 million bricks were used, and 400,000 tonnes of earth had to be excavated. In 1939 only nine airfields had paved runways. Between then and the end of the war, the equivalent of 5,000 miles (8,000km) of three-lane motorway had been laid. Rubble was brought in by train from the bombed cities, but all these miles of runway consumed 45 million tonnes of sand and ballast, and 6.5 million tonnes of cement. Not all airfields could be given paved runways, so a number of types of flexible metal strip roadway were developed to enable grass fields to continue operations throughout the year. By 1945 no fewer than 444 new airfields had been added to the landscape, including 50 built for the USAAF, only 14 of which were constructed by US labour. David Smith has arrived at a total of 740 airfields in use by 1945, in 50 different categories.

The layout of these new airfields was based on the dispersal principle. Suddenly, the bicycle became very important. The lessons of the attacks on airfields of Autumn 1940 were well learned. Aircraft were henceforth to be dispersed around the airfield perimeter, either in hangars or on hard-standings on bomber stations, and in pens with earth traverses, or small, low shelters for fighters. The technical buildings would be grouped together, but away from those with other functions such as instructional. Living or communal sites were dotted around the airfield, but some way away, so messes, accommodation, and recreational facilities were a long way from the aircraft. Defence sites, with their own accommodation huts were placed around the perimeter.

With the new layout came new designs for buildings. There was a new hangar: the T2. In an experiment, two of these were erected by 12 men, working for 20 days with minimal breaks. The resultant 1,200 man-hours would appear to compare less than favourably with the 500 hours claimed for the Bellman, but the T2 was a bigger hangar. There were a number of versions of the T1, T2 and T3, with differing dimensions and different types of cladding, but the most general version (3653/42) known as the 'Home Standard T2' appeared at many airfields. Nearly 1,000 were built altogether. They sometimes appear in coupled pairs or triples. At Barkston Heath (Lincolnshire) there are four in a line, built to house transport aircraft of 9USAAF. Large numbers of T2s still stand, often reclad, and used for storage in both industrial and agricultural contexts. Their transportable nature means that some have migrated. The coupled pair at Duxford, for instance, arrived there from elsewhere after the war, and of the two now at Desborough (Northamptonshire), one was brought from Podington (Bedfordshire), and the other from South Wales, possibly from St Athan.

The 518/40 control tower was constructed in what is sometimes known as 'half-brick', or 'single-brick', but referred to by the RAF as 'temporary brick'. This means that, instead of being 9in (23cm) in thickness, all walls are a single brick's width, and then strengthened by regular brick buttresses, and piers to support the roof. In some cases, to economise on bricks even further, bricks are laid on their sides. When 45 million bricks are needed, even a tiny per cent saving is significant. Such walls were generally rendered in concrete. In the early years of the war, a number of control tower designs were developed, ranging from the single-storey, timber Chief Instructor's Office still standing at White Waltham (Berkshire), or the similar Watch Office (641/41) at Shellingford, in temporary brick with two bay windows, to large, two-storey towers with attached briefing rooms, operations rooms, and PBX. These were put together on a mix-and-match basis so that the components fitted the needs of the station, generally a bomber satellite. There are at least a dozen main drawing numbers which cover this range of structures, but they break down into Type A 7344/40) and Type B (7345/41). Standing examples of Type A include Langar (Nottinghamshire), and of Type B, Long Marston (Warwickshire). A later component of most of these Types A and B was an observation room (13079/41). Further separate designs were used for

94 Framlingham (Parham), Suffolk; the most common of all Second World War watch offices, the type 343/43, with a Visual Control Room on top, and a Nissen hut, crew briefing room behind, now the museum of the Auxiliary Units

95 Langar, Nottinghamshire; squash court in temporary brick construction, around 1941

96 Shepherd's Grove, Suffolk; gymnasium/chapel, *c.*1941

night-fighter stations (12096/41), as at Tangmere (W. Sussex); a new design for bomber satellite (13726/41) as at Seething and Thorpe Abbotts (Norfolk); and various attachments such as an extra control room bolted onto the roof. A new design (12779/41) modified to become the Watch Office for All Commands (343/43) *(94)* finally provided a standard tower that met the majority of needs. These replaced many earlier towers on established airfields, and became the norm on subsequent new ones. Many examples remain, including Wigtown, Debach (Suffolk), Little Walden (Essex), Silverstone (Northamptonshire), Haverfordwest (Pembrokeshire), Duxford,Llanbedr (Gwynedd), and Leicester East, these last three still operating in their original function. At Dumfries, and Findo Gask (Perth & Kinross), third storeys have been added to the design.

The whole range of buildings which had become necessary on airfields was translated into the wartime utility style, either in temporary brick *(95)* or in a variety of hutting types, predominantly Nissen. Some buildings are quite distinctive and can be recognised for their function at a glance, but many are undifferentiated and nondescript. The parachute store, gymnasium/church *(96)*, instructional buildings like the Bombing Teachers and Turret Trainers *(97)*, the Fire and Fuel Tender Houses, and Night-Flying Equipment Stores which clustered round the Watch Office, or the H-shaped Stores *(98)* enclosing the taller Fabric Store, are all instantly identifiable. Often, only an anonymous temporary brick, or Nissen hut presents itself. Occasionally a familiar configuration provides the clue, as in the pairs of Romney Huts which often house the Main Stores or Main

97 Haverfordwest, Pembrokeshire; triple gunnery trainer

Workshops. Sometimes juxtapositioning helps, as in those cases where a small temporary brick structure next to the Parachute Store can, confidently, be identified as the Dinghy Store. Isolated groups of Nissen huts or temporary brick huts with raised towers for water tanks, can usually be accepted as communal living sites. Farms and industrial estates across Britain incorporate the vestiges of wartime airfields in their everyday activities. Particularly well-preserved examples survive at Little Staughton (Cambridgeshire) *(99)*, Drem and East Fortune (Lothian) *(100)*, Haverfordwest, Holme-upon-Spalding Moor, Elvington (North Yorkshire), Tempsford (Bedfordshire), Honeybourne (Worcestershire), and Calveley (Cheshire).

It must be remembered that although the Nissen hut was invented in 1915 by the Canadian engineer officer, Colonel Nissen, and has become one of the archetypal buildings of the Second World War, it continued in production into the 1960s, and there were still huts of that type available for purchase new up to the end of the twentieth century. In 1915 the president of the Royal Institute of British Architects had complained of the waste of talent and expertise caused by the drafting of young architects into Line regiments. Lloyd George was persuaded to agree to the commisioning of such men into the Royal Engineers, and they were enabled to use their initiative in solving problems of materials shortages in innovative ways. The Nissen hut was one such solution to shortages of timber. A whole range of hutting was used on airfields in the Second World War, and many

98 Llandwrog, Gwynedd; Main Stores, *c.*1941

99 Little Staughton, Cambridgeshire; a group of temporary brick structures, dating from 1942–3, on the airfield; the building with the tower is the Parachute Store (9292/42); to its rear is the Dinghy Shed (2901/43); and behind them both, is the Main Workshops (5540/42), consisting of two Romney huts, linked together in an H shape, by an annexe; the Robins hangar, just visible to the right has been relocated from elsewhere on the airfield in recent times

100 East Fortune, Lothian; Main Workshops, *c.*1941

different types, built in a variety of materials: concrete panels, corrugated iron, asbestos sheets, timber planking, plywood and plasterboard sheets, clay blocks etc. can all still be seen on such sites. They ranged in size from the 24 and 30ft (7.2 and 9m) span Nissens, 35ft (10.5m) span Romney, and 45ft (13.5m) span Marston Shed, down to the tiny Igloo Shed, open-ended ammunition storage shelter. Even aircraft hangars were pared down to the minimum, where practicable. The range of Blister hangars found, chiefly on fighter airfields demonstrate this. Blister hangars were also used as gunnery trainers on bomber bases. The synthetic training devices were ingenious attempts to train aircrew in simulated combat conditions. Perhaps the most distinctive of these training buildings was the Anti-Aircraft Dome Trainer, a wooden dome, 40ft (12m) in diameter, and rendered, to give a smooth exterior finish. Only a very few examples survive at Mildenhall, Wyton (Cambridgeshire), Langham (Norfolk), Shoreham (W Sussex) and Pembrey (Carmarthenshire).

Royal Naval Air Stations shared, to a great extent, the building designs of the RAF, up to the end of the Expansion Period. A few designs were different, reflecting the varying needs of the two Services. The Navy could use smaller hangars for folding-wing aircraft, for example, hence their use of the Tees-side Type S (12819/40), and the Main (46691/41) which came in two lengths. There was also a transportable hangar, similar in size to the T2, called the Pentad (3304/43), and a blister-type, the Fromson Massillon. These last two can be seen at Culham (Oxfordshire) and Mains and Pentads at Burscough (Lancashire) and Hinstock (Shropshire). At Evanton (Highland) is an impressive hangar-group which includes a Pentad, four Bellmans, a double and a triple Boulton and Paul VR2 sheds, a B1, F Sheds, reflecting shared use by the Navy and the RAF's armament training school. At Crail (Fife) an almost complete layout survives with an Aircraft Repair Shop, with its north-light roof, and a Bain hangar used as an Electrical Repair Workshop. Amongst the training buildings is a Torpedo Attack Trainer, again, peculiar to the Navy. Perhaps the building which best illustrates the difference is the Control Tower, found on naval air stations. Often of four storeys, incorporating a fire-tender shed, and having balconies and galleries, this building suggests nothing so much as a ship's bridge. Examples survive at Lee-on-Solent (Hampshire), Crail, Burscough, Hinstock *(101)* and Henstridge (Dorset). Many RNAS stations had four runways, most probably in order to cater for the change-able wind-conditions in their, often, exposed locations. Some also had an extra runway for simulating carrier take-offs.

New flying-boat stations tended to use whatever buildings were available, requisitioning them as necessary as at Alness (Ross & Cromarty), and Oban (Argyllshire), where hotels and villas became messes and headquarters buildings. Slipways often remain in civilian use as at Largs (Ayrshire). At the Loch Ryan sites of Wig Bay and Stranraer (Wigtown) relics of the bases are visible in the form of

101 Hinstock, Shropshire; naval type Control Tower from around 1942; the airfield had previously been a SLG for MAP, and there still remains a ruined office bungalow

the jetty used by the local sailing club. Mount Batten (Plymouth), and Calshot (Hampshire), continued to use their First World War hangars. Pembroke Dock retains its two Type B hangars, and some of the buildings of the Victorian dockyard taken over by the RAF, but most of the purpose-built structures have gone. At Hamworthy, Poole, research by Colin Pomeroy has confirmed that the control building still stands, now as a private house. At Fryars Bay, Beaumaris (Anglesey) the Saunders Roe seaplane factory, built to take some pressure off their Isle of Wight home, retains hangars, including a Type B1, and slipways. Loch Ryan was also the location for the RAF's marine craft training, RAF Corsewall, evacuated from the turbulent waters of Calshot. The remnants of its pier still exists. At Lyme Regis (Dorset), the Marine Craft Unit building still stands, now part of a school of boat-building.

We have seen how operational requirements dictated the design of hangars. The aircraft manufacturing process also had an influence. The Ministry of Aircraft Production (MAP) designed a range of hangars for its own needs, and some of these types can be found on airfields. The A1 hangar, gabled with a side annexe, was designed for aircraft production. An example can be seen at the former Fairey works, in what is now a boatyard at Hamble (Hampshire). The B1 Type was a larger hangar, again found on manufacturing sites, but also standard provision on Bomber Stations for aircraft repair workshops. Most bomber bases from 1942 onwards were given one B1 Type and two T2 Type, and dozens of airfields, particularly in East Anglia and Lincolnshire, retain this grouping. Smaller B2 Type hangars appear as coupled pairs at ASUs, and were used for glider storage. Examples survive at Kemble and Wroughton. MAP also used a large R Type hangar still to be seen at Sywell, where Armstrong Whitworth used them, and at Bourn (Cambridgeshire) where a much-modernised triple version stands. Cranage (Cheshire) and Tollerton (Nottinghamshire) retain examples of a MAP side-opening hangar. Robins hangars (2204/41), with sloping sides, and Super-Robins (6910/43) were also used by MAP, but also appear in many other contexts. The aircraft repair site at Horsey Toll (Cambridgeshire) appears to contain a Type A1, a Robins, and a Super Robins.

For the most part, USAAF bases either inherited Air Ministry-designed buildings, or were built with them. The one exception appears to be the Butler Combat hangar, the last surviving example of which, at North Witham (Lincolnshire), was demolished in the 1990s. The Butler Storage Hangar, a much smaller shed, which resembled the Robins Type B, may be represented by a solitary example at Little Staughton, where several Robins also remain.

The rules governing the numbers of aircraft which could be safely stored at ASUs meant that it was necessary to allocate Satellite Landing Grounds (SLG) as extra storage facilities. Around 50 SLGs served the 25 ASUs. Each SLG was given a bungalow watch office *(102)*, a tractor shed, mess hut, and some living huts. Some had a Robins hangar as well, although most stored aircraft were kept in hides, clearings in the trees. Bungalows survive at Wath Head (Cumbria),

102 Rudbaxton, Pembrokeshire; Ministry of Aircraft Production office for Satellite Landing Grounds

Winterseugh (Dumfries) and Rudbaxton (Pembrokeshire) whose tractor shed also stands. Robins hangars remain at Black Isle (Ross and Cromarty) and at Brayton (Cumbria). The ruins of a bungalow watch office at Ollerton (Shropshire) mark the SLG which later became RNAS Hinstock. Some factories initiated their own storage facilities, outside the official SLG programme. Marwell Hall, now a Zoo, retains several out of the 20 Robins hangars put up by the then owner, the managing director of the Cunliffe-Owen factory in Southampton, to safeguard finished aircraft from the constant bombing raids on the factory. Aircraft were flown in and out by ATA pilots, whose administrative base was in the Hall.

The end of the Second World War was the high point for military aviation in terms of numbers of airfields, aircraft, ancillary establishments and personnel. In 1945, Britain was faced with a dilemma. On the one hand was the desire to remain in the select group of nations seen to be taking a lead in the world. On the other, was the recognition that after six years of war, the country was bankrupt, exhausted, and would need every penny and every ounce of energy just to survive. The military dimension of this dilemma related to the choice between a future of conventional or of nuclear weapons. Realistically, once the nuclear box had been opened, there was no choice. It was decided that Britain would retain membership of the nuclear club in order to ensure that she would be both able to influence the deterrent function of nuclear weapons, and to limit their proliferation. The next problem was which delivery system to opt for. Strong lobbying on the part of the RAF and its suppliers, coupled with the prohibitive cost of developing a viable alternative, made an airborne nuclear bomb, to be delivered by a force of bombers, the favoured solution. The RAF was to retain this unique role until 1969. A force of V-bombers, Valiants, Vulcans and Victors, was established in the mid-1950s, based in the old bomber bases associated with the Dambusters and suchlike, and armed with the Blue Steel stand-off bomb. Fighter protection was provided, Javelins initially, then Lightnings, both to protect the bombers, and to intercept intruders. At the same time conventional weapons systems were being run down. AA Command was stood down in 1955, and Coast Defence a year later. In 1961 it was felt that the country's defence spending was still excessive. More cuts were made in personnel and equipment, extending to the reserves and theTerritorial Army. For a a few years from 1961, a land-based rocket delivery system was seen as the answer, and the THOR Intermediate-Range Ballistic Missile (IRBM) system was adopted from the USA for joint use, but based in Britain to be within range of eastern european targets. By 1969, it was obvious that Britain's major nuclear capability should be based on a seaborne rocket delivery system, and, first Polaris, and latterly Trident, have been installed in the nuclear submarines of the Royal Navy. Despite the enormous commitment to nuclear warfare, conventional wars have continued to be fought both during the Cold War period, and since the thaw. Britain's major efforts are divided between the nuclear deterrent, the technological advances in conventional warfare, low-level but high profile international policing operations, and global intelligence gathering. All the developments outlined above are reflected in airfield architecture in the second half of the century.

Even before the advent of the V-bomber, the airfields to be used by heavy bombers required substantial modifications to be carried out. Runways had to be lengthened to at least 3,000 yards. Both Scampton and Waddington saw reroutings of the old Roman road, the A15, in order to accommodate their runway extensions. From the end of the war, a programme of replacing control towers had begun. The 294/45 model, for Very Heavy Bomber Stations, of three storeys with additional Visual Control Room (VCR) on top, still stands at Sculthorpe, Marham and West Raynham (Norfolk), and Lakenheath (Suffolk). Updated versions (5223a/51) can be seen at Biggin Hill (Kent), North Weald (Essex), and Greenham Common (Berkshire). A similar tower for Very Heavy Transport Stations was built at St Mawgan (Cornwall) and Heathrow. In 1955 a control tower for V-Bomber stations was built at Gaydon (Warwickshire) and Wittering (Cambridgeshire), with a modified version at Valley (Anglesey). All of these still stand, as do examples of a much more common design (2548c/55), with local and approach control on two floors with a VCR on top, at Shawbury (Shropshire), Thorney Island (Sussex), Leuchars (Fife), Colerne (Wiltshire), and Benson

103 Thurleigh, Bedfordshire; the Royal Aircraft Establishment Control Tower of 1957; the airfield also retains an interesting group of hangars

(Oxfordshire). Swinderby (Lincolnshire) has the side-by-side version (7378a/55) on one floor plus VCR. Many stations were updated simply by adding a VCR (5871c/55) to a wartime tower, as at Wyton (Cambridgeshire) or Barkston Heath (Lincolnshire). At other stations such as Odiham (Hampshire) local designs for improving earlier towers were produced individually. At RAE Thurleigh (Bedfordshire) *(103)*, a new four-storey tower, with projecting, cantilevered gallery, and VCR, was built in 1957, to a local design. Booker (Buckinghamshire), now in use as Wycombe Air Park, has a small, 1950s tower, with two storeys and VCR, designed for Reserve Flying Training Schools. The Seco control tower (WA15/213/53) at Kirkbride (Cumbria) survives despite losing its attached, 5-bay office hut.

The greatly enlarged aircraft of the postwar period demanded larger hangars. The Gaydon hangar, taking its name from its first appearance in 1954, after the reopening of Gaydon as a Valiant base, is of all-steel construction, with curved roof. Examples can also be seen at Wittering, Coningsby and Valley. The USAF also had a large hangar for its B29s and B47s. Bruntingthorpe (Leicestershire) with its 3,400 yard-long runway, retains a USAF Luria hangar from its refurbishment in 1957. At Greenham Common there remain three of these hangars, and two more at Fairford (Gloucestershire). The problem of accommodating over-large aircraft was not a new one. It had been solved in the First World War by using nose-docking for Sunderland flying boats. Such structures were rediscovered in the

Cold War era, and different types can be seen at Upper Heyford and Alconbury. One overriding feature of the RAF's task in the 1960s was to be able to function as a Quick Reaction Alert force. Thus airfields with V-Bombers permanently had aircraft and crews on short notice, standing on Operational Readiness Platforms. At Binbrook (Lincolnshire) is a QRA hangar of around 1972, twin-gabled, with concertina doors. It was built to house a pair of Lightning fighters, ready, at a moment's notice, to intercept suspect aircraft approaching British airspace. As well as hangars where size was the major design criterion, there was also a need for hangars offering protection against accurate and penetrative bombing. Hardened aircraft shelters (HARS), built to NATO standards can be seen at Honington (Suffolk) and Upper Heyford. At Alconbury (Cambridgeshire) are standard HARS plus specially widened versions for the TR1 Blackbird reconnaissance aircraft.

Many of the airfields of the Cold War were simply Expansion Period ones, modified better to perform new tasks. Coningsby, for instance, closed for refurbishment in order to be re-equipped with Phantoms, rather than the new TSR2 fighter which never materialised, but is nevertheless recogniseable as a 1930s airfield. Marham, Wittering, Cottesmore, Binbrook, Waddington, Mildenhall, Finningley, Alconbury, Kinloss and Scampton, all date from the Expansion Period. Many original buildings remain, often adapted to new uses. At Mildenhall, for instance, the Ready-use Fire-Fighting Motor Transport shed (3681/36) is now a social centre containing a bowling alley. The 1931 Crew Room and Locker Room has been a chapel, and later, offices for the airfield's maintenance department. The old Type A Hangars are now resplendent in their brown and cream USAF livery, shared with neighbouring sheet-steel structures of the 1990s. One, less obvious feature of these Cold War airfields is the reinforcement given to many of the buildings, particularly operations blocks and headquarters, sick bays and decontamination centres. Although not all will necessarily withstand nuclear explosions, many are equipped to resist chemical and biological weapons, and the short-term effects of nuclear fall-out. A number of specialist buildings appeared relating to Blue Steel, the stand-off atomic bomb. The storage, servicing and fuelling buildings, along with associated administrative buildings can be seen at Scampton and Wittering, the only V-bomber stations to be so equipped. In the event of tension, such as the Cuba crisis of 1962, warheads would be issued to the other V-bomber stations or dispersal airfields, either from these two stations by air, or from the PADs at Barnham (Norfolk) and Faldingworth (Lincolnshire).

Over the second half of the century, airfields have generally been seen as the natural locations for land-based missiles. The THOR programme of 1959-63 involved the use of 20 airfields in four groups based in the eastern counties of England. Existing airfields were chosen for a number of reasons. Firstly, substantial buildings such as existing hangars were required for the receipt, inspection and maintenance (RIM) of the missiles. Secondly, the concrete runways and perimeter tracks provided ample hard-standings for the launch platforms. Thirdly, all the workshop, office and living accommodation needs would be met. As well as the

104 Coleby Grange, Lincolnshire; blast walls

RIM building, another hangar was used as the technical storage building. Prior to firing, the rocket was kept in a horizontal position inside a long tent-like cover, on an erector vehicle which ran on rails into the launching bay. This comprised two, very thick concrete blast walls *(104)*, serviced by fuel pipes and power cables contained in open concrete channels. The other structures were minimal. There were fuel tanks, police hut, garages, and fire-tender shed, and not much else as many of the operations were carried out from mobile trailers. Warheads were stored off-site but small ready-use classified storage buildings and pyrotechnic stores behind earth traverses, were provided for each launch site. Each THOR site had three launch pads. Other characteristic structures were cylindrical theodolite pillars, about 12ft (3.6m) tall, with flat mounting plates on top, generally one for each pad, and one concrete cabin for another theodolite. These instruments enabled the gyro-compass in the rocket to be set accurately, an activity of some priority, one must assume. The whole of the launch area was enclosed by double security fences. RAF pilots flying into airfields near the THOR sites during the early 1960s have described the blue lighting which drew their attention. Perhaps this was part of the deterrent principle. The enemy had to know about it before he could be deterred. North Luffenham (Rutland), the main station for the south-western group, probably retains the most complete THOR site layout. Until recently, Mepal (Cambridgeshire) still had all its ducting and channels, but has been cleared away. Harrington (Northamptonshire) has its classified storage buildings and pyrotechnic stores. At Melton Mowbray (Leicestershire) can be seen the theodolite cabin with its central pillar and big windows. The L-shaped blast walls still stand at Polebrook (Northamptonshire), Coleby Grange, Folkingham, Hemswell and Ludford Magna (Lincolnshire), Melton Mowbray (Leicestershire), Feltwell and North Pickenham (Norfolk). Nothing remains at Carnaby or Driffield (East Yorkshire), or at Mepal. It is sobering to think that the evidence of such an important, costly and sophisticated operation could almost be wiped off the face of the earth in the space of less than two generations.

Despite its claim as an AA weapon to be included in Chapter 7, Bloodhound, the surface-to-air missile (SAM) in service with the RAF throughout the Cold War period will be dealt with here as it was deployed exclusively on airfields, and its prime purpose was always to defend the users of airfields, the V-bomber force and the THOR network, although there was some incidental cover for the Midlands. From its initial deployment in 1958, Bloodhound Mark 1 was located at eleven bases in the eastern counties, organised into four wings. Each wing had a tactical control centre (TCC) which was equipped with servicing, maintenance and repair facilities beyond what was present on each missile site. Each TCC also had Type 82 Orange Yeoman radar which enabled data on designated targets to be transmitted to individual missile sites. Each site had two units of eight missiles each. North Coates, the test site had three units. The ten wings are each laid out the same. A large, missile-servicing building stands alongside Station headquarters, and other small test and administrative buildings. Along the road to the hard-standings of the launch pads, are a refuelling building which is a Handcraft hut on a raised brick base, and, further on a mess, presumably located here to cut time spent away from the launch pads. At the far end of the site, is the drive-through arming shed, and, facing east, are the two launch control posts, each with their eight pads in front of them. Next to each launch control post is a works services building containing generators and compressors. Each launch pad received electrical, hydraulic and pneumatic power through service conduits. Almost the entire set-up can be seen at Woolfox Lodge *(105)* and North Luffenham (Rutland). The distinctive guardrooms survive at Rattlesden (Suffolk) and Warboys (Cambridgeshire). There are missile servicing buildings at Warboys and at Dunholme Lodge (Lincolnshire) which also has its launch control posts and works services buildings. Woolfox Lodge has some hut bases which might suggest that the mess and other domestic buildings were temporary Seco constructions or suchlike. Breighton retains a group of BCF huts which may be from this period. Bloodhound Mark II, under development by 1963, was an improved system. It was more mobile, in that services to the launcher were removeable and portable. It had a greater range, and it had better direction from the Type 86 radar, now in service. Between the 1963 trials, and 1991 when all units were stood down, in addition to North Coates, still the main trials site, there were five wings on

105 Woolfox Lodge, Rutland; Bloodhound SAM site, with Works Services Building, and Launch Control beyond

airfields, and a sixth at Bawdsey radar site. West Raynham (Norfolk) was established as the Bloodhound Support Unit, the base for all servicing. Units moved overseas and returned, but once the Rapier was operational in West Germany, in 1983, the units with their Bloodhounds returned to Britain, some being based in locations new to the weapon: Wattisham, Wyton and Barkston Heath. At Woodhall Spa (Lincolnshire), the Mark IIs had been stood down in 1967. Layouts were much less uniform than had been necessary with Mark I, since the enhanced mobility of the Mark II, meant that existing infrastructure could be utilised. At North Coates, the old Mark I pads were recycled. Again, a fair amount is visible at a number of Mark II locations. West Raynham retains its extensive complex of servicing buildings along the east edge of the airfield, and buildings and launch pads remain at North Coates. Some of Wyton's installations are already swallowed up by later structures, but recent photographs show Wattisham's site to be fairly complete. One unusual structure must be mentioned here. That is West Raynham's Air Defence Tactical Training Theatre or ADT3, a later version of the Dome Trainer, and used for Rapier SAM training.

Throughout the 1980s another land-based missile system was accommodated on British airfields. This was the USAF's ground launched cruise missile (GLCM) system with six wings based in Europe, two of them at Greenham Common (Berkshire) *(106)* and Molesworth (Cambridgeshire). On both sites, missiles were

106 Greenham Common, Berkshire; storage bunker for Cruise missiles

stored in earth-covered concrete shelters under conditions of extreme security. Within the guarded and sunken compounds were stored transporter erector launchers, launch control vehicles, and all the servicing and maintenance facilities needed to get the show on the road, and to keep it there. At Greenham Common there are six of the hardened shelters, still behind wire but open to the elements, and visible from what has now reverted to common land. Molesworth never developed as far, but the four shelters there, still overlooked by the tall watch tower, can be seen from outside the perimeter of the, still-active, USAF base.

6

BUILDINGS FOR THE ARMY AND THE NAVY

Most soldiers and sailors began the twentieth century quartered in the same barracks that their predecessors had lived in for the previous 200 years. Certainly the styles had not changed much in all that time, and, in some cases, neither had the actual buildings. The style was a very traditional one. Most line regiments were based in depots built as a result of the Cardwell reforms of the 1870s which localised recruitment, training and home postings. These depots usually included an armoury based on the concept of the medieval keep. Many of these barracks were defensible, with loopholed and bastioned perimeter walls. When Winchester Barracks, the conversion of Wren's baroque royal palace, burnt down in 1894, it was rebuilt around 1900 as a faithful facsimile, complete with Corinthian columns, pediments and a cupola. It has now been splendidly refurbished as apartments. In Portsmouth, the sailors in what is now the shore establishment HMS *Victory*, were given refurbished former infantry barracks in 1899-1903 which are crenelated and machicolated. Across the road, their officers lived in a wardroom (1903) which could be mistaken for a Flemish town hall, quite properly imposing, but, very clearly, from another century. Around the corner, Clarence and Victoria Barracks (late-1890s) were built as French chateaux. One block survived the bombing in the Second World War, and now serves as Portsmouth's museum and art gallery. The gradual professionalisation of the armed forces throughout the second half of Victoria's reign had necessitated a vast building programme, and this was continued over into the new century, with the very definite intention of improving the living standards of the members of the armed forces. As the troops returned from the Boer War more accommodation was needed, and the Royal Engineers came up with simple guidelines for the layout and construction of new barracks, taking account of functional factors, and also other practical considerations of hygiene, health and recreation. It must be remembered that communal dining facilities, and the central cookhouses to service them, were still only a recent replacement for small-group messing in barrack rooms. New barracks, following these principles, were added to Colchester, but, at Tidworth (Wiltshire), a wholly-new establishment for eight battalions, provided a greenfield test bed for

107 Caterham Barracks, Surrey, a barrack block now converted into private housing; this represents a radical new design over the turn of the nineteenth century; other ranks lived in rooms connected by balconies, with access to fresh air, separate dining facilities, and proper sanitation; non-commissioned officers lived in the towers, connected by walk-ways

the new pattern. Detail was important. The two-storey barrack-blocks, for instance, were aligned north–south to allow maximum sunlight to enter. Rooms were smaller than previously to make heating more effective. This was a real advance, for it must be remembered that cavalry-troopers, still living in the barracks of the Victorian era such as Colchester, were required to sleep in lofts above the stables, heated solely by the rising warmth of their horses. These new barrack-rooms at Tidworth, which were inter-connecting, were reached by external verandahs running the length of the building at both levels. NCOs were housed in separate blocks, reached by galleries off the verandahs. A matching block, also accommodating 16 companies of infantry, was linked by the shared dining room and cookhouse/washing/drying rooms, to form an H-block holding half a battalion. A single example of such a block can also be seen at Caterham (Surrey) *(107)*, where the former depot of the Guards Regiments has been imaginatively converted into modern housing. If the layout and internal organisation was new, the appearance of these barracks was little changed. At Llanion Barracks, Pembroke Dock *(108)*, built in 1904 as an alternative depot for battalions of the Welsh regiments, stationed at Wrexham, Cardiff and Brecon, the only apparent gesture to modernity is the absence of a keep. All the other components of the barracks are indistinguishable from earlier examples. Here, barrack blocks are now in use as apartments, administrative buildings are churches or offices, and most of the later, more functional, buildings are in industrial or commercial use. A much grander barracks, but no less traditional in appearance, was built in Edinburgh. Redford Barracks (1907–15), for combined infantry and cavalry is on a monumental scale. This was the first major achievement of a new civilian War Office Directorate of Barracks Construction, set up when it was feared that RE officers were being diverted from their military specialisms by the demands of more domestic activities. Previous experience of building workers' housing qualified Harry Measures for the post of Director, and Redford's Free Imperial Baroque style on such a large scale, probably represents the zenith of the traditional barracks. Redford is still in military use. Other, more modest buildings of this period are attractively if traditionally designed. The School of (Naval) Physical Training (1910), in Flathouse Road *(109)*, Portsmouth, for instance, an L-shaped complex of swimming pool and gymnasium, entered through a domed foyer, and decorated with banded brickwork, stone dressings and turrets, attempts to disguise any innovative internal construction with a traditional external envelope. So solidly built are these late-Victorian and Edwardian buildings, that many, like Redford, are still used by the services. Brock Barracks in Reading, for instance, complete with its faux-medieval gateway and battlemented keep, continues to accommodate units of the Territorial Army (TA). Smith-Dorrien House, in Aldershot (Hampshire), built in 1908, to house Methodist soldiers, continues in a social and community function. Its lantern-topped towers and remarkable

108 Pembroke Dock, Pembrokeshire; Llanion Barracks, built 1904 in a very traditional style; this is the Officers' Mess with the Commanding Officer's house beyond

109 Portsmouth, Hampshire; Royal Naval School of Physical Training in Flathouse Road, *c.*1910; gymnasium and swimming pool form an L-shaped block, with stylish entrance in the re-entrant angle; now a fitness centre

windowed façade could hardly be less martial, and yet it manages to project an image that is clearly institutional, solid and dependable, just like that of the army. If the army was improving the quality of domestic life for its soldiers, then the navy had had further to come. When the first ratings moved into the new Keyham Barracks, Devonport, now HMS *Drake*, between 1890 and 1907, they came from living in hulks, long deemed unsuitable for convicts but still apparently good enough for sailors on shore between postings. Here, a similar arrangement to that at Tidworth is employed, with one essential difference. Each of the four floors of each barrack-block consisted of a large space in which could be slung 125 hammocks. Four of Drake's eight blocks still remain in naval use, along with the accompanying officers' wardroom and some of the detached cookhouses, dining rooms and ablutions similar in conception to those seen at Tidworth.

Another category of building which cloaked itself in the architectural vocabulary of the past was the drill hall. The militia barracks of the 1850s such as Lincoln and Grantham (Lincolnshire), and the Honourable Artillery Company's headquarters at Finsbury in the City of London, had provided the pattern for the quasi-mediaeval fortresses which were built as part of the implementation of the Cardwell programme. Neither the Rifle Volunteers from 1860 in Britain, nor their cousins in the cities of the United States building their enormous castellated Armories, saw any reason to depart from this style. As late as 1907, two drill halls built in Sheffield were given gates from other times. Somme Barracks, home of the West Yorkshire Volunteer Royal Engineers, has a Tudor tower with octagonal turrets with ogee caps, and the Edmund Street base of the West Riding Batteries of the Royal Field Artillery, has a four-storey castellated tower with machicolations. Such apparent anachronisms are far from unusual. Similar drill halls, dating from the early part of the century can be seen at Portsmouth (1901), Winsford, Cheshire (1900), Kings Road, Whalley Range, Manchester (1903), Wrexham, with arrow-loops, (c.1902), and, in Glasgow, Govan (1905 for the Royal Naval Reserve), and Gilbert Street (1901 for the 6 Volunteer Battalion Highland Light Infantry). The enormous upsurge in recruitment to the Volunteer Force which was, most probably occasioned by the Boer War, combined with the escalating costs, and ambiguities regarding accountability, eventually led to a recognition of the need to put the volunteers on to a more official and secure footing. In 1908, the Territorial Force (TF) was established, funded by Government but administered by local, usually County, Territorial Associations *(110)*. Between 1908 and 1914, a large number of drill halls were built, many of them in the Edwardian Baroque style, sometimes dubbed 'Wrenaissance'. It may be noted here that the Old War Office, in Whitehall, completed in 1907, is itself in a very grand Baroque style. It may be that the new drill halls of the TF were designed to be a conscious move away from the anarchic eclecticism of the volunteer movement which drew on, as the War Office may have seen it, outmoded notions of medievalism. Recent reference to over 1500 extant drill halls in Britain, has suggested a move toward uniformity, not previously seen. Whilst local architects continued to design

110 Blair Atholl, Perth and Kinross; the 1907 drill hall of A Squadron, 1st Scottish Horse, Territorial Force

111 Holywell, Flintshire; drill hall, built 1914, for D Company, 5th (Flintshire) Battalion The Royal Welsh Fusiliers, Territorial Force

premises for the local Association, Scorer and Gamble in Lincolnshire for instance, there is, in the form of each building, an observable pattern. A two-storey front block with orderly room, offices for the CO and adjutant, messes, armoury, stores etc. is placed in front of a hall, along one side of which is usually an indoor rifle range. At the back are garages or gun sheds, and often there is a house adjoining for a permanent staff instructor or a caretaker. The components of the complex were well-established, but the uniformity of their grouping was new. Several groups of contemporary drill halls in the Edwardian Baroque style, all dating from around 1913-14, can be seen, along with some amongst the small group of drill halls built during the 1920s: the TF Association offices in Mold (Flintshire) and the drill halls in Holywell *(111)* and Rhyl; the drill halls in Melton Mowbray, Hinckley, Shepshed (Leicestershire), Oakham (Rutland), and Rugeley (Staffordshire), for instance; and Wellingborough and Rushden (Northants), possibly from the later period, and Millfield, Peterborough (Cambridgeshire), dated 1927, all exemplify this particular style. Although no two drill halls are identical, local styles are nevertheless observable from this period, as in Cornwall, (Hayle, 1911, Redruth, 1912, and St Just, 1911). Occasionally buildings stand out as even more individual than normal. The arts and crafts inspired TF Association office and drill hall (1913) at Kirkcaldy (Fife), is a fine example of this.

Naval dockyards were for the most part established during the Georgian period and consolidated through Victoria's reign, the heyday of the Royal Navy. Many of the specialist buildings from this era, often large covered spaces using innovative construction techniques, were simply adapted for new machinery. At Portsmouth, Chatham, Devonport and Sheerness, early buildings were converted, extended or modified for new demands. Occasionally the requirements of the Dreadnoughts necessitated new building, and the factory (1905-7) at Portsmouth was built for this programme. It is 600ft (180m) long, and has two spans, each of 150ft (45m) under gabled glass roofs. Travelling gantries run along the length of each bay. It originally housed machinery, much of which was imported from Germany. There is a certain irony in the fact that it was the threat of the German potential for naval superiority which prompted the need for a new dockyard to be built at Rosyth on the Forth, between 1903 and the outbreak of war. Graving docks, workshops and a fuel depot were built, and largely remain within the present dockyard.

The enormous expansion of the armed forces during the First World War resulted in the creation of vast cities of tents and temporary buildings. The camp for newly-enlisted soldiers at Ripon (North Yorkshire) eventually accommodated 50,000 men in huts, was served by a narrow-gauge railway, and included churches, institutes, canteens and cinema. A new power station was needed to provide electricity, there were 26 miles of roadway, and a military hospital. The entire camp was built in four months by navvies recruited from Ireland specifically for this job. Everything was quickly demolished in 1922, and Claro Barracks now occupies part of the site. Bramshott (Hampshire) was chosen as the location for camps for the Canadian troops en route for service on the Western Front. They were billeted, 25 to a hut with a stove, and slept on beds of planks on trestles. Along the main road there grew up 'Tin Town', all the shops and services for the camp, Salvation Army, YMCA, churches, cafes and so on. The camp occupied nearly a square mile (2.5 sq.km), and included the 630-bed hospital built prior to occupation by the Canadians. They expanded it for their own use, and also found room for 1,000 battle casualties. At the end of the war, Bramshott camp was entirely cleared, once the twin traumas of slow demobilisation and an influenza pandemic had been endured. A handful of huts were re-erected, some as housing, and one as a school cricket pavilion. A row of officers' housing now serves as a terrace of private housing in Haslemere Road, Liphook *(112)* (Hampshire). Ripon and Bramshott were typical of dozens of such temporary camps which for a short while made an enormous impact on a locality. Ripon's occupants, for instance, brought a weekly spending power of £9,000 to the city's shops and leisure facilities. Many of Bramshott's Canadians, far from home, were given generous hospitality by the locals. Early in the war, hutting was built on the spot by labourers. By the second autumn of the war it was apparent that several more Christmases would pass before a resolution was likely, and that shelter was needed not only behind the front line, but also at home, both urgently and in quantity. In August 1915, a revised 'Scale of Accommodation' for the British Expeditionary Force was drawn up, which required a significant increase in huts. A large number of prefabricated designs were tried out. Most involved the use of folding trusses, and timber

112 Liphook, Hampshire; officers' accommodation from First World War Bramshott Camp; now a terrace of cottages on Haslemere Road

panels and floors. All tended to be overshadowed by the two versions of the Nissen hut, one for sleeping, and one, cosily lined with matchboard, for hospital use. The Nissen owed its success to its simplicity. It had floor panels, corrugated iron roof panels, and end panels which came with doors and windows. A sleeping hut for 24 men weighed one ton, could be carried on an army lorry, and assembled in four hours by four men using only spanners. Each component was inter-change-able and could be lifted by two men. The hospital hut was proportionately larger and heavier but used the same parts, plus a roof light. This made it suitable for other applications, as a dining room or recreation hut. All the parts were made in factories and shipped to wherever they were needed. Somewhere between 25,000 and 30,000 huts were produced during the last two years of the war. Once the need was over, the camps disappeared, only a very few like Bovington (Dorset), the home of the new Tank Corps, Royal from 1923, being retained as a permanent base. It should be noted that some of the huts from the original camp became married quarters after the Second World War, and were not finally replaced until the mid-1960s.

The interwar years saw very little building of barracks and camps, apart from on Salisbury Plain. The School of Artillery, at Larkhill, was developed around the mid-1920s, and again, ten years later, during which expansion, St Alban's, its garrison church (1937) was built *(113)*. The major developments at Bulford Barracks also belong to the 'thirties, although its church was completed in 1927. Both these, and Bovington share the neo-Georgian style which we have already met on the RAF's airfields of the Expansion Period. It is interesting to note that the RAF Officers' Mess, to drawing number 7035/30, an example of which still stands at the former RAF Westwood Farm (Peterborough), can also still be seen at Warley Barracks (Essex), now a nursing home, at Deepcut Barracks, still a depot of the Royal Logistics Corps, and at Bordon (Hampshire), most recently used by the MoD Police.

There was, however, one area in which a significant military construction programme was implemented in the 1930s, and that was the drill halls of the Territorial Army (TA), which had been reconstituted in 1920. The accelerating mechanisation of the army required soldiers, particularly part-time ones, with new skills. Volunteers had always been men in steady employment, and now the army needed volunteers from particular types of employment: engineering, mechanical, electrical and civil; automotive trades; wireless technicians. Many TA infantry units, still bearing the names of illustrious line regiments were transformed into AA gunners with the Royal Artillery, or into searchlight operators with the Royal Engineers. Some of the Yeomanry regiments exchanged their horses for tanks and armoured cars, whilst others converted to field artillery. Many remained as infantry, but with mechanised transport, AT rifles, and automatic weapons. All this change made new premises indispensable, for training and for secure storage of the expensive, new kit *(114)*. The AA gunners needed indoor dome trainers; the tankers and transport units needed garages; the engineers needed workshops. The new buildings incorporated all the traditional components plus garages,

113 Larkhill, Wiltshire; St Alban's, the Garrison church of 1937

114 Left Southwold, Suffolk; the drill hall built in the geodetic barrel style and now an antiques centre known as 'The Dome'; it shares its design with a group of Cornish drill halls used by anti-aircraft units in the 1930s

115 Below Sutton, south-west London; Farringdon House TA Centre, built during the later 1930s; now home to a unit of the Royal Logistics Corps

workshops, gun sheds, training rooms, and increased accommodation for the permanent staff needed to maintain equipment, and to train the volunteers. The style chosen for the majority of these buildings was the same neo-Georgian, employed on airfields. At least 210 new or replacement drill halls were built in England during the 1930s, 40 of them in Greater London *(115)*. About 80 per cent still stand, but current cuts in defence spending is seeing a great deal of disposal and demolition. Suburban drill halls often occupy valuable building land, where the added factor of brown-field status makes development of the site for housing even more attractive. Drill halls of this period are much rarer in Wales and Scotland, but there are good examples in Cardiff, Edinburgh, Glasgow and in other places. As well as the traditional neo-Georgian style, there are examples of international modern *(116)*, most notably Aintree Barracks in Liverpool. Sometimes even the more staid buildings can throw up surprises, such as the carved reliefs of searchlight beams which flank the RE crest over the door of the Edgeware drill hall of the 72 Middlesex Searchlight Regiment, formerly infantry. This drill hall was officially opened in 1938 by Leslie Hore-Belisha, then Secretary of State for War. It was Hore-Belisha, incidentally, who incurred the displeasure of the Army's top brass by shipping TA engineers on his own initiative out to

116 Truro, Cornwall; Moresk Road drill hall built around 1936; there was a company of the Duke of Cornwall's Light Infantry in Truro at this time, and also one squadron of the 1st Devon Yeomanry, who converted into a field artillery unit around 1938; one earlier drill hall survives in the city, and the site of another is known

France in 1939, to construct fixed fortifications on the Franco-Belgian border, in order to minimise the problems caused by the premature termination of the Maginot Line. At Millbrook, Southampton, a pair of identical drill halls standing alongside each other were built to accommodate brother units of TA engineers and gunners. At Peronne Road, Portsmouth the new drill hall designed in the 1930s, was delayed by the Second World War, and only built in 1946-7. In the light of the intervening experience, window size was reduced, the line of the roof-tiles was altered, and a service walkway was inserted at parapet level, all as a response to the threat of incendiary bombs.

The sudden increase in the size of the armed forces in the Second World War, recreated a similar scenario to that we have already seen. Camps covered the land, both early in the war to cater for mobilisation, and in the later concentration of troops massing for the Normandy landings. Nissen huts, the similar, but larger, Romney huts, many types of timber, plasterboard, and half-brick huts were used in their thousands, as well as tents. Very few buildings, intended to be permanent were constructed during the war for camps or barracks. One of the few was Quebec Barracks, in Wootton, Northamptonshire. The nineteenth-century Gibraltar Barracks in the town, had long been inadequate as a regimental depot. In both world wars hutted camps had been established on Northampton Racecourse to relieve the pressure, but by 1941, even this expedient was deemed insufficient, and a new barracks was built. This subsequently became the depot of the Pioneer Corps, and then redundancy brought demolition, and it has entirely vanished. Still with us, however, are numbers of hutted camps such as Stainton Camp outside Barnard Castle (County Durham), now, for the most part occupied by an industrial estate, or the abandoned barracks outside Lanark. Many others are used as industrial estates, some have other uses. The timber huts of Weybourne AA Practice Camp (Norfolk) are part of the military museum known as the Muckleburgh Collection. A few, such as Beckingham Camp on the Lincolnshire/Nottinghamshire border are still in military use.

One other type of camp deserves a mention. That is the prisoner-of-war (POW) camp. In the First World War, these tended to be established in all sorts of locations: farms, country houses, schools, rectories etc., many of which were simply bases for work parties. There were hutted camps as well, but, again, these usually followed no fixed pattern. In the Second World War, however, there was an established plan for the POW camp, and they are, therefore, generally recognisable. Eden Camp in East Yorkshire has been opened as a tourist attraction. Another camp, at Harperley in County Durham, has recently been scheduled as an ancient monument. Fragments of camps can be seen all over Britain. They consist of two compounds, one called the 'Guards Section' contains the administration block, CO's quarters, detention cell, quartermaster's stores, armoury, water tower, fuel compound, and messes and living quarters for the staff. The 'Prisoners' Section' contains rows of living huts, ablutions blocks, canteen and dining-room. This layout exists, almost in its entirety, at Harperley, and at Pingley Camp, Brigg,

Lincolnshire. Easton Grey (Wiltshire) and Nether Heaton (Nottinghamshire) survive as industrial estates. Some unique features remain such as Harperley's theatre hut, complete with orchestra pit, and the well-known Italian chapel, crafted inside a Nissen hut on Lambholm, Orkney, as do many other examples of mural decoration. Many of these camps enjoyed an extended existence as international agricultural hostels. That at Fridaybridge, near Wisbech (Cambridgeshire) still fulfils this function, and, for obvious reasons, is gradually replacing the 60-year-old 'temporary' buildings. Surviving huts are built from a variety of materials: timber at Spalding, BCF concrete panels at Retford, clay-blocks at Moorby (Lincolnshire), Pingley and Caunton (Nottinghamshire). There are also Laing huts with timber frames and panels made of corrugated iron and plaster-board. Some camps, at the end of the war took over redundant military premises. One of the communal sites at RAF Kingscliffe, and the prewar militia camp at Ely, for instance, became POW camps.

As an alternative to building from new, all three services throughout the Second World War utilised as many existing buildings as possible, in order to avoid the costs in time, money, labour and materials which new builds incurred. Country houses were popular as training establishments since they were often situated in extensive private grounds with plenty of space for extra, usually hutted, accommodation to be erected, for training exercises to be carried out, and some level of secrecy to be maintained. This last point was often the most important. The training centres for Special Operations Executive (SOE) personnel were based almost exclusively on country estates. Paramilitary training took place in the Scottish Highlands, mainly in Inverness. Finishing schools were in the New Forest, centred on Brockenhurst, and Operational schools and Signals were dispersed around the Home Counties and south Midlands. Parachute schools were in Cheshire, presumably to be close to the main training facilities of Ringway airfield (Manchester), and Tatton Park. The supplies section for preparing drops to agents was based at Holme, in the fens between Peterborough and Huntingdon, close to Tempsford (Bedfordshire) and Harrington (Northamptonshire), the airfields which would deliver the containers. Commando training was similarly centred on Invereray (Argyll), as HMS *Quebec*, close to suitable terrain, and far from prying eyes, with headquarters Combined Operations (HMS *Armadillo*) at Glenfinnan House, and other elements at Rosneath Castle (Dunbartonshire), Achnacarry Castle (Highland), and Inverailort Castle (Highland). The Auxiliary Units' training base was Coleshill (Berkshire) where a practice operational base still exists along with the outhouses used by trainees, but the main house burnt down in 1952. The access was via the Post Office in nearby Highworth, still protected by a loopholed wall. The auxiliaries in Lincolnshire used Dalby Hall as a training base. In Essex the intelligence officer for East Anglia used his father's vicarage at Kelvedon as his base, storing weapons in the coach-house. Suffolk auxiliaries trained at Mill House, Cransford.

The navy had need of a whole range of premises for many different purposes. Billy Butlin's holiday camp at Skegness, HMS *Royal Arthur* for the duration, was ideal for recruit training. Southwick House, behind Portsdown Hill, became the refuge for HMS *Dryad*, the navy's school of navigation after it had been bombed out of its home in Portsmouth Dockyard in Summer 1941. Once the naval Command headquarters had been established in Fort Southwick, and the D–Day planners were looking for a base nearby, Southwick House was the obvious choice, especially as it already provided overflow accommodation for staff from the fort. The navigation school moved out, and, by April 1944, the *Overlord* staff had moved in, using every berth available: neighbouring properties, outbuildings, newly-erected huts, and for the nomadic senior army commanders, personal caravans. Local naval headquarters were necessary the length and breadth of Britain, and these were established in whatever building was available. At Boston (Lincolnshire) the old workhouse was taken over, as was Pitreavie Castle (Fife), and the Royal Hotel at Teignmouth (Devon). Even seaside piers were pressed into service. Weston-super-Mare's Birnbeck Pier, HMS *Birnbeck* for the duration, was used as an experimental rocket-testing station, until fears for its stability removed the activity to the nearby Brean Down. Specific activities, especially deriving from fresh responsibilities, could make enormous demands on premises. The training of gun crew for defensively equipped merchant ships (DEMS) is a case in point. This organisation required a total of 39 offices, one in each major port, and many in minor ones too, and 24 training centres. In many ports such as Grimsby, Hull, Manchester and Dundee, buildings were found in the docks. Southampton and Bristol already had naval offices which proved suitable. In other places, hotels had to be used, the Grand, in Sunderland, the Imperial in Falmouth, and the St Enoch in Glasgow.

Many country houses were requisitioned by the army for use as formation headquarters or as unit depots. For instance, the airborne forces, prior to the Arnhem operation were based at Fulbeck Hall and Harlaxton Hall (Lincolnshire), and Braunstone (Leicestershire), close to the troop carrier bases of the 9 USAAF, who would fly them into action. Many houses such as Moor Park (Hertfordshire) and Stoke Rochford Hall (Lincolnshire) claim to have hosted the planning processes for such operations, but this merely reinforces the point that so many grand houses were pressed into service. A number of intelligence units occupied houses in the Bedford Triangle, including Woburn Abbey, Bletchley Park and Chicksands. Southern Command headquarters was at Wilton House, outside Salisbury, and the headquarters of the 3rd US Army was at Peover House (Cheshire). Prior to the Dieppe Raid, Canadian troops were based in country houses in Surrey and Hampshire. There were Free French units based in Northamptonshire houses such as Finedon. Wentworth Woodhouse in South Yorkshire was the depot for 1 Corps, and the base for 10 Battalion Duke of Wellington's Regiment. In a number of cases, installations went underground. In Reigate, General (later Field Marshall) Montgomery had his Southern Command headquarters in tunnels which, themselves were the inspiration for an extensive headquarters complex in Newhaven (E. Sussex). Here a RE Tunnelling Company,

in the second half of 1941, excavated a tunnel system under the Guinness Trust
Holiday Home, built on the Heighton Hill cliffs in 1938. These tunnels housed
the Canadian Corps Coast Artillery, but chiefly, HMS *Forward*, evicted from the
Sheffield Hotel in the town. It was the co-ordinating headquarters for the naval
establishments at Hove, Littlehampton, Eastbourne, Newhaven, and Shoreham,
along with their support depots at Burgess Hill and Lewes. It very quickly became
a sophisticated communications centre, gathering information from its entire
sector at regular intervals, and controlling all naval activity, including the Channel
Dash by German capital ships, and the Dieppe Raid, both in 1942. These are only
two examples of many other such subterranean structures. No wonder that there
was genuine anxiety, however far-fetched it may seem to us today, over the possibility of a German channel tunnel, starting from the abandoned workings near
Calais, and then dividing into a myriad of branches, all to be blown in one
synchronised operation as had been the mines on the Western Front in the
previous war. Serious estimates of the time needed, ranged from six months to
twelve years. Newhaven's tunnels were shut down in 1945, but part of the
Guinness building remains, watching over its secrets.

After the end of the Second World War, the country was no less reluctant to
embark on a programme of buildings renewal than it had been 25 years previously.
As we have seen, the RAF took the lion's share of defence expenditure, in order
to provide the infrastructure for the nuclear deterrent. Barracks were replaced only
if absolutely necessary. In 1938, the local MP had described Harewood Barracks,
Leeds, as a disgrace, and the worst in Britain, but it was 1962, before it was demolished and replaced by Churchill Barracks in Regent Street. In the same year,
Chelsea Barracks was demolished, and replaced by long two-storey residential
blocks in concrete. Ten years later Knightsbridge Barracks *(117)*, home to the
Household Cavalry, and itself a Victorian replacement of a Georgian building was
demolished. Sir Basil Spence's five-storey brick and glass range gives comfortable
accommodation over ground-floor stabling. It must, here, be pointed out that the
heating arrangements are not based on the traditional expedient. Most of the nineteenth-century barracks at Aldershot were also demolished in the 1960s and
replaced, for the most part by curtain-walled blocks. At Maidstone, where only
the officers' mess, now a public house, survives of the eighteenth-century timber
barracks, the new Invicta Park Barracks (1962-5) was built in two phases using
industrial housing systems, CLASP for the first phase, and NENK for the second,
producing low-rise, tile-hung and weather-boarded buildings, some in stepped
terraces, designed to be as unlike barracks as was possible. Howe Barracks,
Canterbury, depot of the Royal Irish Regiment, has largely replaced all its old
buildings with modern ones. The extensive barracks at Aldershot (Hampshire)
date almost entirely from the 1960s. Only one Victorian barrack-block remains as
the museum. Some of these modern rebuilding schemes are already deemed superfluous, and the postwar Deysbrook Barracks in Liverpool has already been vacated
by the military. Some Victorian barracks have been updated *(118)*, Woolwich

117 London; Sir Basil Spence's new Knightsbridge Barracks, built 1967-70; it provides the London headquarters of the Household Cavalry, and incorporates stables, riding school, messes, and accommodation for officers and troopers

118 London, Wellington Barracks; behind the refurbished buildings completed in1854, are new five-storey blocks built in 1979-85; they are finished in cream-painted concrete

receiving new accommodation blocks in the early 1960s, and Imphal Barracks, York, a new North Eastern District headquarters building in the early 1980s. At Ballater on Royal Deeside, the barracks built to house Queen Victoria's personal guard still stands like a charming but oversized cottage orné. At the back of the courtyard new accommodation blocks have been added for the company of Royal Scots who are now based there. Attempts have been made to translate the traditional into the modern. The entrance gates of Goojerat Barracks, Colchester, for instance, imaginatively incorporate onion domes. Barracks complexes were also seen as suitable sites for some of the bunkers, built to provide protection against radioactive fallout, for regional and dispersed government in the event of nuclear war. Brecon, Imphal Barracks in York, and Fulwood Barracks, Preston, all received underground reinforced concrete bunkers in order to accommodate Regional Seats of Government in the 1960s. There is a bunker underneath the former Cowley Barracks, once depot of the Oxfordshire and Buckinghamshire Light Infantry, and now part of Oxford Brookes University. No doubt a fine location for student socialising, but once a symbol of nuclear insecurity. Fortunately for the army, as these regimental depots decayed on urban plots with no room for expansion, reorganisation in the RAF freed up a large number of well-built Expansion Period airfields. Kirton-in-Lindsey (Lincolnshire), North Luffenham (Rutland), Ouston (Northumberland), Thorney Island (West Sussex), and South Cerney (Gloucestershire), are home to RA units and Waterbeach (Cambridgeshire) provides a home to RE airstrip construction troops. Amongst former Royal Naval Air Stations, one, Arbroath (Angus) is a base for Royal Marine Commandos, and an infantry unit is housed at another, Bramcote (Warwickshire). The Army Air Corps is at Wattisham (Suffolk) and Middle Wallop (Hampshire), and other army units are based at Driffield and Leconfield (East Yorkshire).

Successive reductions in the size of the TA after the Second World War have been mirrored by corresponding shrinkage in the estate. Around 5 per cent of all drill halls in use since the 1860s in England, and smaller percentages still in Scotland and Wales, were built since 1945, and some of them have already been relinquished. Most of the newer ones are in the larger cities where smaller units have consolidated in centres of employment and housing. Several, notably Cardiff *(119)*, St Cuthbert's Keep, the Northumbrian Universities OTC building in Newcastle, Rutherglen in Glasgow, and Southall, west London, are adventurous buildings architecturally. Most are merely functional and anonymous. In some areas, particularly in the north-east of England, but elsewhere as well, factory-style buildings have been used. They are flexible spaces which can easily be adapted for alternative uses once superfluous to the TA's requirement, as has already been demonstrated at Long Benton, Newcastle. In the meantime they proudly carry the insignia of units with histories stretching back up to 150 years.

Many of the Victorian buildings of the dockyards have seen new developments come and go. Most of the naval support facilities since the nuclear deterrent was transferred, in 1969, to the nuclear submarines carrying first Polaris missiles, and

119 Cardiff, Morgan Street drill hall, built in the 1990s and replacing several older buildings around the city, one of which was demolished to make way for the Millennium Stadium

then Trident, have been geared to keeping these vessels at a state of readiness. Most of them are in Scotland, at Faslane and Coulport (Strathclyde) and at the refitting yard at Rosyth on the Forth. Faslane had long been a minor submarine base, but was established as HMS *Neptune* in 1966, acting as the base for the submarine depot ships HMS *Maidstone* and HMS *Adamant*, and the nuclear submarines of *Dreadnought* and the Third Squadron, and the four Polaris boats of *Resolution*'s Tenth Squadron. A whole new town housing up to 7,000 people by 1972, was constructed at Faslane, and the bleak, rain-swept environment coupled with the uninspiring 1960s architecture spreading up the hillsides, caused the inhabitants to refer to their home as 'Moon City'. In the 1980s, Faslane was further extended to accommodate the new Trident boats of the *Vanguard* class. Whilst some facilities grew, others had short lives. The nuclear refuelling depot at Chatham, completed in 1968, has already been demolished, its functions having been long duplicated at Rosyth. Other installations have been built for specific purposes. Given that HMS *Dolphin* at Portsmouth was considered too cramped, Submarine Central Command was followed to Northwood (Greater London) by the Polaris Command Centre, both being accommodated in a secure underground bunker with a new dedicated communications system. Devonport's Frigate Complex, Fleet Maintenance Base and Submarine Refit Complex, the latter incorporating two earlier dry-docks, all built in the 1970s, are noteworthy for their monolithic size. Similarly, the massive Trident submarine building at BAE's Barrow-in-Furness yard entirely dominates the town's waterfront from every direction *(120)*.

120 Barrow-in-Furness, Cumbria; BAe Systems 1980s facility for constructing nuclear-powered submarines, equipped with the Trident Inter-Continental Ballistic Missile, dominating the waterfront

This was built specifically for the construction of the new generation of missile-carrying nuclear submarines, laid down in 1985. The four boats of the *Vanguard* class, equipped with the Trident ICBM, were launched between 1993 and 1999. It may be that, apart from these monolithic constructions, built with one specific purpose in mind, budgetary constraints and, maybe even a desire to keep a low profile by employing building designs from the civilian world, suggest that, whilst the application of innovative engineering and architectural designs may continue, never again are we likely to see the stately magnificence which so often characterised the Royal dockyards of earlier times.

7

AIR DEFENCE

The twentieth century saw an entirely new dimension added to warfare. Ultimately it was to transform all that had gone previously on land and sea. Initially few saw the possibilities, and many amongst the hide-bound and conservative military establishment dismissed the idea of air warfare as a diversion or a fantasy. Just as books such as *The Battle of Dorking* predicted invasion across the seas, another succession of writers including H.G. Wells in his *War in the Air* foresaw the threat from the skies. Although it was to take a while for the aeroplane to ascend over the airship, this threat was, indeed, to materialise in the First World War, both in the bombing of targets in mainland Britain, and in the air war over the Western Front. By the 1930s there was an unchallenged assumption, famously articulated by Stanley Baldwin, that the bomber would always get through, and that measures were necessary to protect against such attack, even though total prevention was unfeasible. As the century unfolded mass bombing was for the most part superseded by targeted nuclear strikes, and aircraft themselves were replaced by rockets, and the charade of a viable defence against attack from the skies was maintained. This chapter will examine the diverse elements which made up these defence systems, and point to some of what remains on the ground.

Prior to the outbreak of the First World War, there was a lot of discussion amongst the military planners, who all recognised the need for AA defences, but were divided about their form and organisation. As ever, there was the search for a single solution, so choices had, apparently, to be made between putting resources into guns to shoot down aircraft from the ground, fighters to shoot down aircraft in the skies, or bombers to destroy the enemy's aircraft on the ground. It was recognised that each of these solutions presented equally complex technical challenges, and little progress was made beyond the development of two dedicated AA weapons for ground use. One was the 3in (75 mm) 20 cwt (1 tonne) AA gun, only two of which were in service by the start of the war, and the other was a cobbling-together, by the navy, of a 1-pounder pom-pom on a high-angle mount. Much effort went into improvising temporary solutions. Field guns, for instance, were jacked up at improbable angles on piles of logs, and lighter guns were mounted on

164

waggon wheels fixed horizontally on axles stuck in the ground. It was the navy, whose ammunition and fuel depots were perceived as most at risk from aerial incendiary attack, which took the lead in AA defence, installing guns and manning them with naval personnel. Once aerial attacks by airships on civilian targets began then AA defences were demanded for central London. A number of guns were mounted, supported by searchlights manned by special constables and firemen. One of the subsidiary quandaries was between static and mobile AA guns. Two mobile forces were formed based on Newmarket and Caterham, ready to respond to incursions by airships when alerted by police. A mobile force in London soon replaced the former southern one. The headquarters of the London defences was Kenwood House in Hampstead whilst the lorry-mounted guns were based at Ladbrooke Grove and fired from the Artillery Ground at Moorgate, a traditional practice area used by the Honourable Artillery Company. By 1915, targets other than London and the naval depots were gradually given AA defences. These included ports, manufacturing centres, airship stations and airfields. A large number of guns were being deployed, both purpose-built weapons and adaptations, including 6in howitzers firing shrapnel. By the middle of 1916, through a combination of improved spotting and reporting systems, the provision of search-lights, and the increasing skill of both fighter pilots and AA gunners, the airships, having suffered heavy losses, and, more importantly, anticipating even heavier ones in the future, were deterred from raiding. Many were shot down by the fighters of the RNAS, later RFC, Home Defence Squadrons, but some were victims of the AA gunners. As in most situations, it was a mixed economy which prevailed. The searchlights helped the fighters, the ground gunners had an advantage over the pilots in that they were able to hear their targets coming, which the pilots could not, and the spotters helped everyone. In Cleveland in November 1916, a contemporary account of a Zeppelin raid demonstrates how the several elements operated together. The approaching Zeppelin was tracked by the Wireless Station at Stockton-on-Tees, which was then able to issue a warning through the civilian telephone system. Police officers on bicycles with placards and blowing whistles then passed on the warning to the civilian population. Meanwhile, the searchlight at Hutton Henry illuminated the airship as it crossed the coast en route for indus-trial targets. The local observer network or, indeed, the three acoustic mirrors mounted on this coast could equally have given warning. As it happened, the AA guns stationed locally in four batteries probably did not engage the airship, but a BE-2c from 36 Home Defence Squadron, based at Seaton Carew, intercepted the Zeppelin, L34, and shot it down.

The defeat of the Zeppelins meant that the enemy was forced into an alterna-tive strategy. The Gotha bomber had just about the range to make direct flights from airfields in the Low Countries. It could deliver 1,000lb (455kg) of bombs from 12,000ft (3,600m), and had a radius of 125 miles (200km). From Spring 1917 fleets of between 16 and 24 Gothas raided targets in the south-east of England including London. The British reaction to this was to set up the London Air

Defence Area (LADA) based on fixed zones of activity. There were patrol lines for fighters, areas near the coast and around central London where only guns operated, and barriers (known as aprons) of tethered balloons. These forced enemy aircraft into a narrow slot above 11,000ft (3,300m) at which height the AA shells were fused to explode. As the Gothas were pushed into night operations, the RFC pilots perfected their night flying, and, once again, the searchlights came into their own. It was claimed that large numbers of enemy bombers were deterred by the barrage produced by the 300 guns, and the 400 searchlights emplaced in the LADA by early 1918. The truth was that enemy numbers were overestimates, as were kills. The volume of AA shells caused more actual harm to people on the ground than they did to the enemy. It has been suggested that the major lessons to be learned were to do with integration, organisation and co-operation. The final improvements to the AA defences in the final year of the war, after the threat had, in fact, disappeared, was the installation of telephone lines to increase the warning times given by the spotters, and the pruning of the detailed information, they had, hitherto, been expected to pass on. This could then enable the guns and fighter aircraft, in their separated zones, to tackle intruders more efficiently, by breaking up formations thus rendering individual aircraft more vulnerable, and by denying them whole areas of the sky. The LADA spotter system was eventually spread to other areas, by which time, spotters had been given a basic instrument which enabled them to work out a compass bearing for the approaching bombers' predicted target. This information, passed quickly to the control centre at Horseguards, Whitehall, would inform the despatch of intercepting fighters.

By the end of the war, around 400 AA guns were in service in addition to those in LADA. Of these, 50 or so were with the nine AA Mobile Batteries on the east coast. The rest were scattered across some dozens of locations. The Tees and Tyne AA Commands, for instance, in June 1917, had a mixture of 3in and 18-pounder guns in 42 different locations, plus an out-station, with eight gun sites, at the big munitions works at Gretna. In contrast, Western Command's Manchester AA defences consisted of just 16 guns, reflecting the fact that, after the Zeppelins had virtually ceased operating, air raids were unlikely at that distance from the enemy's airfields. The Vickers yard at Barrow-in-Furness had one gun in 1914, and, three years later, still only two. Half the guns outside LADA were the preferred 3in 20 cwt, but these were deployed almost exclusively down the east side of the country.

There are few visible remains from this period. Many of the AA guns were truly mobile, rather than transportable as in later wars. This meant that they spent their working lives on the backs of lorries. Some of the London guns were mounted on timber towers, as were some of their accompanying searchlights. Crew quarters were in temporary wooden huts. When the London mobile batteries were temporarily moved to the Norfolk coast in 1916, they were emplaced in fieldworks with dug-outs, designed by their commander, drawing on his prior experiences on the Western Front. Obviously, all traces have long gone, especially when one considers that their locations included King's Cross, Hyde

121 Waltham Abbey, Essex, TL386024; First World War anti-aircraft gun position, designated 'Cheshunt'; platform with shelter, and hold-fast for 3in 20 cwt AA gun

Park Corner, and the Foreign Office. Outside London, a much larger number of guns were mounted on pre-existing fortifications, particularly coast batteries. Most of the 25 AA guns emplaced around Portsmouth Harbour, for instance, in 1916, were mounted in the forts which already stood there. Many of the guns were simply adaptations of standard weapons, using standard mountings. On the West Demi-bastion of Hilsea Lines, however, which is known to have been equipped with a 6-pounder Hotchkiss AA gun, is a holdfast, with eight mounting bolts, embedded flush in the concrete platform. Although it is not quite the same as other, positively-identified mounts for this gun, it may yet be one. Different patterns were used, and whilst virtually all Hotchkiss guns, reused in the Second World War, were mounted on nine bolts, at least one example (near Formby, Liverpool) used 12. There are also records which state that a 1-pounder pom-pom was mounted in this location. Some of the outer LADA fixed AA defences included permanent mountings for AA guns. On a hill east of the River Lea but probably representing the AA site designated as Cheshunt *(121)*, is a brick and concrete platform with a brick hut at one end. In the centre of the platform is a circular steel mounting plate, probably for a 3in 20 cwt AA gun. The hut may be a crew shelter. The platform is hollow, and may contain ready-use ammunition lockers. Cheshunt is one of 18 sites forming the Northern sector of LADA, in 1917, each having a 3in gun. At Purfleet *(122)*, on the former military ranges of the Thames marshes, is a cylindrical, brick tower with, formerly, five embrasures

122 Purfleet, Essex, TQ793538; pre-First World War submarine-spotting tower with iron shields over the loopholes; in the First World War a 1-pounder pom-pom anti-aircraft gun was mounted on the roof; this contributed, along with the other guns defending the Purfleet powder works, to the shooting down of a Zeppelin in 1916

with iron shields. It was built around 1905 as a submarine-spotting tower, but by the First World War, had been equipped with one of Purfleet powder-magazine's two 1-pounder AA pom-poms. It was with this gun that the gunners of 3 Company, Essex and Suffolk Royal Garrison Artillery helped to shoot down Zeppelin L15 on 31 March 1916. There are further odd vestiges of AA installations from the First World War in many coast defence forts. At Grain Fort (Kent), for instance, a fragmentary structure built into a former gun-position has been tentatively identified as the ammunition store for the AA gun whose holdfast, probably for one of the 3in 20 cwt guns with which the Medway positions were generally equipped, is just discernible in aerial photographs.

Incidentally, it should be noted that the government felt no responsibility for the protection of the civilian population against the effects of air raids. Although there were nearly 5,000 casualties, a third of them fatalities, in the raids, shelter was left to the individual. Most people's solution seems to have been to hide under the bedclothes and hope for the best, but some took more positive action. In Cleethorpes, on the north-east coast of Lincolnshire, there still stands a surface air-raid shelter built by a local pharmacist. Early in 1916, a raid on the town by Zeppelins, had killed 31 soldiers billeted in a chapel, so maybe this shelter was a reaction to that. It is now used as a lock-up garage.

The Y-Station at Stockton-on-Tees still stands, now converted to a private house. It consists of a control-block with operations room, office, and accommodation for a crew of around five. In the upper floor, reached by external ladder was the battery-storage. A separate building held a generator, all the battery-charging equipment, and trolleys for moving them between the two blocks. The site, containing the anchorage points for five masts, is surrounded by wire fences fixed to concrete posts bearing the fouled anchor emblem of the navy. Controlled from Room 40 at The Admiralty, a chain of these wireless stations used for listening in to enemy radio traffic, extended from the Orkneys to Cornwall, with one or two outliers on the west coast and in Ireland. At Culver Battery (Isle of Wight) the boundary markers for the signal station, bearing their fouled anchor emblems, can still be seen.

A number of sound mirrors also survive. In the North East, there are mirrors at Fulwell *(123)*, north of Sunderland, Boulby, near Loftus, Redcar, and Kilnsea on the Holderness coast. These, although they differ from each other in minor ways, are all slab mirrors, designed to allow the operator to locate aircraft by collating the sounds reflected in a network of mirrors via microphones. A further group survives in Kent, mainly dating from 1918 onwards and developed through to the 1930s as a complement, or, in extremis, an alternative to radar. There is an integrated group of three types of sound mirror on Romney Marsh, which includes a 200ft long (60m) curved wall, or strip mirror, a slab mirror and a bowl mirror. Another slab mirror, like the earliest examples, survives at Capel, and a

123 Fulwell, Sunderland, NZ389596; First World War sound mirror for picking up the noise of incoming aircraft, and attempting to predict their course and intended targets, in order that anti-aircraft guns and fighter planes might be alerted in time

bowl mirror at Hythe. Others, mainly slab mirrors, as at Fan Bay which probably dated from the last years of the First World War, have been destroyed. At Capel, an ancillary building holds a cylindrical, concrete pillar, which may have provided the base for a compass which would have helped to determine the approaching aircraft's intended target.

In the aftermath of the First World War, the air defence system which had evolved to become steadily both more efficient and more effective, and from which so much had been learned, was dismantled. The responsibility for actually manning AA guns and searchlights was largely devolved onto the new Territorial Army (TA), but there were very few men and little equipment. Although the Steel-Bartholomew Report of 1923, put forward an Air Defence Plan strikingly similar to that of LADA, temperamentally, those concerned with national defence, veered toward the bomber as deterrent option, backed up by fighters to protect our own bombers and to destroy those of the enemy. An AA school was established at Biggin Hill, the infrastructure of an AA Command was retained, but only cadres of the actual TA units existed anywhere but on paper. It was not until the breakdown of the League of Nations' Geneva conference at the end of 1933, that anxiety about a likely future conflict with Germany injected some sense of urgency into AA defence planning and provision, resulting in the establishment of stores to hold searchlights and AA guns near the units who would use them in wartime. The expansion of the TA units to bring them up to strength was accelerated, and their training intensified. A new heavy AA gun, the 4.5in (115 mm) was developed to be emplaced in permanent two-gun batteries, but with two further empty emplacements on each site for instant reinforcement if necessary. The 3.7in HAA gun, developed throughout 1935, and being trialled as a mobile gun in April 1936, was to become the standard HAA gun of the Second World War, but as common on fixed mountings as on the mobile one, intended as the norm. It is interesting to note that in order to speed up the production of this new weapon, and in light of the urgency with which rearmament was now regarded, the Director General of Munitions Production, realising that Woolwich Arsenal could not cope with the flood of orders for new models in quantity, ordered 500 of the 3.7in barrels from private industry. He was overruled by the Treasury, who had not authorised the order. Eventually, it went through but it becomes obvious why, in 1938, the AA Commands had received only a fifth of their guns. They were also persuaded to accept the static model of the new 3.7in gun in a greater proportion than had been planned, as it was cheaper and quicker to manufacture. The revised plan was to convert these static guns into mobiles as more 4.5in static guns were delivered, but this hardly happened. What it did mean was that an AA defence based on the flexibility of transportable equipment had to be jettisoned for an alternative plan based on static guns in fixed sites. As well as new heavy guns, the 40 mm Bofors LAA gun was acquired to replace the ageing pom-poms and previous improvisations, but they only appeared in small numbers to begin with, and most of them went to the field army. New practice camps for AA gunners were established on the north Norfolk coast, and at Manorbier, South Wales, joining that at Watchet (Somerset), in use since 1925. The AA defence plans of the 1920s and early 1930s had envisaged a continuous belt of guns and searchlights up the eastern side of Britain, with concentrated defences around London, the major cities, the main ports, and a few specific military targets. In the event, it became apparent that the number of targets requiring AA protection was more or less infinite, and that attempts must be made to protect as much as possible with what was available. Once again, there would be improvisation, and many batteries started the war equipped with reconditioned 3in 20 cwt guns, and, long after the beginning of the war, the most common LAA weapon was still the old Lewis light machine-gun.

The permanent HAA sites were built to War Office plans by contractors working under the loose supervision of RE officers. A battery consisted of four octagonal concrete gun pits in an arc, with each gun anchored to a central holdfast which was embedded in the concrete base of the pit. Behind the guns was the command post, basically a bunker for the telephonists, with, alongside, open positions protected by blast walls, for the Predictor and Height-finder. Further back were the magazines, gun store, and, behind them, guardroom, offices, stores, garages, workshops and the huts to accommodate the 100 or so men needed for a four-gun battery. As the war progressed and direction and fire-control relied less on visual instruments, the command post became a larger, better protected building with more overhead cover. The earlier octagonal emplacements were supplemented, or often replaced by squarer positions fitted for the remote control of the guns. Sometimes, the old positions were retro-fitted with conduits for the necessary cabling. Early gun emplacements had insufficient ready-use ammunition storage, and no crew shelters. On cold nights the former doubled as the latter, but eventually, shelters were provided and locker-space for shells increased. It must be remembered that the original intention was to have a preponderance of mobile guns, jacked up on temporary hard-standings, with a sandbag command post and open, sandbagged instrument positions. Accommodation would presumably have been tented. As new technical improvements were developed, sometimes in order to meet new threats, then the battery structures and layout had to change. New designs for 3.7in emplacements (Type DFW 55414) in 1943, incorporated both crew shelters and generous ammunition storage. By the time that the flying bombs were coming over, between June 1944 and March 1945, there had been a number of improvements in design and operation. Britain's AA supremo, General Pile, moved as many guns as he could mobilise to the south and east coasts to combat these rocket attacks. These positions were known as the Kentish and Coastal Gun-belts, the Diver Box, Diver Strip, and Diver Fringe. Together, they stretched from Brighton to Bridlington. The HAA guns mounted in these positions were served by gun-laying (GL) radar, optical instruments mounted on a scaffolding platform called a Tracker tower, and plotting rooms in Nissen huts. The radar and predictor working together, allowed for automatic tracking of targets, remote control of the guns, and hence smoother traversing. In order to speed up the redeployment of so many static guns, it was necessary to solve the problem of remounting them, without having to replicate the concreted holdfast method. A platform, often known as the Pile Mattress, was developed which locked the standard holdfast between layers of railway sleepers and lengths of rail, making a very stable and strong mounting. The parts were simple to source, and were often produced in workshops and distributed as kits to be made up on site. The other innovation, one might notice on these later gun sites was the semi-circular anti-clutter screen which surrounded the radar and the tracker tower, to prevent nearby buildings from interfering with the signal. There were crew shelters on site, but we must remember that all but the Kentish belt were on the coast and were manned right through the winter of 1944/5. The main living accommodation was in huts on a separate, adjacent site. Many of these sites were manned by mixed units, so separate living huts for male and female personnel had to be provided. Throughout AA Command, mixed batteries with Home Guard or ATS representation received superior, heated command posts (Type DFW 55402). The final HAA weapon to come into service before the end of the war was the 5.25in (133 mm) naval gun, often intended, as at South Shields (Tyneside), to be mounted in a dual AA and CD role. Some twin turrets were mounted in London as early as 1941, in order to provide the capability to reach 40,000ft (12,000m). Both single and twin versions were turret-mounted atop a deep, circular, concrete pit, which held all the power cables and operating mechanisms. Adjoining this emplacement was the power house, entered by double doors, and easily recognised by the distinctive ventilator on one side, and proud of the roof line. It is likely that somewhere around 200 guns would have been mounted, had original plans been fully implemented.

So many of these HAA emplacements were built, many of them in out-of-the-way places, that it is inevitable that a good number survive. Virtually complete layouts of gun pits, command post, magazine, gun store and power house can be seen at Western Heights, Dover; at Stranraer in south-west Scotland; at Synah Common, Hayling Island; at Stone Creek on the north bank of the Humber; and at Gloucester Lodge *(124)*, below Blyth on the Northumberland coast. At the Stranraer site there is an example of a Nissen hut covered in 6in (15cm) of concrete, probably for use as a magazine. Similar structures can be seen at coast batteries in the Orkneys. At Trimley St Mary (Suffolk) *(125)* there is a complete 5.25in battery, built in 1945. In addition to its four gun emplacements, there are a combined gun shed/power house, a radar tower with sloping ramp, and adjoining command post. These are only a sample of the many sites remaining, many of which are heavily overgrown, or difficult of access. In some places only parts remain. Outside Nottingham there is a mobile home park laid out around the magazine of a former HAA site, and at Elvaston (Derbyshire), the campsite occupies the former HAA battery, two of whose gun pits now form caravan standings. Also remaining are the gunstore, motor-transport shed, and the later

124 Blyth, Northumberland; Gloucester Lodge Heavy Anti-Aircraft Battery; three of the four emplacements for 3.7in guns are visible

125 Trimley Heath, Suffolk, TM277360; emplacement for 5.25in heavy anti-aircraft gun, showing the ventilator with short pillars, and the gun pit beyond; this battery, dating from 1945, is almost complete

operations room. There are undoubtedly many sites, apparently built over which, nevertheless, retain some remnant of former structures. At Lizard Lane, Marsden (South Tyneside) the HAA site overlooking the site of one of the Tyne Turrets, is marked by the usual gun pits and associated buildings. Next to the (modern) tearoom, however, the bungalow is recognisable as the officers' quarters. Beyond this, is a gun store and adjoining MT garage, still in use, the garage that is, for its original purpose. Very occasionally, hutting, associated with HAA sites, survives such as the Nissen huts on Maker Heights (Cornwall), or the BCF huts at Stanground, near Peterborough.

LAA emplacements are much less uniform than those we have been looking at for HAA guns. This is due to a number of factors. The whole point of LAA artillery is its flexibility. It must be deployed and operated with minimal restraints. Targets are spotted and fired on instantly. Guns are moved around, and expected to go into action with the minimum of preparation. However there were occasions when Bofors guns, for instance, were required to operate in fixed positions. Although many fieldworks for Bofors were locally designed, there were drawings issued by DFW for holdfasts, and individual Commands designed emplacements. Unlike its HAA equivalent the Bofors emplacement was a simple pit, revetted with concrete blocks, with a holdfast in the middle, recesses for ammunition in the sides, and provision for a predictor in one corner. Earth was mounded up around the sides to minimise blast. Bofors and other guns were often mounted on the roofs of factories, or arms depots, where the height of surrounding obstructions prevented effective deployment at ground level. Here, a sandbagged emplacement would contain a holdfast, with, usually four, ammunition boxes embedded in the sandbag walls. An example is Fort Dunlop in Birmingham. A third alternative was the Bofors tower. These were built to a variety of designs and heights, ranging from 15-60ft (4.5-18m). They were, in fact, twin towers as the gun and the predictor occupied separate platforms to prevent the vibrations caused by gunfire, disrupting the operation of the sensitive predictor. Although the basic design was a skeletal structure of reinforced concrete, some of these towers had the open walls bricked in, to give a solid structure, often then pierced by loopholes for small-arms. These occur in a number of settings: airfields such as West Malling, Gatwick and Weston-super-Mare all had high, solid towers; there were lower, skeleton towers at the Vickers, Brooklands (Surrey) aircraft factory and the Admiralty cordite factory at Holton Heath (Dorset); Dunkirk Radar site (Kent), Waltham Abbey explosives factory and the Admiralty compass factory at Iver (Buckinghamshire) all had low, concrete, solid towers; Filton airfield (Bristol) and Portishead Docks *(126)* had low, brick, solid towers. All the above examples survive save Gatwick and Weston. Ultimately, the lower-level tower designs were to be replaced by a steel alternative, probably resembling scaffolding. At Newark (Nottinghamshire) a Bofors tower survives in the corner of a Council Depot. It consists of a reinforced concrete frame supporting a platform with the gun position on. At each corner is a ready-use ammunition locker. The frame is hidden under

126 Portishead, Somerset, ST474766; tower for 40mm Bofors light anti-aircraft gun; the lower level is loopholed for close defence; similar towers can be seen on the River Lea at Waltham Abbey, at Dunkirk CH station, and at Filton airfield, Bristol

a brick skin with garage doors. Only eye-witness reports make the discovery of such structures possible. A ground-level version of the twin platform design can be seen near Hamble, on Southampton Water. Here a Bofors gun is mounted in its half of the structure, while the cylindrical concrete pedestal which held the predictor, occupies the other half. A number of similar concrete pits with holdfasts for Bofors guns exist around Rugby. Many LAA weapons, however, relied on very simple mountings. We have already seen how a number of pillbox types incorporated concrete pillars to carry LAA machine-guns. The Stork mounting for twin machine-guns simply needed a slot at ground level in which to plant itself. Often around airfields may be seen waist-high sewer pipes, joined together in pairs to form figure-of-eight shapes. In the base of one will be fixed a short, cylindrical pipe, into which would fit a Stork mount. Adrian Armishaw has found a purpose-built pit for a Stork mount at Sywell (Northamptonshire), and several examples of the sewer-pipe model *in situ* at Kingscliffe (Northamptonshire). Another type of emplacement, thought to be for an Oerlikon 20 mm LAA gun can be seen both at Methwold (Norfolk), next to the BHQ, and at Dunkirk *(127)*. It is an octagonal, concrete pit about 15ft (4.5m) across, whose outer walls descend in three tiers to a central space with a circular holdfast in its middle.

127 Dunkirk, Kent, TR076593; mounting for light anti-aircraft gun at this Chain Home radar site; there is also a Bofors tower

By 1942, attempts to provide an easily-operated weapon with which the Home Guard could be equipped, resulted in the 3in (75 mm) unrotated rocket projectile generally known as ZAA. Projectors had anything from one to nine barrels, and were grouped in large numbers to benefit from the scatter effect of their rockets. Standard groupings, for instance, were 64 two-barrel launchers, or 12 nine-barrel ones. Launchers were generally spaced 10 yards apart, in a regular grid formation. Between launchers were corrugated iron covered magazines and crew shelters within earth traverses. Since there was never very much to be seen, and sites tended to be in built-up areas, such sites have totally disappeared, and only their former locations may be remembered.

From the very first, the Barrage Balloon had been seen as a useful component in the AA armoury. These were crewed largely by the WRAF, and organised from regional headquarters. Quite large depots were required to store, maintain, and mend these ungainly balloons. The regional headquarters was often in a separate location. Thus in the Derby GDA, for instance, the depot was at Alvaston, and the headquarters, nearer the city centre on the corner of Midland Road and Carrington Street. Very little evidence of the balloons remains. Some sheds stand at Pawlett (Somerset), Pucklechurch (Bristol), and Rollestone Camp (Wiltshire). Some huts, now used as a children's nursery, in between the tower blocks at Kidbrooke (south-east London) may represent all that remains of the depot there, but the similar Hook (Surrey) depot, covering south-west London, has been completely cleared for housing. A number of mystery objects: octagonal plinths standing about 3ft 6in (1.1m) high, and 4ft (1.2m) across exist. One at Abinger

(Surrey) has now been positively identified by a long-term resident, as an anchorage for a barrage balloon put up against V1 attack. This now means that another similar structure at Gerrards Cross *(128)*, retaining its central, threaded bolt, can be identified as another. There must be many more.

The most impressive structures of the AA campaign are not on dry land at all. Two river estuaries, the Thames and the Mersey, were defended by forts out at sea. Known after their designer as the Maunsell Forts, they are of two types. There were four naval forts in a line between Harwich and Margate. They consisted of two 24ft (7.2m) diameter, hollow, concrete tubes, sitting on a pontoon, and joined by a deck. The pontoon was towed out to sea, and then sunk onto the seabed. The deck carried two 3.7in HAA guns, and two Bofors guns along with predictors and GL radar. The magazines, crew's quarters and generators were housed in the seven floors of each tube. On the deck were officers' cabins, a control room, and galley. Two lifeboats were slung on ship's davits. There were a number of objectives for the naval forts, but it has been suggested both by civil engineers and the military, that their main achievement was in extending radar cover far out into the estuary. The army forts were quite different in appearance and construction methods. Whereas the naval forts sat on the sea bottom, the shifting sands of Liverpool Bay, for which the army forts were originally designed, and where three were sited off Formby, demanded a different approach. The army forts were three-storey concrete boxes, with open upper decks, on four hollow, reinforced concrete legs. The legs were anchored into a square of hollow concrete beams which were sunk into the sand. When filled with seawater, they then stayed there. The towers,

128 Gerrards Cross, Buckinghamshire, SU998885; octagonal concrete block for tethering a barrage balloon; there is a threaded steel pin in the centre

in groups of seven, joined by walkways, were laid out like a battery on the ground. A control tower sat in a semi-circle of four towers, each equipped with a 3.7in HAA gun. Beyond one of these was a searchlight tower, and behind the control tower was a Bofors tower. The argument was that troops trained on conventional HAA batteries could adapt to their new surroundings better, for not having to learn new layouts. All the accommodation, magazines and so on were contained in the two main floors of each tower, with much more space than in the naval forts. The garrison of each fort was around 120 men. Most of the construction was carried out by assembling prefabricated units in a shipyard, and then floating the completed fort out to its station between barges. The base section was then flooded and it was lowered gently onto the seabed. As well as the three Liverpool examples, all long since broken up as hazards to shipping, there are three army forts on a line running south-west from Foulness to Grain. Three of the naval forts and two of the army ones in the Thames estuary survive, having enjoyed varied lives since the war as pirate radio stations, and, one, outside territorial waters, as the independent state of Sealand.

At least two AA structures have been excavated by professional archaeologists. Prior to its demolition around 1993, the HAA battery at Coldra Woods, Newport (Gwent) was examined by the Glamorgan-Gwent Archaeological Trust. Emplacements of two different designs for six HAA guns, and a seventh for a Bofors gun were found, along with a command post (Type DFW 55402), and the bases of 30 Nissen huts. The presence of two types of 3.7in gun emplacement appears to conform to the normal pattern of increasing the battery from four to six guns, sometime after late 1943, when the second type of emplacement, present here, became the standard for 3.7in guns. In 1997, Birmingham University Field Archaeology Unit dug a small complex of semi-buried structures from the Second World War at Brockhill, Redditch (Worcestershire). They found a concrete platform containing a standard Bofors LAA mounting, a rectangular, loopholed structure, presumably for close defence, and a hexagonal building, probably used as a magazine. The individuality of the site suggests a date, late in 1940, when local initiative was encouraged in the urgent need to defend against both air and ground attack.

Searchlight sites have left hardly any traces at all. Some of those, subject to the injunction, in July 1940, to build a pillbox on site, may have left that as the sole remnant. Most have left nothing to show for, maybe, months of occupation. The essential mobility of the equipment enabled sites to be moved regularly, either to respond to need, or to experiment with alternative operational techniques. There were linear layouts, clustered lights, concentrations in belts, the searchlight equivalent of a barrage, and single lights. Literally hundreds of sites may be plotted in quite small areas, all those occupied by any one single unit in one year, having entirely removed to new sites by the next. After the Phoney War period, the only fixed points appear to be the headquarters of formations, many of them being in country houses, village halls, or new army camps with grandiose names such as Gaza and Loos Barracks, respectively in the Kent villages of Hildenborough and

Staplehurst. The sites themselves consisted of one or more lights, a generator, a couple of huts or tents, and a sandbag pit with a LAA weapon mounted. In the early days this would have been a Lewis gun, but, later on, some sites received Oerlikon guns, and, in 1942, those in Hampshire were given powered aircraft turrets with twin Browning machine-guns, bucket-seats, and binocular sights. Searchlight sites often show up on aerial photographs and have been mistaken, amongst other things, for disc barrows and windmill mounds.

Despite the political reluctance to rearm, the conservative nature of some of the military establishment, and the penny-pinching of the Treasury during the 1930s, it can be argued that, in 1939, Britain had the most effective air defence system in the world. There were a number of reasons for this, but the prime one was radar. This invention, still, at that time called Radio-Direction-Finding (RDF) had been pioneered at Orfordness and Bawdsey on the Suffolk coast. Although the aerials have gone, many of the buildings used in these experiments remain on both sites. Particularly prominent at Orford, is the Black Beacon *(129)*, built in 1928 to house an experimental navigation beacon. During the Second World War, work continued at Malvern (Worcestershire), Worth Matravers (Dorset), and in Dundee. By the mid-1930s, work was advanced enough to provide a viable early-warning system, which might alert home defence fighter squadrons to approaching enemy bombers, and thus enable them to be intercepted before they could reach their target. The race was on to build the necessary radar stations to girdle the east and south coasts. The original 20 Chain Home (CH) stations in the network stretched from Netherbutton on Orkney, as far as Ventnor on the Isle of Wight. The vulnerability of the south-east corner of Britain is reflected in the fact that 12 of those original Chain Home stations are south of the Wash. These East Coast type stations consisted of three basic elements. The receiver block, well-protected by earth traverses sat in the middle of a square of four 240ft high (72m) timber aerial towers. The transmitter block, similarly protected was placed beside a line of four 350ft high (105m) steel towers *(130)*. The power for all the equipment came from generators in stand-by set houses, again protected by earthworks. These were the key components of the site. Duplicate equipment for use if the main kit was put out of action, was housed in the buried reserve, another earthed-up bunker. A guard room, of standard pattern, a house for a caretaker, and administration blocks completed the site. A sturdy fence and close defence pillboxes and weapons pits ensured against small-scale raids. The camp which accommodated the technicians and other staff, was some distance away.

One major problem, not accounted for by the CH stations, was that of enemy aircraft flying under the radar cover. This was met by a complementary network of CH Low (CHL) stations, stretching from Rosehearty (Aberdeenshire) down to Dover, one of only two sites to co-locate CH and CHL, all open in early 1940. The layout of a CHL site was entirely different to that of the CH one. At first, separate transmitter and receiver aerials, in the shape of rotating mesh screens, 20ft (6m) high, were mounted on the ends of brick or timber huts around 150ft (45m)

129 Left Orfordness, Suffolk; the Black Beacon, erected here in the mid-1920s by RAE Farnborough, in connection with aircraft homing beacons and radio direction-finding

130 Right Stenigot, Lincolnshire, TF256826; steel Transmitter tower, 350ft high, one of an original line of four, at this Chain Home radar station

apart. By 1941 most had been altered into a single gantry over a brick hut containing both transmitting and receiving equipment. A variation on this was the Coast Defence/CHL station intended for the army to plot enemy ships, in order to feed this information to coast defence batteries. This was soon seen as an unnecessary duplication of effort, and these army sites reverted to RAF control, being run as Triple Service CHL. From this was developed CH Extra Low (CHEL) whose sites used either a wooden gantry straddling a Nissen hut or, in low-lying areas such as Cresswell (Northumberland), and Humberston (Lincolnshire), a 184ft high (55m) tower. Many CHEL equipments were mobile, mounted on the backs of trucks.

As the war unfolded, the CH network was enlarged both to provide denser cover in the areas already established, and also to extend the coverage to areas not hitherto reached. By 1942, there were ten CH and eight CHL stations extending the network around the south-west coast, and on towards Bristol. Wales was covered by nine CH, nine CHL and four CD/CHL sites. Scotland's tally included a further 13 CH sites, additional to the original four, 31 more CHL sites, and five CD/CHL sites. West Coast CH stations were different in layout to the East Coast version. Here, the components tended to be dispersed rather than buried. Duplicate transmitter and receiver blocks are spread across the site. Between the two receiver blocks are two timber masts like their eastern cousins. A line of four steel, 325ft high (97.5m) transmitter masts, supported by guys, stand equidistant from the two transmitter blocks. The receiver and transmitter blocks are revetted in earth but lack the thick, gravel-filled roofs of the east coast bunkers.

The final link in the radar chain was the Ground Control Interceptor (GCI) station, which was designed to guide individual fighter aircraft onto specific targets. The sites comprised a single, 30ft long (9m) aerial gantry, known as a cheese aerial since it resembled nothing so much as a piece of Edam, fixed over an underground chamber which contained the motor for rotating the aerial. Some sites had a large parabolic dish aerial mounted on a concrete plinth. All the other functions of the site were accommodated in a single operations building, 150 by 40ft (45x12m) nicknamed the 'Happidrome'. These GCI stations numbered over 50 by the end of the war, and stretched from Cornwall to the Orkney Islands.

Since many of these radar sites occupied coastal locations there is a high level of survival. A number of sites enjoyed an extended life into the Cold War period, and, although often much altered, elements of their Second World War structures often survive. Masts or towers are rare. One steel transmitter mast survives at Stenigot, a CH site on the Lincolnshire Wolds, and at Swingate, Dover, two transmitter towers, and a replacement still stand. Dunkirk (Kent) retains a transmitter tower. The transmitter and receiver bunkers of the East Coast CH stations are quite plentiful, surviving, as well as at Stenigot, Dunkirk and Swingate, for instance at West Beckham (Norfolk), Canewdon (Essex), Drone Hill (Borders) *(131)*, and Ottercops Moss (Northumberland). Examples of surviving CHL sites include Bempton (East Yorkshire), Happisburgh (Norfolk) and Strumble Head (Pembrokeshire). The distinctive buildings of the CD/CHL station can be seen at Scremerston *(132)* and Hartley Crag (Northumberland), and Skipsea (East Yorkshire). At Greyfriars (Suffolk), along with other structures, are the rectangular blast walls which originally protected the Nissen hut, straddled by the aerial gantry, of one of the first GCI stations. Many sites retain simply the concrete blocks upon which, the legs of the radar towers formerly stood, and these are often the key to the interpretation of the site.

Under the umbrella of radio-direction-finding there is a further group of related devices which were just as vital in their contribution to the air war, and have left a few marks on the landscape. The hardest part of a bomber's task is finding the designated target. The German air force developed a way of transmitting a signal which enabled their bomber pilots to locate their target by following

131 Drone Hill, Borders, NT849665; guardhouse for Chain Home radar site *c*.1939; note pillbox alongside; this site was defended by nearly a dozen of the big octagonal type often found on Scottish airfields and radar sites

132 Scremerston, Northumberland, NU008501; the Transmitter/ Receiver block of this Coast Defence/Chain Home Low radar site; the other building on site held the generator

133 Clipston, Northamptonshire, SP703825; in the background is a Second World War Royal Observer Corps visual spotting post; its raised brick platform has steps down to a shelter; in the foreground is an underground nuclear attack monitoring post from around 1960

the radio beam. The system was code-named Knickerbein. Once this had been discovered, the British response was initially to corrupt the signal, but, eventually, the signal was intercepted, and a fresh signal transmitted with parts substituted, to confuse the enemy navigators. This operation was known as Aspirin, and receiver and transmitter stations were built across the main bomber routes. The British system, equivalent to Knickerbein, was called Gee. Many of the Gee transmitters shared their sites with radar, but some were free-standing, as is the one at Ulceby Cross (Lincolnshire). The later V-bombers used a development of the system known as Gee-H, operating from radar sites in the south-west.

If radar represented the high-tech approach to air-defence, then the Observer Corps, Royal from 1941, (ROC) epitomises the other end of the scale. The informal, and largely unorganised spotter screen of the LADA, had more than demonstrated its worth, and when the air-defence system was being recreated in the 1930s, this dimension was seen as essential. ROC posts take all sorts of shapes. Many were located in high buildings, particularly church towers and windmills, but also such buildings as maltings, as at Sleaford (Lincolnshire). Working from anywhere that was suitable, using a plotting instrument introduced in 1934, and still in use in the 1950s, hundreds of ROC observers all over Britain developed specialist skills in difficult conditions. There were a number of dedicated structures which appeared for ROC use. There are a few survivors *(133)*, Sutton Bassett (Northamptonshire), is one, and Porlock (Somerset) is another, of a two-level post with accommodation below, and a part-covered platform above. At Epworth (Lincolnshire) is a single-storey design with a plinth under a large hatch in the roof. These, however, are the exceptions, for the normal provision was a timber shed with an open annexe, often referred to as the rabbit hutch. Local variations on this produced stilted timber towers and sheds. Sometimes such a structure was erected on top of a more permanent building, and then removed at the end of the War. Group headquarters tended to be located in city centre post offices and telephone exchanges, in order to access communications systems freely. Many of the RAF Filter Rooms, such as Watnall in Nottinghamshire, or Blakelaw Quarry (Northumberland), into which news of approaching enemy aircraft was fed, and from which, orders to intercept were issued, survived for a while as part of later air-defence systems. Some are lucky enough to have found new tenants, such as the Sea Cadets at Blakelaw, but the shooting club at Watnall has been and gone.

We have seen how attempts were made to produce a system which might provide early warning of the approach of enemy aircraft, and information about numbers and types of aircraft and the direction in which they were travelling. We have seen how this information was used to activate guns, searchlights and inter-ceptor aircraft in order to destroy those enemy aircraft. There was another element in the system which was devoted to fooling the enemy aircraft into unloading their bombs onto non-targets. This was one of the major deception plans of the war and consisted of a network of specialised bombing decoys. The leading bombers in a raid use visual cues to reach their targets and to drop their bombs. Those following behind assume that their leaders have dropped their bombs in the right place, and gratefully add theirs so they can turn for home as soon as possible. Bombing decoys set out to present false targets to the bombers. There were a number of types of decoy, at first designed to protect airfields. For daylight use there was the K site, a convincing dummy airfield, complete with realistic aircraft built by the film industry technicians from Shepperton Studios. A small crew of airmen moved the dummies around to simulate a working airfield. Perhaps a few sheds would suggest habitation, with more almost hidden in the trees. A QL site operated at night by mimicking runway lights. As the enemy were heard to approach the lights were (not too) hurriedly extinguished, to tempt the enemy into an attack. Lights were operated electrically from a control blockhouse on the edge of the fake airfield. Here, a much smaller crew was needed. Most prewar airfields had one or two decoys. As the need for more and more airfields increased then decoys were often developed as real airfields, but, by then, much of the danger of enemy bombing had passed. The apparent success of the K and Q sites led, as the Blitz intensified, to the provision of decoys for the cities and for industrial targets. Starfish (SF) sites were large open areas studded with braziers of combustible materials, again, electrically ignited from a control blockhouse. As enemy bombers approached, then the fires would be lit in order to convince them that the first bombs had already been dropped there and that the raid was progressing satisfactorily. These basket fires became steadily more sophisticated through the war, and their operators learned to replicate many of the characteristic behaviours of urban fires, with sudden eruptions and explosions. Even more sophisticated were the industrial decoys. Here particular processes were simulated such as the sparks from a loco's furnace in the railway marshalling yards, or the particular flame patterns of the steelworks. Oil depots had to strike the right balance between convincing the enemy he had started oil fires burning, and not doing his job for him. Some specific targets had decoys based around their shape. Hull Docks had a very distinctive outline, delineated by lights fringing the basins. By hanging lights on poles planted in the ponds of the marshy ground skirting the Humber estuary, it was possible to suggest the characteristic shape of the docks and to entice enemy bombers to drop their loads in harmless places. A further refinement reproduced the sparks given off by the trams local to the docks. Sometimes this would work, sometimes not. On one occasion, the Nottinghamshire village of Plungar in the Vale of Belvoir had 500 wholly unexpected bombs dropped one night. The only possible explanation was that the Cropwell Butler SF site had been mistaken by the bomber pilots for a burning Nottingham. Plungar was therefore translated, in their mental maps, into the part of Derby containing the Rolls-Royce factory. During the Second World War, 300 of Britain's 800 bombing decoys received hits, and that had to mean fewer hits on the intended targets. Bombing decoys had only minimal buildings so it is some of the control blockhouses which survive *(134)*. Several can be seen on the extensive Farlington marshes, where a number of different decoys were built to lure bombers away from

134 Wormegay, Norfolk, TF653126; blockhouse for a bombing decoy, to drawing number 367/41; generators were housed in the chamber to the right, and a headlamp was mounted on the platform on the left; the Nissen section housed a stove and the controls for the crew's various lighting tricks

Portsmouth, across the water, and many airfield decoy blockhouses can still be traced. In built-up areas this is more difficult and most of those such as Glasgow's nine SF sites will have long been built over.

If all the possible ways of preventing bombs falling on their intended targets failed, then damage limitation became the priority. Although the effects of bombing civilian targets with modern technology had been known for some time, there was a reluctance on the part of government, generally because of the enormous costs involved, to embark on a programme to provide communal shelters. The intention was that employers would provide shelters at work, and householders would provide shelter at home. Public shelters would be built, only to accommodate those people caught out in the street by an air raid, but this was not always understood. Legislation in 1939 made it mandatory for employers to make provision for Air Raid Precautions (ARP) in the workplace, and for local authorities to provide materials and expertise to enable householders to do the same at home. Ideas of dispersal through evacuation and children's camps were current and it was still envisaged that public shelters would cater for no more than 10 per cent of the population at any moment. Local authorities would provide the infrastructure: ARP wardens, gas decontamination centres, casualty clearing stations, and reporting centres. They would also distribute kits to enable house-holders to strengthen basements, or the small, household shelters named for Sir John Anderson, Lord Privy Seal, whose responsibility Civil Defence had become, free to those on low incomes, and at cost to others. These two schemes were expected to afford enough protection for 10 million people. A handbook of Structural Defence was finally issued, containing detailed constructional and engineering advice, but apparently overtaken by the events listed above. In the event, large numbers of personal shelters were in use. In some places, natural or pre-existing facilities were used: the Nottingham caves or the London Underground, for example. What remains tends to be evidence of the ARP operation, and a few institutional shelters, particularly on school sites. A number of communal, surface shelters survive, along with many examples of Anderson shelters, often used, now, as garden sheds. There are some Wardens' Posts extant, as well as Reporting Centres, and Decontamination Units, often still in use as local authority or health authority offices. A number of personal, one-man shelters were developed for fire-watchers or security guards at factories. These were usually steel, cylindrical cabinets with steel doors and shuttered windows. The Consol is a conical steel shelter with just one letterbox slit in the front. It was made by Constructors of Erdington, Birmingham, and widely used at factories to shelter the man on the gate. The contemporary advertisement shows a masked and helmeted figure emerging like an alien from a space capsule, very *War of the Worlds*. Another similar design, but with a circle of 15 vertical slits at head-height, came from Rustons of Lincoln, who had built tanks in the First World War. Morrison shelters were steel frameworks with wire-mesh sides designed for indoor use. They were intended to accommodate a bed for two adults and two children, and could withstand the weight of two collapsing storeys. Nearly 500,000 were made, to shelter over a million people. Stanton shelters, mainly found on military property were made up of curved concrete panels bolted together along the ridge, and then covered with earth. Only a chimney-like escape hatch shows, proud of the mound. ARP reporting centres and decontamination centres usually consist of single-storey asbestos, concrete-panel, or temporary brick hutting with a water tower at one end. Wardens' posts are very similar to Home Guard explosives/inflammables stores, rectangular with a single door, 4in (10cm) concrete roof, and two small ventilator grilles. Whilst many of the anti-invasion defences of the early part of the war were redundant by 1943, air-raid shelters were needed right up to the Spring of 1945 when the flying-bomb threat finally ceased *(135)*.

One consequence of the air raids on London was the need to protect the functions of Government from the effects of bombing. Protected accommodation was built both below ground and on the surface. The Cabinet War Rooms were installed in extensive storage basements under the former Office of Works building. Tunnels under Whitehall brought telephone cables into all government offices. Plans were made to evacuate central London altogether, and underground citadels were constructed for the Admiralty in Cricklewood, for the Air Ministry in Harrow, and for the Cabinet in Dollis Hill. There is some doubt that the Whitehall provision was as strong as people thought, but, at the time, it was felt bad for morale to voice such doubts. The Admiralty Citadel still stands on the

135 Princes Park, Liverpool; sign showing the way to the Emergency Water Supply, in Belvidere (*sic*) Road

north side of Horseguards Parade and displays loopholes, gun positions and large chunks of solid concrete. Other London buildings were either strengthened, such as the basement of Curzon House for use as the Royal citadel, or adapted as already protected sites, such as Goodge Street Underground Station *(136)*, which became Eisenhower's London headquarters of the Chiefs of Staff, during the D-Day planning process. The Rotundas in Horseferry Road, Westminster housed vital telephone exchanges servicing Whitehall. Both the Cabinet War Rooms in Whitehall, and the contemporary tunnels under Dover Castle, known as Hellfire Corner, are now open to the public.

After the end of the Second World War Britain's defences against air attack largely consisted of the network of AA guns, early-warning radar, and interceptor fighter aircraft which was already in existence. The 3.7in and the 5.25in dual-purpose HAA guns remained emplaced, along with GL radar, and all the technical refinements which had been developed through the war years. The Bofors LAA gun remained in use with the field army. By 1947, the international situation demanded a closer look at Britain's defence plans. The ROC was re-formed, and committees began to formulate the AA Defence system known as ROTOR. This consisted of a network of CH, CHL, CHEL, Centrimetric Early Warning (CEW), and GCI radar sites, reporting to Sector Operations Centres (SOC). Although many of the locations of these radar sites were the same as those used in the Second World War, by 1954, many had been completely rebuilt to new building standards and designs. The main radar sites were along the east and south coasts reporting to four SOCs. One of these at Box, near Bath, the Southern Sector SOC was an updated underground control centre of wartime origin. The other four at

136 London, Goodge Street Underground station, used as a headquarters of Chiefs of Staff Supreme Allied Command (COSSAC), led by General Eisenhower; in the background is the Post Office Tower, built as part of the defence communications network, sometimes referred to as 'Backbone'

Kelvedon Hatch (Essex), Bawburgh (Norfolk), Shipton (North Yorkshire), and Barnton Quarry outside Edinburgh, were all new, purpose-built, three-storey, underground structures in R4 reinforced concrete bunkers. The radar sites themselves were given a range of single-storey (R1 and R2), and two-storey (R3 and R6), semi-sunken and underground buildings. The Type 80 Radar was mounted atop a Modulator building, and individual radar sets sat on cubical concrete plinths, dispersed around the sites. The underground blocks were entered through guardrooms built to resemble gabled bungalows with frontal verandahs. A tunnel ran from the back of the guardroom down to the operations room. Accommodation was remote, and only the minimum construction appeared on site. Whereas the other five Sectors were at permanent readiness, at least in day-time, the Western Sector, with SOC at Longley Lane, Preston, was largely at a state of stand-by. Warning of approaching enemy aircraft was also sent via telephone lines to Anti-Aircraft Operations Rooms (AAOR) in order to activate the HAA guns of the 32 designated Gun-Defended Areas (GDA). Many of these were two-level, semi-sunken reinforced concrete bunkers. Some, however, were established structures, upgraded for reuse, such as the tunnels at Dover, or the Brompton Road tube station in west London. However, ROTOR was not to last as a system, as accelerating obsolescence brought a constant and costly need to upgrade, in order to keep up with the known or imagined technical improvements in the enemy's capabilities. In 1955, AA Command was stood down, and much of the radar network was gradually shut down as new equipment was developed to bring cover to increasingly wide areas. Although many of the structures were adapted for other defensive purposes, a number of structures survive relatively unchanged from this period. The SOC of the Metropolitan Sector, Kelvedon Hatch is open to the public, as is the GCI radar station at Anstruther (Fife) *(137)*, with its stone guardroom bungalow, and some radar sets mounted for display. The Type 80 Modulator building at the Bempton CEW station in East Yorkshire survives along with radar plinths. There is an improved Type 80 Modulator building at Hope Cove (Devon). Langtoft (Lincolnshire) GCI station retains its surface R6 bunker along with radar plinths and guardroom, now a house. Also at Hope Cove is a semi-sunken R6 operations room, and at Truleigh Hill (West Sussex) the sunken R2 bunker of the CHEL station. The R3 control room of Wartling (East Sussex) GCI station is derelict, with its guardroom converted into a private house. Kelvedon Hatch retains its gabled generator building and tower with saddle-back roof. A number of the purpose-built AAORs also remain, unaltered by subsequent defence use, as at Gosforth, for the Tyne GDA, now the local Record Office, West Cross, adjoining a TA centre, for the Swansea GDA, and Elvaston, for the Derby and Nottingham GDA, now derelict, in the middle of a campsite.

The ROC had remained in existence through the life of ROTOR as a traditional aircraft-spotting organisation. For this purpose a new construction had been developed to bring some uniformity in place of the *ad hoc* local solutions which had sufficed during the Second World War. This was the Orlit Post, a part-covered concrete box containing the plotting equipment which observers used to work out the directions of raiding aircraft, in order to alert the SOCs. Orlit A posts were at ground level, and Orlit B posts were mounted on concrete stilts, and were reached by a built-in ladder *(138)*. There were a very few posts built at this time which were not of the Orlit design, but which shared the same characteristics. However, by the mid-1950s it had become apparent that, in view of the increasing speed of modern aircraft, it was not realistic, any longer, to retain confidence in purely visual spotting. There was, nevertheless, still a role for the volunteers of the ROC. In conjunction with the United Kingdom Warning and Monitoring Organisation (UKWMO) the ROC was given the task of monitoring fallout in the event of nuclear attack. New underground posts were designed to accommodate three observers and their equipment. It was felt, by Government, that even though there was no shelter provision for the general population, in the event of a nuclear strike, people would still be better under cover until the immediate fallout had blown over. The few minutes warning that the radar network might achieve, coupled with information about the exact location of the bomb blast (Ground Zero), and the direction and speed of the prevailing wind, constantly monitored and updated, would assist people in avoiding unnecessary exposure. The new ROC post measured 19ft (5.7m) long, by 8ft 6in (2.55m) wide, by 7ft 6in (2.25m) high.

137 Above Anstruther, Fife, NO568089; guardhouse of ROTOR ground-control interception radar site, dating from the 1950s; this stone version retains all the usual features: the porthole window, verandah, and rear tower enclosing the access down a ramp to the underground operations rooms; this example is now a museum

138 Left Swallow, Lincolnshire, TA177024; an ORLIT B elevated Royal Observer Corps spotting post dating from around 1953

Access was down a ladder from the entrance hatch, which, along with two venti-
lators, and two pipes holding instruments, was the only part of the structure above
ground. In the buried concrete chamber were bunks, chemical toilets, work-
surfaces on which to process data from the recording instruments, and some food
and water storage. Posts were grouped in threes and fours. Each had a telephone,
and one in each cluster had a radio. The ROC was organised in 29 groups in six
Regions. Each group had a protected headquarters building where information
from the posts was collated and passed on. Some of these headquarters were
surface and some were semi-sunken. A few were accommodated in existing
buildings. Inside was a two-storey deep well with a mezzanine balcony. Plots were
received and transferred onto glass screens for the plotters to record on a master-
plot, and pass on to the different military and civil authorities who needed particular information. By the time the programme was completed in 1965, there were
over 1,500 posts, with nearly 300 in the vicinity of the nuclear bases in the eastern
counties, retaining visual-spotting posts. Despite a sweeping cull of posts in the late
1960s, many continued in service up to 1991. A large proportion of all these posts
remains. One at Dersingham (Norfolk) is opened to the public regularly, and re-
equipped with all its instruments for the occasion. Some are now being bought as
rural *pieds à terre*. Some of the ROC headquarters also survive. Examples of the
semi-sunken version, often referred to as Aztec Temples, remain at Acomb, in
York, at Fiskerton, outside Lincoln, and on the northern ring road, at Norwich.
A surface example stands behind the Drill Hall in Horsham.

In the 1970s, a new air-defence plan named the improved United Kingdom
Air Defence Ground Environment (UKADGE) brought about a significant
reduction in the large number of radar stations involved in ROTOR. There were
now just eight radar stations reporting to the headquarters at High Wycombe
(Buckinghamshire). Mobile radars enabled the sites to operate with minimal infrastructure. Remote early-warning systems both terrestrial and airborne had
reduced the reliance previously placed on coast-based installations. Pooling of
establishments and the increasing value placed on shared signals intelligence
through NATO, have made further reductions possible. Spectacular constructions
of the Ballistic Missile Early Warning System (BMEWS) like the Fylingdales
radomes, the Cobra Mist antennae at Orford Ness, or the parabolic dish aerials of
ACE High at Stenigot, have all been and gone. The radar stations of UKADGE
however remain in military use at Buchan (Aberdeen), Boulmer
(Northumberland), Staxton Wold (North Yorkshire), Ash (Kent), Neatishead
(Norfolk), Portreath (Cornwall) and Ty Croes (Anglesey). Neatishead hosts a
museum devoted to air defence in the Cold War. The Bloodhound surface-to-air
missile systems, of which there survive extensive remains, have already been
examined in a previous chapter *(139)*.

Whilst Britain's nuclear deterrent was being deployed during or after a nuclear
attack, it was expected that orderly national life would continue as before. Given
that London might be expected to be hit early on in a nuclear conflict, national

139 West Raynham, Norfolk, TF849251; Air Defence Tactical Training Theatre or ADT3, a development of the Second World War Dome Trainer, but for use with Rapier missiles

and local government facilities were established on a dispersed and protected basis. In the 1950s, War Rooms were set up for emergency use located in twelve regions across Britain, with four in London's suburbs. These were built of reinforced concrete and were designed to accommodate civil and military planners and liaison officers centred on a map room, and communications staff to receive and transmit situation reports and directives. It quickly became apparent that there was insufficient space in these war rooms to accommodate all the people necessary to keep things ticking over for the length of time it was now felt would be needed. Britain was next split into ten regions each to be run by a commissioner with a staff of around 150 civil servants. The new buildings were called Regional Seats of Government (RSG) and were either added to existing war rooms as at Cambridge, or converted from suitable buildings as at Drakelow (Worcestershire) where the underground Second World War factory was adapted. This national network was quickly supplemented by sub-RSGs, many of which, such as Hack Green (Cheshire), Kelvedon Hatch and Mistley (Essex), Anstruther (Fife), Barnton Quarry (Edinburgh), Skendleby (Lincolnshire) and Hope Cove (Devon), were converted from buildings of the ROTOR scheme, though one, at least, at Loughborough (Leicestershire), had been an emergency Cold Store in the Second World War. As ROC Group headquarters became vacant, some, like Lawford Heath (Warwickshire), and Wrexham were also adapted for use in the RSG network. Most of these buildings were simply bombproof, underground or semi-sunken, and equipped with independent power sources. Some attempt at renderering them proof against chemical and biological weapons was usually made, but, primarily it was radioactive fallout that was seen as the major threat to be countered. Decontamination facilities are therefore prominent in all the buildings in RSG use. Although, many commentators perceived a thaw in the Cold War during the 1980s, the Thatcher government nevertheless encouraged local authorities to construct underground fallout shelters by offering generous grants. Many local authorities incorporated such constructions underneath newly-built Civic Centres. Leicestershire County Council's Glenfield complex, for instance, along with other such buildings built in the 1960s, already had a nuclear bunker in its basement, but so now would neighbouring Melton Mowbray, built in around 1988, and many more including Huntingdon (1983), Horsham (1984), the offices of the Highland Region at Gareloch (1988), Dover (1989), and Southend (1992). All these bunkers survive, although most are used for storage, with, perhaps, a possible role as emergency control centres in the event of natural or man-made disaster. Other surface constructions such as the war rooms at Cambridge or at Brislington (Bristol) survive but with uncertain futures. Some such as Hack Green and Kelvedon Hatch are museums.

One of the keys to maintaining the operation of government during a nuclear attack was seen to be a robust communications network. The BBC was provided with studio facilities and transmitters in the RSGs in order that what remained of the populace might be kept informed of developments. The BBC facilities in the Government bunker at Corsham (Wiltshire), which had, by the 1950s, replaced Dollis Hill as the underground base for the Cabinet, were expected to be used for keeping the Queen in the public consciousness as a morale-booster. Telephone lines are vulnerable, and only in central London had any real attempt been made to protect them by burying lines serving the government offices, mainly in Whitehall, in tunnels, up to 100ft (30m) down, and by the construction of an underground telephone exchange known as Kingsway, but actually in Chancery Lane. The answer lay in a network of inter-visible microwave towers, the best known of which stands in London's Tottenham Court Road, known as the Post Office Tower when it was built in 1961. At the time, few realised the significance of these towers, and, for many years, they were explained in a context of bringing colour television to the nation. This network, whose central spine is sometimes referred to as Backbone, extends across the whole of Britain, linking radar stations, radio and television transmitters, RSGs, military communications systems, air traffic control systems and so on. Many of the towers are strictly utilitarian, but others have some claim to aesthetic distinction. Alongside this essentially strategic communications system of microwave towers, was the Home Office network of hilltop radio stations, designed for tactical use by the police, ROC, and emergency services. Many of these installations remain, some of them as masts for mobile 'phone networks. Other sites such as Bawburgh (Norfolk), former ROTOR site, and former RSG, are used by private communications firms.

Large numbers of bunkers for a whole variety of purposes still exist all over Britain. Many of them will, most likely, have been part of one of those schemes outlined above, but we will meet a whole range of other uses in the final chapter.

8

LOGISTICAL SUPPORT

Napoleonic armies may have marched on their stomachs, but twentieth-century armies could not fight by bread alone. Already by 1900, the successful prosecution of war was dependent on the extent to which the protagonists had managed to industrialise the production, distribution and development of materiel, the efficiency of its mobilisation systems, and the degree of total commitment to the war effort by military and civilian alike. Armies might be raised, trained and delivered to the fighting front, but unless they could be kept supplied with ammunition, food and water, medical support and replacements for losses, both human and material, their endeavours would be in vain. This chapter examines some aspects of the physical monuments underpinning these very practical considerations. As well as the more tangible assets, such as munitions, food and fuel, which needed protection, it must be noted here, how intelligence and communications continued to become steadily more important through the century. A significant reminder of this can still be seen at Porthcurno (Cornwall), where the terminal for the submarine cables connecting Britain with the USA and the Empire, is contained in a large blockhouse still bearing camouflage paint, and protected by pillboxes.

In peacetime, training may be the major occupation of the military, and has often been portrayed as a leisurely way of whiling away a few hours of each day in order to justify the existence of expensive manpower and technology. In times of war, training suddenly assumes a frantic urgency. At the beginning of the century training tended to consist of endless drill, with the occasional, often only annual, large set-piece manoeuvre. Prior to this, only engineers and gunners, at Woolwich, had received anything approaching a technical education. Prospective naval officers, often as young as 12, had joined ships in order to learn their trade on the job. Until the Cardwell reforms of the 1870s, the majority of commissions in the army were obtained by patronage or purchase. As the increasing demands on the professional officer became apparent, then preservice training was instituted, and the now-familiar institutions for training officers gained in prominence. Although the Royal Military Academy at Sandhurst, traces its origins back to the

Napoleonic period through establishments in High Wycombe and Marlow (Buckinghamshire), Richmond-on-Thames, and particularly Woolwich the new college developed through the late 1800s, but underwent significant expansion between 1922-37. The Britannia Royal Naval College, Dartmouth, replacing a number of previous naval training establishments, notably Queen Victoria's Osborne on the Isle of Wight, was built in 1899-1905. The youngest service saw the necessity for an officer-training school instantly on its foundation as the RAF, in 1918. From 1920, the RAF Cadet College at Cranwell (Lincolnshire) *(140)* built on the pilot-training function begun on the site by the RNAS in 1915. The grand, neo-Baroque buildings were finished by 1933. It is worth noting that Aston Webb's Dartmouth, West's Cranwell, and Martin's Sandhurst extensions, all with their pediments, columns and domes, seem to look back rather than forward. Clearly nothing but traditional styles would do for the Services' new officers, however innovative they might be expected to be. The fourth wing of Cranwell's College Hall was finally added in 1960, and, clearly had to conform to the rest of the block. However, the entirely new Whittle Hall, opened in 1962, retains this neo-Georgian look. Not until the new Trenchard Hall of 1966 was built, designed to accommodate the technical training facilties being transferred from Henlow, do Cranwell's buildings begin to project a contemporary image of living alongside the new universities in the white heat of technology. Of course, in the emergency conditions of the Second World War, officers would be trained wherever there might be space, and Officer Cadet Training Units (OCTU), were set up all over the country, some in the regimental depots, and some in requisitioned country houses. The naval college annexed Eaton Hall (Cheshshire) for the duration. Pilots were trained at elementary flying training schools (EFTS), often run by civilian firms such as Marshall's at Cambridge, or Airwork at Perth. Many flying clubs, some of which had always been involved, through such schemes as the Civil Air Guard, in training pilots, with half an eye on the international situation throughout the 1930s, now assumed an entirely military orientation. Small, hitherto private airfields such as Desford (Leicestershire), or Sywell (Northamptonshire), were suddenly transformed into busy military airfields. At Cambridge, alongside the art deco hangar, control building and hotel, can be seen the MT block, Blister hangars and Handcraft huts, hurriedly added around 1940.

We have seen the requisitioning of large houses in several contexts now, as bases, depots, or training camps for army units; as out-of-the-way locations for secret or clandestine activities; and as headquarters for naval units. Country houses were also used widely by the RAF and the USAAF. If, as at Rackheath (Norfolk), the big house was on the airfield, then it would be integrated into the life of the base, often along with the squire and his family, in the case of Rackheath, the Straceys. At Woodhall Spa, the officers' mess was in the Petwood Hall Hotel. At Hendon, the former London Aerodrome Hotel, of 1917, was pressed into service as an officers' mess. Bawtry Hall (South Yorkshire) was headquarters of 1 Group, Bomber Command throughout the Second World War, and such houses provided

140 RAF Cranwell, Lincolnshire; the grand portico of College Hall, completed 1933; dismayed by official plans for a cross between a gothic railway station and a Scottish hydro, Sir Samuel Hoare had taken the eventual architect to see the Royal Hospital Chelsea for inspiration

the headquarters for most of the other RAF Commands. The US 9th Army Air Force used Sunninghill Park (then in Berkshire, now in Surrey) as its headquarters, and the Combat Wing headquarters of the 8th USAAF were spread across the stately homes of East Anglia including Elveden Hall (Suffolk), Ketteringham Hall (Norfolk), Sawston Hall (Cambridgeshire), and Walcot Hall near Stamford.

The authority for this wholesale requisitioning of private property in the national interest was vested in a piece of legislation from the First World War, called the Defence of the Realm Act (DORA), of 1914, reinforced by the 1920 Emergency Powers Act, and then by the Defence (General) Regulations of 1939. Through this legislation the government was able to establish a coastal exclusion zone in 1940, and also to commandeer land for training purposes. Whole villages in Dorset, around Lulworth and Tyneham, and large tracts of land around Thetford (Norfolk), now the Stanford Battle Area, were taken, and never returned. In 1938, a register of suitable houses was set up, in order for government departments to put in their bids. Houses were earmarked for hospitals, the safe storage of museum collections, and schools, as well as the military applications we have seen. Existing hospitals, government buildings, food stores and buildings used by transport organisations such as railway or canal companies were exempt, as were any houses with less than four rooms on the ground floor. As a rough guide to the level of demand for requisitioned properties, the Admiralty took over 2,800 during the course of the war. At the end of the Second World War, most houses were returned to their owners, but many, in a condition unfit for further human habitation. The 'live now, for tomorrow brings who knows what?' attitude of many wartime occupiers relegated the care of private property to the bottom of their list of concerns. The combination of the introduction of high death duties, the reluctance of former domestic staff to return to a life which now seemed to many of them anachronistic, and the general unavailability of building materials in the late-1940s, spelt the end for large numbers of country houses. In many cases, owners, faced with all these problems, felt that they had little option but to demolish.

One training facility which needed plenty of space was the range. Outdoor rifle ranges gained in importance at the beginning of the century with the adoption of the Lee Metford 0.303in (7.7 mm) rifle. This would develop into the short magazine Lee Enfield (SMLE) rifle, used, in its various marks, in two world wars. There had been ranges at Bisley and Pirbright for some years prior to this but they were under enormous pressure. New ranges were necessary to train regulars and territorials with the new weapon. The marksmanship of British troops had been compared unfavourably to the virtuoso performance of the Boer riflemen in South Africa, and practice on a better weapon was seen as the answer. Musketry camps such as Purfleet on the Thames marshes were established. Here, extensive ranges were served by light railway. Opened around 1908, and expanded in 1914 to train some of the million plus recruits on their way to the Western Front, Purfleet had five lengths of Butts, allowing up to 70 riflemen to fire at once. In front of the Butts, but in trenches protected by earth banks, markers would raise and lower targets on pulleys, and indicate hits with long wooden pointers. These Butts at Purfleet are of a more lightweight construction than many, owing to their location on the marshy ground. At the similar range at Long Eaton (Derbyshire), on the banks of the River Trent, the Butts, only one third of the width of Purfleet's, contain 45,000 tonnes of earth, but on more stable ground. Other

141 Left Stirling, central Scotland; a stretch of simulated Atlantic Wall, at NN838037, built for troops to practise attack techniques prior to the D-Day invasion of Normandy; note the Tobruk shelters

142 Right Drigg, Cumbria; quadrant tower on Vickers artillery range

similar ranges from this period, survive at Middlewick, outside Colchester, and at Hythe. At Whitburn, on the coast above Sunderland, there is a range, built in 1912 for the Territorial Force. Although the huts have now been upgraded, the original offices and warden's house remain. Now Purfleet has been sold to the Royal Society for the Protection of Birds to be returned to natural habitat, but other ranges still operate at Beckingham Camp on the Nottinghamshire/ Lincolnshire border, at Hornsea (East Yorkshire), at Altcar, above Liverpool, at Barry Buddon Camp near Dundee, and many others.

Apart from ranges, there is little visible evidence to remind us of infantry training sites. At Penally (Pembrokeshire), there are practice trenches, used for training purposes at this Infantry School in the Second World War. Similar trenches survive on the hills above Sheffield, where the Pals Battalion of the York and Lancaster Regiment prepared themselves for the trenches of the Somme. A number of structures remain from training exercises prior to the D-Day landings in the Second World War. These range from lengths of AT-wall in the woods at

Hankley Common, near Tilford (Surrey), to a stretch of the Atlantic Wall, complete with Tobruk shelters and underground bunkers, on the moors at the west end of the Ochil Hills, north of Stirling *(141)*, to German beach-defence pillboxes along the shores of Croyde Bay (Devon). Besides the traditional training areas of Aldershot, Castlemartin (Pembrokeshire) and Salisbury Plain, all still in use, tank training has left little trace. On the north Devon coast, Roger Thomas has identified tall, concrete walls in the form of portals, simulating landing-craft ramps and doors. Allied tank drivers practised reversing through them, in order to be able to speed up embarkation on D-Day. The area around Dunwich (Suffolk), is criss-crossed by ditches and other obstacles, used to test the 'funnies' of General Hobart's 79th Armoured Division, with its flail, flame-thrower and bridging tanks.

Gunnery ranges were largely on Salisbury Plain, near the School of Artillery at Larkhill, although it has been suggested that there were AT gun ranges on the Thames marshes. Shoeburyness in Essex was the main proofing range, and there were permanent emplacements for heavy guns. At Drigg, on the Cumbrian coast, guns were fired from the Vickers works at Barrow-in-Furness, and the fall of shot measured by observers in concrete bunkers in the sand-dunes backing the beach. A similar exercise was attempted in 1943, when a Vickers prototype 13.5in (340mm) gun adapted to fire 8in (200mm) shells, was sited next to one of the super-heavy guns mounted at Dover. With a range of 100,000 yards, it fired towards the range at Shoeburyness. Unfortunately, three quarters of the rounds burst in flight, and the barrel was worn out after only 28 rounds had been fired. At Drigg *(142)*, range shelters can still be seen in the dunes. Shoeburyness remains in MoD use.

Bombing ranges have left more remains, mostly in the shape of quadrant towers. These were vantage points from which observers could provide immediate feedback to pilots and bomb-aimers. Many were on the coast serving RAF and RNAS armament training schools (ATS). In Galloway, the bombers from West Freugh used ranges in Wigtown Bay and Luce Bay, where there are traces of targets. The ranges around the Wash and the Lincolnshire coast, served Sutton Bridge and North Coates. Holbeach and Wainfleet Sands, where a new range control tower has just been built, are still used for bombing practice. Leuchars, in Fife, used the Tentsmuir range below the Tay estuary, and, here there are stilted, square and pentagonal, quadrant towers built astride the AT blocks and pillboxes of the anti-invasion defences *(143)*. At Druridge Bay (Northumberland), used by 7 ATS at Acklington, there are range shelters. Two high, three-storey quadrant towers remain at Goswick Sands (Northumberland). One is built on top of a beach-defence pillbox. The other, a mile further down the beach, has mock battlements, perhaps to disguise itself as a church tower. As well as these bombing ranges on the shore, they were also sited inland. There is a single-storey quadrant tower in Grimsthorpe Park (Lincolnshire), and two-storey ones at Preston Capes (Northamptonshire), and at Grandborough (Warwickshire). Other testing facilities have been used over the century. Blue Streak, the IRBM, developed in the 1950s

143 Left Tentsmuir, Fife; quadrant tower on the Second World War bombing range

144 Below Portsdown, Hampshire; Royal Navy experimental radar establishment, built post–Second World War; later, Dry Land Test Site for radar and other weapons

was tested at Spadeadam Moor in Cumbria, prior to its full testing at Woomera, in Australia. At Spadeadam, the enormous concrete missile stand remains. An associated project, the Black Knight rocket, was tested on a track built by Saunders Roe, at the Needles (Isle of Wight), and now standing on National Trust land. In Wales, there are rocket-testing facilities at Aberporth (Ceredigion), and Pendine Sands (Dyfed), where the officers' mess was, until its recent disposal, located in Llanmiloe House, a mansion dating from 1720 and taken over by the RAF in 1942. The imposing building up on Portsdown Hill next to the naval headquarters in Fort Southwick *(144)*, was built in the 1950s as the offices of the RN radar experimental establishment, and has since served as the Dry Land Test Site for weapons and radar, which once occupied a site on Whale Island.

Throughout the nineteenth century, the move to the production of munitions on an industrial scale had dominated the development of gunpowder mills. The end of that century saw a move from gunpowder to cordite as the main military propellant, and a consequent change in both the location and the design of plant. At the start of the First World War, there were four major cordite manufacturing centres. The long-established royal gunpowder factory at Waltham Abbey on the banks of the River Lea (Essex), the old Faversham mill with its newer off-shoot at Cliffe (Kent), and the Chilworth (Surrey) plant. All had undergone extensive rebuilding for their new task. Also involved in the new chemical processes of producing explosives were Nobel's with plants at Ardeer (Ayrshire), Pitsea (Essex), Faversham (Kent) and Stowmarket (Suffolk). Research continued to be carried out at Woolwich Arsenal. The navy ran its own cordite production, from 1914, at Holton Heath (Dorset). Hayle (Cornwall) continued in business producing nitro-glycerine, gun-cotton and cordite, originally for the mining industry, but available for military purposes. The start of the First World War brought a pressing need not only to increase production on a massive scale, but also to ensure that all aspects of munitions production should be under the control of the government. DORA ensured that existing plants were brought into the fold, and the National Factory programme made sure that new ones were part of a planned effort from the start. A strip of land north of Carlisle, and stretching along the north bank of the Solway Firth, embracing Longtown, Gretna, Mossband, Eastriggs and Dornock, became home to a vast complex of cordite factories and magazines, all linked together by railway. Whilst the navy continued to favour Lyddite, as the war progressed the major explosive was TNT. Both new plants and established ones in the traditional industrial cities, produced the constituent chemicals. Once the raw materials had been processed, the need was for shell-filling factories. Lloyd George, first Minister of Munitions appointed to prevent the recurrence of shortages, went to great lengths to short-circuit the bureaucracy inherent in any monolithic system. One of his moves was to appoint the dynamic industrialist, Lord Chetwynd, to bring varied industrial processes to the problem. With no previous experience of explosives, he nevertheless combined existing technology from other fields, into a successful shell-filling plant, at Chilwell (Nottinghamshire). He also developed steel-framed magazines with travelling cranes on gantries, and an unique, underground magazine. A large number of new factories were constructed during the First World War, exclusively for the production of shells filled with explosive or gas. Remains of many can be seen either incorporated in later factories, or occupying their original greenfield sites, in locations not subsequently developed, often due to their remoteness. The Billingham plant on Teesside, for instance, ultimately formed the basis of ICI's chemical factory, Cliffe remains derelict, and Waltham Abbey is open to the public.

In the First World War, the production of aircraft and guns was in the hands of their established manufacturers, but supplemented by engineering factories acting as sub-contractors. It was Foster's at Lincoln, that developed the first tanks. Whilst Rolls-Royce (Derby), for instance, having begun the war building French-designed aero engines on licence, quickly developed their own range of designs, manufacturing in such quantity as to meet 60 per cent of demand by the end of hostilities. In Lincoln, Ruston's, Clayton and Shuttleworth, and Robey's produced thousands of aircraft and more engines than anywhere else, necessitating the construction of two Aircraft Acceptance Parks (AAP) in the city. By the end of the war, the Bristol aircraft factory at Filton had 3,000 employees. At Hendon, the Graham-White factory, along with the neighbouring works of de Havilland, and Handley Page, produced around 8,000 aircraft of all types. Hawkers, on their three Kingston-on-Thames sites, built 16,000 Sopwith aircraft themselves, or using other firms, under licence. Aircraft were built under such licences all over the country, and these were delivered to AAPs prior to their delivery to units. The AAP at Castle Bromwich (Birmingham), for example, took delivery of locally-built Handley Page 0/400s. The Royal Aircraft Factory was established at Farnborough (Hampshire). Short Brothers, and Samuel's on the Isle of White, May, Harden & May, building flying-boats at Hythe, Fairey's at Hamble, and Noel-Pemberton-Billing, the forerunner of Supermarine, all clustered around the Solent. The giant Vickers-Armstrong Works at Newcastle and at Barrow-in-Furness turned out enormous numbers of warships, as did the yards on the Clyde. Many of the buildings of this period remain, surprisingly, often embedded in later construction. The Graham-White factory at Hendon is currently being moved within the RAF Museum site to allow for a reorganisation. The BSA factory at Armoury Road, Smallheath, Birmingham occupied three revolutionary long concrete-trussed blocks built in 1914. These were derelict, when last seen, around the turn of the century.

After 1918, much of the munitions industry was dismantled, some of it because its efficiency presented too much of a challenge to the private sector. Queensferry, the new national factory in Flintshire, producing 500 tons of TNT per week, was closed, while the ageing Waltham Abbey was retained. Several of the factories of the First World War era, such as Irvine (Ayrshire) were put on a care and maintenance basis, to be reactivated if necessary. Although the post of Director of

Ordnance Factories was revived in 1926, the prevailing economic climate precluded what was seen as unnecessary expenditure, and it was another ten years before much began to happen as a response to the need to rearm. Vulnerability to aerial attack suggested that the new Royal Ordnance Factories (ROF) should be built in the west of the country, away from those places which might more easily be bombed from across the North Sea. Thus the new ROFs coming on stream early in the Second World War, were Bishopton (Renfrewshire), Irvine (Ayrshire), Drigg and Sellafield on the Cumbrian coast, Wrexham (Denbighshire), Pembrey (Carmarthenshire), Bridgwater (Somerset), and Ranskill (Nottinghamshire), the only one in the east of the country. Holton Heath was remodelled, and a new RN Propellant Factory opened at Caerwent (Gwent), where a copious supply of water was assured from the operation of permanently pumping out the Severn railway tunnel. Twenty shell-filling factories were proposed of which, one at Hereford, was an up-grading of a First World War establishment, and 15 were new builds. Four of the planned factories were never built. Most, again, were on the west side, with three in Wales and a further five in the border counties. Two were built in the North East in order to tap into available labour. The layout of these ROFs was standardised, but buildings differed on the basis of the operations which were carried out there. If at all possible, parallel plants were built in order to minimise disruption if one were put out of action. Certain production was carried out in parallel between sites, so that Caerwent was intended to compensate for any inter-ruption in production at Holton Heath. Design also responded to individual circumstances. At some factories, for instance, only small amounts of explosive were actually held on site, and the buildings were deemed to merit less protection. Apart from those ROFs whose prime concern was producing explosives and filling shells, there were others, such as Yeading in west London, Capenhurst (Cheshire), and Hirwaun in the Rhondda, producing small-arms ammunition. In all, some 206 new ROFs and private, ordnance factories had been built by 1945. Most were intended to produce one specific item. ROF Creekmoor (Dorset), and ROF Burghfield (Berkshire), for instance built 20mm cannon, mainly Oerlikon, under licence from the Swiss company. BMarco in Grantham (Lincolnshire) were producing the same weapon both on their main site, and at the nearby shadow factory at Hungerton Hall. Also making Oerlikons was BSA in the requisitioned London Transport sheds at Ruislip (west London). All production was controlled by the Ministry of Supply, who set the permitted levels of production. In 1939, the Admiralty were allowed 300 Oerlikon barrels per month. BSA also had a factory making Hispano-Suiza cannon at Newcastle-under-Lyme (Staffordshire). At Weymouth (Dorset), the firm of Whiteheads, previously during the First World War, a subsidiary of Vickers and Armstrong Whitworth, reopened in 1926 as a manufacturer of torpedoes, both for the Royal Navy and for foreign navies. From 1939, all work in progress was requisitioned by the Admiralty, and new orders placed to supplement the output of the RN Torpedo Factory at Alexandria (Dunbartonshire). Peter Brotherhood, in Peterborough, also manufactured

145 Fakenham, Norfolk; Mobilisation Depot, holding guns and vehicles for Territorial Army units, particularly anti-aircraft, in the run up to the Second World War

torpedoes, amongst other things, and theirs were taken by rail, to the RN Armaments Depot, in a disused brick-pit in Warboys near Huntingdon, for storage and distribution. For such high-volume items as the SMLE Mark 4 rifle, the standard issue weapon in all services, complex arrangements had to be made. ROF Fazakerley (Merseyside) made the entire rifle from parts made in-house, as did the BSA plant at Shirley (Birmingham). On the other hand, ROF Maltby (South Yorkshire) made up complete rifles from parts made by the dozens of sub-contractors scattered across, mainly, London, and the Midlands. Many of the shoe manufacturers of Leicestershire and Northamptonshire made large quantities of particular parts for assembly in one of the ROFs. Other firms, used to making anything from Addressograph machines to Zip fasteners, found themselves turning out rifle-bolts or safety-catches by the million. The Royal Enfield Works upgraded older models to Weedon Repair Standard, and even worn rifles were given minimal renovation to enable them to fire grenades from a cup-discharger. The BSA factory at Smallheath (Birmingham) made machine-guns and AT rifles. Other BSA factories at Redditch (Worcestershire), at Leicester, and at Mansfield (Nottinghamshire) were equally busy. ROF Fazakerly had a separate department manufacturing sten guns.

Prior to the actual outbreak of war, there was a need to stockpile certain items. It was obviously possible to issue much of the new equipment being produced direct to units, but in the field of AA this presented a problem. The gun emplacements were not yet built and could not, therefore, receive the guns or their supporting searchlights, predictors and height-finders. Neither were the territorial units who would man them, yet embodied. Although practice equipment was made available, and stored in the TA drill halls, the bulk of the equipment had to be accommodated elsewhere. The answer was a network of Mobilisation Centres, many of them exclusively for the AA units of the TA, but others, intended for the storage of arms, uniforms and equipment generally. These centres were built to a common design, and can be seen all over Britain *(145)*. The most prominent element is the vehicle shed, two storeys in height, with low, glazed, hipped gables, and roller doors along one side. They came in a range of sizes, seven bays at Fakenham (Norfolk), Topcliffe (North Yorkshire), and Oundle (Northampton-shire), but only three bays at Ellesmere and Tern Hill (Shropshire). Similar buildings may be seen at some regular army barracks, for example Deysbrook (Liverpool), and Llanion (Pembrokeshire), so it was either a standard building, or else some mobilisation centres may have been incorporated into existing secure sites, when their end-users were within easy distance. This would make sense in the two examples cited, since both Liverpool and Milford Haven had strong AA defences, manned by TA units. Each centre also has a bungalow for the caretaker, garages, offices, workshops, boiler room and stores. Some, as at Tetbury (Gloucestershire) had brick-built accommodation for a permanent cadre of Royal Artillery staff to maintain and service the equipment, and prepare it for issue to TA units. Others, like Killingworth (Tyne and Wear) had large magazines for AA ammunition. Some of these centres continued in use into the Cold War period, some fulfilling their original purpose as at Killingworth, storing AA ammunition. Others were given new purposes, as at Caxton (Cambridgeshire) which became an emergency food store. Many are now in use as commercial premises, as factories, haulage and storage yards, or leisure facilities.

Clearly, the policy of dispersing producers and stockpiled equipment around the country, and having a number of firms producing the same item, was motivated by the need to avoid losing total production or stock through bombing. Although the underground magazine at Chilwell had been abandoned after the end of the First World War, as it was felt, with only 200 tons capacity, to be too small for modern needs, the concept itself was still valid. In 1939, a supply of small arms ammunition (SAA) sufficient for three months' projected use by the armed services, was held in the disused Spring Quarry at Corsham (Wiltshire), known as the Central Ammunition Depot (CAD), and it was felt that there was a lot to be said for putting other vulnerable key production functions underground as well, particularly in the field of aircraft production. Recognising the fact that existing facilities would not be able to meet the demands generated by wartime conditions, most aircraft manufacturers had established shadow factories by the late 1930s. The Bristol Aircraft Company (BAC), for instance, co-ordinated a consortium of car makers to make aero engines. Rover Cars ran shadow factories at Solihull, Acocks Green (Birmingham) and in Helen Street, Coventry. When that Coventry plant was badly damaged by bombing in 1940, Rover dispersed much of its work across the country and staked a claim on the new underground factory to be built at Drakelow, near Kidderminster (Worcestershire), in which to continue building aero engines. BAC had already transferred some of its work from Filton, to an underground plant at Spring Quarry, Corsham. By the time that these factories were up and running, the danger was well past, and production figures never reflected the vast sums of money spent on a project which should have been abandoned. During the war more than 100,000 BAC engines were built, less than 0.5 per cent of which were produced by the £20 million Spring Quarry plant. Drakelow fared no better. A crippling combination of delays in both construction and fitting-out, more delays in product-development of the Centaurus engine, and a recognition by Rover that the whole scheme was overtaken by (non-) events resulting in a distinct lack of management enthusiasm, all contributed to low productivity. Much of Drakelow, in the end, was used for secure storage of aircraft components. Only towards the end of the war, and subsequently, when Rover handed aero engines back to Rolls-Royce and concentrated on tank engines, did Drakelow really pay for itself. It ultimately became a RSG as did Warren Row, at Henley-on-Thames, also developed as an underground factory for aircraft components late in the war.

The problems of creating these underground factories appear to have convinced most aircraft manufacturers that dispersal was as good a solution as any to the threat of aerial attack. When the Southampton aircraft factories at Woolston, Itchen, Swaythling, and Eastleigh were destroyed by bombing in autumn 1940, production of Supermarine Spitfires was shifted to Worthy Down and Hursley Park, and the Cunliffe-Owen conversion operations to the managing director's own estate at Marwell Hall, all in Hampshire. The First World War airfield at Chattis Hill (Hampshire) was also brought back into service for the assembly of Spitfires. It was hoped that the gallops used by race horses, would disguise the activity. There was also a MAP operation at Aldermaston (Berkshire), assembling Spitfires in hangars alongside the OTU based on the airfield. In 1941, the Vickers-Armstrong works at Hawarden (Flintshire), producing Wellington bombers, established a shadow factory at Byley (Cheshire). Completed aircraft were towed along a taxi-way to the adjacent airfield at Cranage, to be flown off. Many of the shadow factories were located in the North West, in order to be out of the line of fire as perceived in 1939. Rolls-Royce had a shadow factory at Hillington (Glasgow), and other local firms such as W.D. & H.O. Wills at Alexandra Parade, and the lace factory at Thornliebank were brought in to help in the work of producing and reconditioning Merlin aero engines. Avro's factories at Chadderton, Newton Heath, and Metropolitan-Vickers at Trafford Park, produced aircraft components, most famously of Lancasters, for final assembly and flying off from Woodford (Cheshire). Speke (Liverpool) was the site for Rootes' factory, building Blenheims and assembling Hudsons, brought over from the United States by sea. Later, vast numbers of US aircraft were flown in, across the Atlantic, by the civilian pilots of the Air Transport Auxiliary (ATA) and stored at airfields such as Burtonwood (Lancashire), and Kirkbride and Silloth in

Cumbria. The shadow factory at Squires Gate (Blackpool), was built as a double of Vickers parent factory at Brooklands (Surrey) building Wellingtons. Brooklands was severely damaged in a raid in September 1940, the month that the first Wellington rolled out of Squires Gate. As it happened, there were to be no more raids on Brooklands, and over 2,500 Wellingtons had been built by the end of the war. In anticipation of such air attack, Hawkers had already moved from Brooklands to Langley, and their Kingston plant had continued in use from before the First World War. Over 15,000 Hurricanes were built by the end of the war. Leavesden and Hatfield, the successor to Stag Lane, Edgeware, overtaken by suburban development in the early 1930s, were used by de Havillands throughout the war. When the Mosquito development contract was unaccountably cancelled by MAP, Geoffrey de Havilland continued privately at Salisbury Hall, near London Colney (Hertfordshire), and, in the end nearly 4,500 were built there, at Leavesden, and at Hatfield. Cricklewood proved inadequate for Handley Page's manufacture of, first the Hampden bomber, and then, the Halifax, and they were forced to expand their operation out to Radlett (Hertfordshire). Over 6,000 Halifaxes were built by Handley Page themselves, English Electric, Rootes, Fairey, and London Passenger Transport. Rootes' shadow factory at Blythe Bridge (Staffordshire) used the nearby Meir airfield, half-a-mile away, to fly off their Blenheims and Beaufighters. Boulton–Paul's Wolverhampton factory, opened in 1936, built Defiants, and then Blackburn Rocs and Barracudas under licence from the parent company based at Brough on the vulnerable north bank of the Humber. At Sywell (Northamptonshire) first Wellingtons were repaired or converted into transports, and then Armstrong Whitworths set up a factory to assemble Whitleys, then Manchesters, and ultimately, Lancaster lls. This last operation appears to have been based almost on a local network of cottage industries producing the components for assembly here, and at the Bus Depot in Northampton. Many smaller companies, rather than making components for larger aircraft, produced entire single models throughout the war. Examples of this are Percival's Proctors at Luton, and Taylorcraft who graduated from building Tiger Moths, to developing and producing their own Auster army co-operation aircraft at Rearsby (Leicestershire). Such firms were often lodgers on operational airfields. Martin Hearn assembled aircraft manufactured in the USA and Canada at Hooton Park (Liverpool) for instance. There remain countless relics of these great aircraft factories and their shadows. MAP hangars can be seen near Cranage (Cheshire), at Langar and Tollerton (Nottinghamshire), and at Bourn (Cambridgeshire), where three R Type hangars survive. Sywell is almost completely preserved with hangars from both the Brooklands, and the Armstrong Whitworth operations. Some of the aircraft factories such as English Electric at Luton (Beds) are long gone. Others, as at Brough and Woodford, remain in operation. The Saunders Roe, Columbine Hangar, built in 1935, stands at Cowes, Isle of Wight, and Salisbury Hall is now a museum dedicated to the Mosquito.

Despite Britain's lead in the development and use of tanks in the First World War, and the primacy of British tank warfare theorists such as Fuller and Liddell Hart in the interwar years, efforts to improve and rearm were confined by the Treasury to the RAF and the navy. The Tank Design Department of the War Office was shut down, and Vickers-Armstrong were left to meet whatever short-term needs that the army identified. The rearmament push of the mid-1930s led to a traditional structuring of the armoured units employing light, medium, and heavy tanks, in traditional, but discredited infantry support roles. After the campaign which culminated in the miracle (or disaster) of Dunkirk, 700 tanks had been lost, and Britain's counter-punch to the anticipated German invasion, lay with small numbers of light tanks, largely unsupported by motorised infantry and artillery. Suddenly, it was all hands to the wheel. Motor manufacturers and the workshops of the railway companies were pressed into service in a frantic effort to build up tank numbers. In addition to the obvious problems of design, labour, materials and premises, there was one of competition. Most of the British army's AT-guns had been left behind in France. Not one of the anti-invasion formations sitting on the coast was adequately supplied with artillery, and especially deficient, was the 2-pounder AT-gun. It was this gun, however, which was also needed for the main armament of the Matilda, Valentine, Crusader and early Churchill tanks. Cruiser tanks were developed by Lord Nuffield's Morris Car Company of Cowley (Oxfordshire) and he was able to obtain the Christie suspension system from the USA, by importing a tractor, and parts labelled as 'grapefruit' to circumvent the neutrality laws. Cowley built Cruisers, and others, particularly Covenanters, were built by the LMS Railway workshops. These workshops in Derby, employing 44,000 workers in seven locations, were involved in the production of all types of armour, artillery, aircraft, and landing-craft. Engines for tanks came from AEC, Meadows, Bedford, and Morris. By 1941, the Cromwell and Comet tanks had been developed with bigger guns and Rolls-Royce Meteor engines. It was these engines which Rover Cars produced in their underground factory at Drakelow. Until 1936, the War Office relied on Woolwich Arsenal, Vickers-Armstrong, and William Beadmore and Co. to supply the army's artillery. It soon became apparent that they had nothing like the capacity to satisfy wartime demand, and contracts were given to many other firms to produce guns. Throughout the war, engineering firms produced the vast quantity of ordnance needed by the British army and its allies. A good example is Baker Perkins at Peterborough, which built Twin 6-pounder QF guns, 6 and 17-pounder AT-guns, 25-pounders and 5.5in medium guns. The barrels were supplied by ROFs, but everything else was done in-house. Very often, just as Chetwynd had shown in the First World War, experience from other contexts could be applied to new problems. A new way of producing recuperator mechanisms for 25-pounder guns was developed by Baker Perkins saving months of complex processes and consequent labour costs. It became standard on the new 17-pounder AT-gun across all the engineering firms making it. Whilst many of the wartime factories have been redeveloped, some buildings do remain.

As with aircraft production, there was an element of cottage industry in all armament production. A collection of sheds, for instance, at London Colney (Hertfordshire), now used as storage by a car auction firm, was originally part of an operation assembling tank-turrets. Many established firms with no obvious links to the armament industry have fascinating wartime histories. Who would have thought, for instance, that Peterborough's corset factory made parachutes, with the ripcords produced by a neighbouring braid manufacturer? Similarly it comes as a surprise to find that amongst the firms contracted as managing agents for ordnance factories in the second half of the Second World War, were Lyons, Co-op Wholesale (CWS), and Imperial Tobacco. Maybe the line between shelf-filling and shell-filling was but a narrow one for the Co-op's versatile managers, running a bomb-factory outside Nottingham. Other Co-op ventures included the production of AA rockets and steel cables at the Shieldhall steelyards in Glasgow, and the construction of 750 giant tank-transporters by the Scotland Street motor-body works. The Cambuslang works of Hoover made aircraft parts.

Whilst many industries were expanding their product ranges, the ship-building industry was required merely to expand output. Lithgow's on the Clyde built 1.2 million tons of shipping during the Second World War. In neighbouring yards, John Brown's built everything from battleships to escort vessels; Stephens of Linthouse built aircraft carriers and minelayers; Fairfields built capital ships; D. & W. Henderson built landing-craft; Denny of Dumbarton built hybridised merchant ship/aircraft carriers (the so-called Woolworth carriers) and McGruers the yacht-builders produced gunboats and motor-torpedo boats. This scale of production was replicated on the Tyne and the Tees, whilst many smaller yards around Britain produced smaller numbers of smaller vessels. The Essex boatyards of Wivenhoe and Brightlingsea produced wooden minesweepers based on traditional trawler designs, as well as many of the assorted motor-boats, dinghies, refuellers, seaplane-tenders and steam-pinnaces which fulfilled some of the Navy's more mundane functions.

If the dozens of automobile manufacturers were producing armoured and soft-skinned vehicles by the thousand, then there was a need for a nationwide system of distribution, linked to a similar network of repair facilities. Based on the ordnance depot ot Chilwell (Nottinghamshire) such a network spread across each Command of the army. The map of Chilwell's network includes known ROFs such as Elstow (Bedfordshire) and Bridgend (Glamorgan); major Ordnance Depots such as Bicester (Oxfordshire); RAOC depots such as Peterborough; REME depots such as Mill Hill (London); Mobilisation Depots such as Setchey (Norfolk); and then two other groups of sites. Firstly, a number of AFV Depots in the West Midlands, Manchester area, and Glasgow area, which may be points at which the output of factories were assembled, much like the AAPs of the RAF. The second group seems to be of dumps and includes several brick-pits, including Stewartby (Bedfordshire), and Whittlesey (Cambridgeshire), where vehicles could be stored in some safety. Eventually there was to be a network of REME Command

Workshops across the country. One at Newark (Nottinghamshire) is now a motor-caravan dealership, two more at Warminster (Wiltshire) and Norton Fitzwarren (Somerset) are industrial estates.

As well as the army's CAD at Corsham, much of the other services' reserve stock of explosives went underground. Both the army and the RAF shared Chilmark quarry, near Salisbury for explosives storage. The navy had underground storage facilities for ammunition, optical equipment, and aircraft spares at Dean Hill, near Salisbury, and at Copenacre in the Corsham complex, this latter replacing several garages and a slaughterhouse which had previously been requisitioned for the purpose in Bath, and subsequently found to be vulnerable to bombing. In 1939, the RAF had established No. 42 Group, a system of storage and distribution based on four ammunition depots each storing 15-20 kilotons of explosives built at Chilmark, Fauld (Staffordshire), Harpur Hill (Derbyshire) and Llanberis in Snowdonia, all in underground disused mines or quarries. Constituent RAF units were known as Maintenance Units (MU). The Ammunition Depots were run by civilians under RAOC control but directed by RAF personnel. Ten Air Ammunition Parks, each holding 750-1,250 tons of explosives, and four specialist parks for SAA, gas, and pyrotechnics, served as distribution points for the operational airfields. Thus Brafferton (North Yorkshire), for instance, served 4 Group (north), later 6 Group, bomber airfields such as Dishforth, Dalton, Tholthorpe, and Linton-on-Ouse. As more airfields opened, and demand increased, the system was reorganised into Reserve and Forward Ammunition Depots (FAD), and Advanced Ammunition Parks (AAP). Each of the FADs was given satellite units, often on airfields themselves, one of Brafferton's, being at Dalton. After the catastrophic explosion at Fauld, in 1944, stocks were moved to neighbouring airfields at Tatenhill and Church Broughton. Whilst the underground sites were relatively safe from air attack, if not from accidents, the dispersed sites were much more vulnerable. The main SAA depot in East Anglia, 53 MU, was in the enormous airship hangar at Pulham (Norfolk), presumably the twin of that moved to Cardington in 1927 or thereabouts. The application of camouflage seemed only to intensify the attacks. The FADs and AAPs gradually moved away from concentrating the bombs in large storage sheds, mounded in earth and surrounded by earth traverses, as remained in general use on airfields, to a system of dispersal, in smaller quantities, hidden in woodland. This approach can still be seen in Morkery Wood, part of 100 MU's South Witham FAD. The 8 USAAF had Ordnance Depots in Bedfordshire and Suffolk, and Lords Bridge (Cambridgeshire) now part of the University Observatory, was a chemical weapons depot.

Fuel depots were also often buried underground, particularly by the Admiralty, at Plymouth, Portsmouth, Harwich, Immingham, Dover, Invergordon (Highland), and Lyness (Orkney). Throughout 1939 and the Phoney War period, stocks were built up, but consumption had been consistently under-estimated, prior to the outbreak of war. Subsequently, demand was over-estimated, leading

146 Haughley Junction, Suffolk; emergency grain silo for use in a nuclear emergency

to stockpiling, but the problem was not basic availability, but the location of storage in the west, and the lack of rolling-stock to get fuel to the airfields in the east. By 1943, pipelines linked the receiving refineries of Ellesmere Port to the Air Ministry's storage depots of Sandy (Bedfordshire), Aldermaston (Berkshire) and Misterton near Doncaster. This pipeline continued on down to Southampton, presumably, after D-Day, feeding PLUTO. The RAF also used facilities such as disused brick pits, as at Yaxley (Cambridgeshire) to hold stocks of aviation fuel, in addition to storage tanks on airfields. During the course of the war, the consumption of aviation spirit rose from 10,000 tons per week at the beginning to 112,000 tons per week by the end. Even a brief run of the FIDO system had devastating effects on fuel reserves. All this had to be shipped to Britain in the first place, then distributed to its point of use. At Kelham (Nottinghamshire) oil-wells were opened up by Texan oil-field engineers, who lodged, in what must have been a novel experience for both parties, with the local monks of Kelham Hall.

Agriculture provided a few additions to the landscape beyond that of the transition of every available bit of land, public and private, into vegetable patches. In order to minimise waste, new food-processing plants were built in food-producing areas, drying eggs and potatoes, and canning fresh vegetables. Silos *(146)* were built to store bulk crops for distribution or processing, and cold stores were built by the Ministry to stockpile otherwise perishable foodstuffs. Across the countryside, hostels were provided to accommodate members of the Women's Land Army. Some of these hostels were conversions of existing buildings, others were purpose-built, often in the familiar temporary brick hutted style, with a raised water tank on the roof. A number of these remain, usually in agricultural or industrial use *(147)*.

We have seen how the need to move fuel imposed a heavy burden on the railways, which, added to the other demands of troop movement, delivery of

147 Whaplode, Lincolnshire; Land Army Hostel

munitions, the delivery of rubble from the bombed cities, and other building materials, to new airfield sites, made it imperative that the system kept going. Emergency control rooms were built at strategic locations to ensure that, even under fire, the trains continued to run. Examples of these buildings remain. A compilation of official documents of 1942 listing sidings specially provided for depots, airfields, munitions facilities, camps, foodstores, and so on, runs to 33 pages, with details of around fifty installations on each page. This gives some idea of the extra traffic the railways were expected to cope with, in addition to all those pre-existing establishments which already enjoyed easy rail access.

It is still possible to see evidence of the preparations for D-Day. At Cairnryan near Stranraer in Wigtownshire, the military port, some of whose buildings remain, was used for the construction of the pontoons for the Mulberry Harbour. These were tested off Wigton Bay, where the beach and tidal action were very similar to those that would be encountered in Normandy. Remains of smaller 'Beetles' can be seen on the shore. Other pontoons were built in Leith, in the Menai Straits, and around the ports of the south and east. At least 70 hards, or slipways, were constructed from Cornwall to Felixstowe to enable landing craft to load tanks, vehicles, infantry and stores, prior to assembling off the Isle of Wight for the final run in. Many of these survive, along with the roads which it was sometimes necessary to construct, in order to give heavy vehicles access to the hards. There were more D-Day hards in south Wales, at Milford Haven, Port Talbot, and Swansea. The D-Day hard at Stone Point, within Lepe Country Park, where some of the Mulberry Harbour caissons, the Phoenix permanent inshore breakwaters, were built and launched, can still be seen along with associated structures. Concrete beach-hardening mats, the construction platform, and the slipways, down which the caissons were launched sideways, all remain. There are also hards for launching loaded landing craft, and, just offshore, two dolphins, iron platforms on legs, used as jetties for loading up ships carrying supplies or reinforcements to the Normandy beaches. Following a survey, steps have been taken to consolidate the remains, which are constantly in danger of erosion, by the tide.

After the end of the Second World War, everything was scaled down, and many depots, factories, and munitions stores were closed. Not only was the volume of such facilities no longer necessary, but, with the detonation of the atomic bombs over Japan, the whole nature of war appeared to have changed. Suddenly, there was more need, not less, for research and development, testing and experimentation, and the production and stockpiling of new breeds of weapon. Some of the deep storage facilities did continue in use, most notably, RNSD Copenacre. The RAF, however, maybe mindful of the disastrous history of their underground stores, most of which had suffered some sort of calamity, ranging from the explosion at Fauld, the discovery of structural faults at Harpur Hill and actual roof-falls at Llanberis, leaving only Chilmark an unqualified success story, opted for new stores for their atomic warheads. Barnham (Suffolk) *(148)* and Faldingworth (Lincolnshire) were chosen as the new Permanent Ammunition Depots (PAD), with the USAF eventually settling on Welford (Berkshire). Visits to both PADs reveal them to be virtually identical in layout. Three perimeter fences with tall

148 Barnham, Norfolk; one of the atomic bomb storage units at this Permanent Ammunition Depot; the bombs were delivered by truck and unloaded by a crane on the overhead gantry; each store could accommodate about 20 bombs, which would be assembled, when necessary, in a separate building; the complex is now an industrial estate

watch-towers define the pentagonal perimeter. Guardroom, offices and a barrack-room cluster around the gate. Inside an oval access road leads to three atomic bomb stores, inside high earth traverses, where the bombs, weighing 10,000lb (4,545kg) were swung via gantries into the store. Also on this road is a maintenance workshop, and access to the 57 brick fissile core stores, each about the size of a privy, individually alarmed, and entered through a steel door. These are in groups of about a dozen. The plutonium core was set into the floor in a lead-lined tube. Some huts held one core, and others, two. Without this, the initiator, the Blue Danube bomb was harmless. Bombs were shuttled backwards and forwards to the RAF airfields on ordinary lorries with RAF Police outriders on motorcycles. Bombs were armed on the airfields, which were provided with parallel facilities, called unit stores. Since Cottesmore had no assembly building, Wittering would arm its bombs. Gradually, nuclear weapons have become ever more compact, and the storage facilities for them, have similarly contracted, some, under the floors of Hardened Aircraft Shelters, and others, in semi-sunken bunkers, mounded in earth.

The end of the century had seen a shift in emphasis toward intelligence gathering almost as a goal in itself rather than as a means to an end. A number of structures are dedicated to this task. At Chicksands (Bedfordshire), a circular forest of aerials facilitates the reception of signals from all directions. At Menwith Hill (North Yorkshire) recently a target for Greenpeace protestors, and at Croughton, on the Northamptonshire/Oxfordshire border, domes cover the listening apparatus. Until very recently, the TR1 Blackbird reconnaissance aircraft flew from their specially-widened hardened aircraft shelters at Alconbury (Cambridgeshire) bringing back data to be analysed on site in the Magic Mountain, a semi-sunken bombproof bunker, a big advance on the surface film-processing laboratories which previously handled the product of the Victor and Canberra photographic reconnaissance sorties from Wyton (Cambridgeshire). Other associated sites are Edzell (Angus), and, of course, GCHQ at Cheltenham.

It is perhaps unsurprising that, having seen the subordination of the railway to the road, in the second half of the century, this should have been reflected in military thinking. Whilst the anti-invasion planners in 1940 felt it necessary to obstruct London's arterial roads, sparse though they were, against troop-landing aircraft, and Germany's autobahn network was not only a means to relieve unemployment, but also a way of ensuring that the Wehrmacht would enjoy optimum mobility and the new Luftwaffe would always have somewhere to land their aircraft, Britain, for good reason, stuck with the train. The German invasion of Belgium and France in 1914, had been predicated on the efficient scheduling of German trains, and on the inability of Russian ones to expedite mobilisation. We, in Britain, simply needed to move a lot of stuff around. By the 1950s, times had changed. Before the M6, in the shape of the Preston Bypass, Britain's first motorway, opened, it had been tested as an airstrip by the RAF. It is said, no doubt with more than an element of truth, that the A14 road, long awaited as an A1-M1 link, was primarily designed as a quick way of getting the Cruise missiles out of Molesworth and into their dispersed, and secret, launching sites.

In peacetime, the medical needs of the armed forces were met by a network of hospitals, many of which had been built early in the nineteenth century, and the balance, in the post-Scutari period after the Crimean War. As soon as the outbreak of war came, then premises were either assembled from temporary buildings, or suitable buildings were requisitioned for the duration. Thus, in 1914, for instance, the 5th Northern General Hospital at Leicester, was set up in the empty County Lunatic Asylum, supplemented by hutting. It had 60 affiliated establishments, and these included civilian hospitals, stately homes, and Voluntary Aid Detachments. These dealt with some 80,000 patients, mainly casualties from the Western Front, of whom only around 500 died. A nucleus of staff came from the Territorial Force, but was greatly increased by civilian trained staff and willing volunteers who learnt on the job. Much of the hutting operated on the open-air basis, by having canvas screens instead of windows. Whilst the army and navy continued with mainly long-established hospitals, the RAF was able to start anew. Halton (Buckinghamshire), Wroughton (Wiltshire) and Ely (Cambridgeshire) were all built between the wars, the latter two in the international modern style. Once again, in the Second World War, the hutted hospital came into its own. Entire hospitals of Nissen huts were constructed, such as that for the 8USAAF at Wymondham (Norfolk). A similar arrangement was constructed at Nocton Hall (Lincolnshire) for the RAF, who also took over the nearby Rauceby Mental Hospital. Many stately homes resumed their wartime role as hospitals. During the Cold War period, a number of hospitals were established to receive air-lifted casualties from European battlefields during the anticipated conventional prelude to nuclear war. One such is Upwood (Cambridgeshire), still in service with USAF. Nocton Hall was mothballed, but retained in case. The first Gulf War involved the resuscitation of such facilities, and a number of hangars, on active RAF and USAF bases, were equipped as emergency hospitals, to receive large numbers of chemical and biological casualties. Fortunately, these facilities were not needed in either Gulf conflict. Although the armed services now tend to integrate much of their medical provision into the National Health Service, a number of military hospitals continue, but in civilian use. These include Ely, and Chatham's Edwardian naval hospital. Incidentally, from the Victorian period, although the enormous Netley hospital on Southampton Water, apart from its imposing chapel, has been demolished, the innovative Herbert Hospital, built for the Royal Marines at Woolwich, south London, has now been converted into housing, the former military hospital at Devonport is now a school, Haslar RN hospital at Gosport is part of local NHS provision, and the Cambridge military hospital in Aldershot continues to serve the garrison.

One topic not previously addressed is housing. There is a long tradition of living on the job in the defence industry, and examples abound. RAF married quarters were an integral part of the Expansion Period airfields. At Mildenhall

(Suffolk) are terraces of houses built in a rural, almost arts and crafts style, with tiled dormers and overhanging eaves. By 1935, there was a range of married quarter designs which clearly reflected the heirarchical structure of the Service. At the bottom of the pyramid were two-storey blocks of six airmen's flats. Next were pairs of semi-detached houses with room for families. Larger, semi-detached houses were designed for warrant officers, but the officers' houses are in a different league. All are detached, and progress through simple square blocks, to L-shaped, T-shaped, culminating in a splendid neo-Georgian mini-mansion. A half-hexagonal, two-storey bay-window projection, and canopied, stone door surround, make this an extremely desirable residence. Postwar, the construction of RAF housing has continued, but much has now been disposed of into the public sector, and much of the character of the earlier housing has disappeared under double-glazed windows, porches, and other improvements. Good examples of RAF housing can be seen in many places including Watton and West Raynham (Norfolk), Newton (Nottinghamshire), and Langtoft (Lincolnshire). Housing was also provided for many of the larger munitions factories. Dating from 1914, the Well Hall Estate in Eltham (south London) was built to house workers from the Woolwich Arsenal. It is a very carefully planned garden suburb development of 1,000 houses and 200 flats, executed in an arts and crafts style, and incorporating a wide variety of materials and layouts. It was intended to be a showcase, from the start, pointing the way to a solution to London's suburban development, using public housing to emulate the earlier, private development of Hampstead Garden Suburb (1906). At Gretna, a similar development took place in 1916, and included houses, hostels which could be converted into housing after the war, and public amenities, many of which, such as the Institute, are still in use. Here, the chosen style was neo-Georgian, and this proved to be the universal model for public housing in the postwar years. Other schemes, albeit on a much smaller scale, followed these, for example at Langwith (Derbyshire), where four houses and 38 cottages, housed essential personnel at the National Ammonium Perchlorate Factory. Some 300 employees of Hendon Aerodrome were housed in a formal square of cottages, with neo-Georgian details, known as Aeroville, and built in 1917. Workers at Queensferry (Flintshire) were also provided with housing, built 1916-18, by theHousing Department of the Ministry of Munitions under Sir Raymond Unwin, the architect of Gretna. This scheme of housing in pairs and short terraces, also included social facilities and a hospital. At Cardington, workers at the airship works were accommodated in a purpose-built garden village, known as Shortstown, after the factory owners, and built in 1927, when the works was expanded to develop the R100 and R101. Terraces of houses are grouped around greens, opposite the factory gate. A social club and a shop were included. Early in the Second World War, similar schemes, tied to ordnance factories, were, again, undertaken. The Central Ordnance Depot, established at Donnington (Shropshire), was provided with a housing estate for workers. Between the beginning of the war and 1953, 2,000 houses had been built. Owing to the

149 Orfordness, Suffolk; one of the Pagodas at the Atomic Weapons Research Establishment; it was used, between 1953 and 1971, to test the non-nuclear components of atomic bombs

scarcity of timber, the houses were built with flat, concrete roofs, and concrete staircases. Communal shelters and a parade of shops were provided. Different ROFs had different needs. Swynnerton employed a higher than normal complement of imported labour living in hostels, so cinemas and other social amenities were provided. Other factories built semi-detached bungalows for families. Heirarchical considerations remained evident in the architecture, since only certain grades were entitled to bay windows. At Ranskill (Nottinghamshire) virtually the entire ROF has been demolished, so the only reminder, now, is a row of workers' bungalows between Lound and Sutton. At Monkswood (Gwent) a row of 19 pebbledashed formal houses with hipped roofs, projecting gables and chimney stacks, were built in 1939 for the workers at ROF Glascoed. The garden suburb, begun in 1915 to house workers at the Royal Dockyard at Rosyth (Fife), never properly developed because of the interruptions caused by the closure of the dockyard between the wars.

With the end of the Cold War around 1990, much of the defence superstructure has been dismantled *(149)*. Many of the vast depots such as that of the REs at Long Marston (Worcestershire) have closed, others like the REME depot at Old Dalby soldier on. The stores at Bicester (Oxfordshire) and Kineton (Warwickshire) continue in service, but every year brings a new crop of MoD closures, as elements of procurement and supply are privatised. Some ROFs like Summerfield (Worcestershire) remain in operation, but Woolwich Arsenal, and the navy's Priddy's Hard, are now museums. It would appear that much of Britain's military heritage is going the same way as its industrial heritage has gone.

CONCLUSION

As we have seen, it is difficult to avoid encountering relics of our twentieth-century military past in any part of the British landscape, and yet this is often barely acknowledged, even in history-based guidebooks, and material aimed at tourists. It has been suggested that more is known about most aspects of the Roman occupation of Britain, nearly two thousand years ago, than is known about some aspects of our recent military past. There would appear to be a number of factors which might have combined to bring about this situation.

The first cluster of factors relates to values. Very simply, the old is more valued than the new. A Roman fort is seen by many historians, archaeologists and heritage bodies as having a greater importance, both intrinsic and extrinsic, than, say, a First World War coast defence battery, simply by virtue of its age. It is automatically seen as being rarer; it is felt, almost intuitively, to be capable of telling us more; and that what it is able to tell us must be more important than anything that might be learnt from the more recent monument. All this may obtain regardless of the facts of the individual case. There may be another, more insidious element in the values question. Mediaeval castles, for instance, were, in Britain at least, for the most part built by royalty, or what passed for an aristocracy at any given time or place. Twentieth-century fortifications may be seen to be much more democratic. The conscript soldier cannot compete with the medieval knight in the romantic warrior persona, and the governments who grudgingly financed defence works were unlikely to regard them in the way that medieval kings might have taken pride in their constructions. Then there is the aesthetic dimension. Hadrian's Wall, Carnarfon and Edinburgh Castles, and even Tilbury Fort or Fort George are undeniably beautiful, picturesque, and romantic, and rightfully hold iconic status in the British landscape. At the end of the Second World War, local authorities were quick to draw up programmes of demolition, to clear, especially the coastline, of what they perceived and designated as eyesores. This had an economic angle to it, in that, it was felt that holiday-makers would want to forget the war, and seaside towns relied on trippers for their prosperity. There was, no doubt, some consideration of public safety, to be taken into account. Norfolk, for instance, assigned three priority

150 Pevensey Castle, East Sussex; A Second World War strongpoint built into the defences of the Roman fort, originally intended to repel Saxon invaders in the third century AD; although some of these works were destroyed at the end of the war, many remain in both the Roman and medieval parts of the fortress

categories, to its war relics, with immediate demolition for category one, through degrees of urgency until everything had gone. The key word there is, of course, *everything*. It seems not to have ever occurred to anyone that anything might be worth sparing, about which, future generations might be curious. The same went for almost all eyesore clearance programmes. It is pretty safe to say that anything that remains of the First or Second World War coast defences, is there by default, by oversight, by chance, or by being missed by the demolition gangs. There is, however, one other factor which aided preservation, but, again, more as a result of chance rather than of policy. Many earlier fortifications, because of their location, continued to have successive layers of defence works added over the centuries. Obvious examples of this process are Dover, Plymouth, Falmouth, the Firth of Forth, the Bristol Channel and the estuaries of the Tyne, Tees and Humber. This, in itself, is no guarantee of survival. The Second World War pillbox added to one of the bastions of Deal Castle, for instance, was removed at the earliest opportunity, as was one from the esplanade in front of the Tower of London. At Pevensey Castle *(150)*, the pillboxes so effectively hidden in both the Roman masonry of the fort walls, and in the medieval keep, have been allowed to stay, but the anti-tank block-house built in one of the gateways was demolished, according to the Ministry's guidebook (1952, revised 1960) because it obscured the foundations of the Roman gate, and obstructed the public footpath. It is easy to see how the tensions between structural purity and messy continuity of use can arise. It is equally easy to see how such tensions are usually resolved.

The next factor affecting the survival of threatened twentieth-century monuments relates to their perceived quantities. Little effort has been made to preserve monuments which appear to be plentiful. Problems have occurred when this plenty has proved illusory, or when structures which may superficially have appeared the same, have in fact, and often too late, been shown to be quite different. Sadly, it is often the unique which has been demolished. There are conservation professionals who still use the old argument that, having once been misled about the uniqueness of a structure, never again will they believe any defence work to be worth saving on that criterion alone. The question of populations is further exacerbated by the lack of information relating to twentieth-century structures, in many Sites and Monuments Records (SMR). It would appear fairly obvious that without actually recording monuments, we are in a difficult position when it comes to assessing survival. There are still SMRs which record every last find of Roman or medieval coin, but continue to be unable to find the resources to record structures from recent military history. A generation ago, the industrial archaeologists were facing the same attitudes.

The final factor concerns development. No landscape stands still. Changing lifestyles, the different demands of evolving industry and commerce, the changing nature of cities, the application of new methods in agriculture and horticulture, and the demands of new transport systems, have all contributed to the disappearance of military monuments. Recent policies promoting the development of brownfield sites over virgin countryside for house-building and commercial development have also come into play, affecting, particularly airfields and camps. The rundown of armed forces since the thaw in the Cold War, has also meant that fewer military sites are needed, and the Ministry of Defence has been active in shedding sites which might produce revenue as areas for commercial development. This process appears, still, to be accelerating, and preservationists have found it difficult to produce arguments against that of the developers, that they are not only saving the taxpayer large sums of money, but they are also saving greenfield sites for posterity. Balance is the most that can be sought. Heritage bodies are, however, attempting to identify sites which merit preservation.

That said, there is much still to be seen, and not only in a derelict state. One of the side-effects of the gap between supply and demand in the housing market, possibly encouraged by the vogue for the grand design genre of TV programme, has been the reluctance of some home-seekers to reject anything as a potential domestic paradise. As early as 1967, Sam Scorer, the Lincoln architect, was commissioned by Peter and Kari Wright, to transform the Northern Command RE command post at Canwick, outside Lincoln, into a family home. His treatment gained the property, by then known as Lindum House, the additional local name of Canwick Cathedral, owing to the soaring glass projection. In 2003, it was on the market for £375,000, and described by the estate agent as 'a converted Second World War command post with truly impressive cathedral-style shaped window to the front elevation'. It is not always so easy to wax quite so lyrical over such conversions, or changes of use. The

Old Repeater Station on the A1 near Grantham, may have Brazilian hardwood and brass fittings throughout, but it remains a 1939 bungalow. Whilst Annington Homes have been selling off much of the MoD's more conventional housing stock, a number of oddities have appeared on the market. RSGs at Drakelow and Skendleby, one a converted underground car factory making aero engines in the Second World War, and the other a converted radar station from the ROTOR system of the 1950s, have both been available recently. Such bunkers are often developed as secure storage, and companies are charged £36,000 per year (2003 prices) for keeping their data in nuclear bombproof storage, such as the former RAF Ash, ROTOR site at Sandwich (Kent). But there are other uses to which imaginative, and wealthy people will put them. The former South-East London War Room at Kemnal Manor built in 1951 on a site requisitioned by the War Office in 1939, and in use up until the 1970s, has been converted into a 'party pad' with swimming-pool, five bedrooms, roof-level glass living room and terrace. Marketed for around £3m in 2001, as the 'Glass House', it was clearly a challenge. Cutting a hole in the 5.5ft (1.65m) thick reinforced concrete, to take the new glass roof cost £250,000. However, a Cold War bunker need not be quite so costly. A telecom company which bought 200 ROC underground posts in the early 1990s as possible sites for mobile phone masts has recently disposed of some of those surplus to requirement. Auctioned through eBay, with reserve prices around the £2-4,000 mark, they fetched between £7,510 and £25,100. When one realises that many are in locations such as National Parks, where planning permission is unobtainable, it becomes clear why an underground chamber, 15ft by 8ft (4.5m x 2.4m) is so attractive. This matter of planning permission appears to apply especially in coastal locations. The BOP at Bawdsey battery (Suffolk) was on the market for £180,000 in April 2003, and at Felpham, near Bognor Regis (West Sussex), an imposing three-storey villa with bow-string roof, called The Old Gun Post, sits atop the gunhouse of a 5.5in emergency coast defence battery. Apparently less attractive properties continue to find new uses. Pillboxes are used as gazebos, bat hides, and fishing shelters, and sea front gunhouses are public conveniences or sheltered seating. Wherever we might travel in Britain, it will not be long before we come across some reminder of Britain's twentieth-century military heritage. Perhaps, one day, we will learn from the Channel Islands, who have managed to retain their twentieth-century military monuments as a constituent part of their historic landscape, and to benefit from those tourists who visit the islands specifically to see them. A start has been made in several parts of Britain. Kent, for instance, has collaborated with their tourist board partners across the Channel, to promote coast defences on both shores as elements of the historic landscape. It will, however, only be possible to emulate such initiatives while there are monuments surviving to be promoted. Spurious commemoration as seen at the former Hook Balloon Depot in Surrey, with its new residential streets named for Tedder and Gibson, or the former Second World War GCI Radar, and postwar ROTOR site at Langtoft (Lincolnshire), where the roads are equally inappropriately called Lancaster, Blenheim, Shackleton and Wellington, can never stand in for the authentic, or, indeed, the real thing.

GAZETTEER

NOTES

All map references are given as six-figure national grid references using OS 1:50,000 or 1:25,000 maps. Where a number of monuments occur in a compact area, references to the containing square are given, e.g. TM35-40; i.e. spread over the grid square TM35 eastings and 40 northings. Monuments spread over a number of grid squares are shown: NT43/47-76/80, i.e. NT43-47 eastings and 76-80 northings.

CHAPTER I: COAST DEFENCES

Aberlady area (Lothian) AT blocks and slotted blocks for RSJs at NT43/47-76/80

Abbotsbury (Dorset) pillboxes, AT blocks, 75 mm gunhouse at SY54/6-83/5

Aldeburgh (Suffolk) gunhouse and BOP in mill at Fort Green at TM464561

Alderton (Suffolk) two circular First World War pillboxes at TM345424

Alnmouth (Northumberland) pillbox on top of earlier gunhouse NU252112

Angle (Pembs) East Blockhouse Bty: Twin 6pdr, 9.2in and 6in gun pits at SM841028

Aylmerton (Norfolk) circular First World War pillbox at TG183404

Bacton (Norfolk) L-shaped section post at TG349337 and Broomholm Priory 351331

Balmedie (Aberdeen) 3 locally-designed pillboxes NJ976176

Bamburgh (Northumberland) local design 6pdr position and AT blocks NU178355

Barrow-in-Furness (Cumbria) batteries on Walney Is: Hilpsford at SD231620 and Fort Walney (two 6in guns and CASLs) at SD173691; also pillboxes around town

Bawdsey (Suffolk) gunhouses, CASLs, BOP, magazines, engine room etc. and First and Second World War pillboxes at TM35-40

Berrow (Somerset) around a dozen assorted pillboxes at ST293/300-522/540

Bishopstone (E. Sussex) pillboxes on roof of Art Deco BR station at TV469999

Blue Anchor Bay (Somerset) section post at ST021436; around 12 assorted pillboxes, some camouflaged, between SS984464 and ST013436

Blyth (Northumberland) Fort Coulson, First/Second World War, complete 6in battery at NZ32-79

Blythburgh (Suffolk) two double machine-gun posts at TM456747

Brancaster (Norfolk) ruins of battery and pillboxes near Golf Club at TF77-45

Brixham (Devon) one 4.7in gunhouse, BOP and 6pdr position at SX922569

Broughty (Dundee) two 6in positions and BOP and mg loops in Castle at NO464304

Budle Point (Northumberland) gunhouse for 4in gun at NU162358

Burghead Bay (Moray) eight pillboxes, some in pairs and AT blocks along shore

Burnham (Essex) XDO post at Holliwell Point at TR017958 and sea wall pillboxes

Calshot Castle (Hants) 12pdr positions at SU488025

Camber Sands (E. Sussex) local design mg posts and AT obstacles at TQ964184

Carnoustie (Angus) gunhouse for 4in or smaller gun at NO572345

Clenchwarton (Norfolk) Kings Lynn 6in battery at TF589241

Coalhouse Fort (Essex) battery on roof of 19th-c. fort and XDO post at TQ691768

Corton (Suffolk) many local design pillboxes and 6pdr emplacements at TM55-95

Cramond Island (Forth) battery etc. at NT196785

Cuckmere Haven (E. Sussex) pillboxes and AT blocks at TV51/2-97/8

Dale (Pembs) West Blockhouse First and Second World War batteries at SM817036

Dover (Kent) Castle: AT emplacement in wall and AT pimples in moat at TR324420; St Martins Bty: two 6in gunhouses and Type 23 pillbox at TR315408; Citadel Bty. Later additions to 1895 work at TR303403; Wanstone Bty: site of heavy, cross-Channel guns at TR354429; Langdon Bty: gun pits at TR339424

Druridge Bay (Northumberland) pillbox disguised as cottage at NZ283946

Dymchurch (Kent) gunhouse and pillboxes etc on roof of Napoleonic redoubt and Type 28a gunhouse at TR129322

Earlsferry (Fife) Kincraig Battery, gun pits, BOP, CASLs etc. at NT465997

East Tilbury (Essex) Radar Tower on Thames foreshore at TQ689763

Fairbourne (Gwynedd) 1.5 miles of AT wall and blocks and pillbox at SH60-12/14

Falmouth (Cornwall) Pendennis Castle: Half-Moon 6in Bty. and Crab Quay 6pdr Bty. below castle remain and other defences at SW82-31

Felixstowe (Suffolk) Landguard Fort: Twin 6 and 6in gun positions, DELs, XDO post BOP, pillboxes, AT blocks etc. at TM28-31

Flamborough (E. Yorks) machine-gun and rifle pillboxes at TA25-70

Flotta (Orkney) Buchanan Bty: Twin 6pdr and director tower, magazine, shelter, CASLs etc, also Stanger Head PWSS

Folkestone (Kent) Copt Point 6in battery: gunhouses, BOP etc at TF240366

Formby (Mersey) Types 28a, 23 and local design pillboxes along line east of town

Forth Bridge Carlingnose Battery gun pits, BOP etc at NT134804 and Inchgarvie Is

Fowey (Cornwall) St Catherines Castle: two gun pits for 4.7in guns at SX118509

Fraisethorpe (E. Yorks) mg posts, AT blocks, pillboxes and beach light at TA16-63

Freiston Shore (Lincs) two 6in gunhouses, CASLs, magazines, engine room, pillboxes etc. astride Seabank at TF39-32; more pillboxes to north and south

Gedney (Lincs) pillboxes, some of local design and AT blocks at TF40-33

Gibraltar Point (Lincs) AT blocks, pillboxes and CASL at TF56-57

Grain (Kent) AT obstacles and other defences at TQ88-77; Twin 6 on late Martello; chain for boom around base of Grain Tower

Gravesend (Kent) New Tavern Fort: 19th-c. fort with restored First/Second World War battery with 6in, and 12pdr guns *in situ* at TQ653742

Greatham (Teesside) pillboxes and AT blocks at NZ49-27

Great Yarmouth (Norfolk) pillboxes around town and TG524106 on end of barn

Hartlepool (Teesside) pillboxes, section post and AT blocks at Hart Bay NZ49 36 and 6in/9.2in Heugh Battery at NZ528340

Hartley (Northumberland) Roberts Bty. Fort House at NZ341759

Harwich (Essex) Beacon Hill Fort; Twin 6, 6in and 9.2in batteries, XDO post, radar

Heacham (Norfolk) Type 28a, Type 28, spigot, and roadblock at TF662/4-366/75

Holkham (Norfolk) Two pairs of double mg posts and AW turret and AT rails at TF87/9-44

Holyhead (Anglesey) circular castellated pillboxes at Trearddur at SH25 79; gothic follies converted into strongpoints at Soldiers Point at SH237837

Holy Island (Northumberland) double lines of AT blocks by causeway at NU080427

Humber Estuary (Lincs/E. Yorks) Bull Sand Fort at TA370093 and Haile Sand Fort at TA349062

Hurst Castle (Hants) 12pdr, Twin 6 and CASLs on 19th-c. casemates at SZ315897

Inchcolm Island (Forth) 12pdr, Twin 6, and 4.7in batteries and DELs, etc. at NT18/9-82

Inchkeith Island (Forth) 6in and 9.2in batteries at NT29 82

Inchmickery Island (Forth) battery etc. at NT207805

Isle of Wight Brighstone: prefab pillbox with machine-gun table at SZ413823; Fort Albert: Twin 6pdr battery on roof at SZ340899; New Needles Bty: 9.2in gun pits, PWSS, DEL with searchlight in place at SZ239849; Culver Bty: two 9.2in gun pits and boundary stones of Admiralty Signal Station at SZ638855

Kilnsea (E. Yorks) battery on (over?) cliff edge at TA418160 and lozenge pillboxes

Loch Ewe (Highland) complete Second World War 6in gun battery at NG815920

Mainland (Orkney) Ness Bty: BOP and 6in gunhouses at HY248079; Links Bty. Twin 6pdr and CASL at HY252077; Cara Bty: 12pdr gunhouse and BOP and CASLs at ND480946; Houton Bty: two 12pdr gunhouses, BOP, DELs, magazines etc. at HY295062; Holm Bty: Twin 6pdr and two 12pdrs, BOP, magazines, DELs, shelters etc. at HY494017; Hoxa Bty: two 6in gunhouses, BOP, shelter, gun pits of First World War 4in guns etc. at ND404925; Balfour Bty: two Twin 6pdr with director towers, shelter, CASLs etc. at ND403930; Rerwick Bty: two 6in gunhouses, BOP, magazine, shelters etc at HY541119

Mersea Island (Essex) gunhouse and DEL of 4.7in battery at TM020124

Minsmere (Suffolk) BOP and engine room of 6in battery and spigot pit at TM47–68; also strongpoint in ruined chapel at TM478661

Montrose (Forfar) two 18pdr gunhouses and two Armco pillboxes at NO724568

Mundesley (Norfolk) complete 6in emergency battery at TG300372

Newbiggin (Northumberland) at Beacon Point, gunhouse for 6pdr at NZ314895

Newgale Bridge (Pembs) AT blocks at SM847224

Newhaven (E. Sussex) 19C fort with Second World War 6in battery, BOP, 12pdr position, pillbox, field gun emplacement, CD radar; and separate 6in gun pits and BOP at TQ44–00

Nigg Bay (Highland) batteries at N. and S. Sutor defending Cromarty Firth naval base

Padstow (Cornwall) battery for two 4in guns at SW918766

Paull Fort (E. Yorks) 19th-c. fort with later batteries, BOP, DELs etc. at TA170255

Pett Level (E. Sussex) BOP and remains of Toot Rock battery at TQ893137

Pevensey (E. Sussex) Second World War pillboxes built into fabric of Roman fort at TQ64 04

Plymouth (Devon) Fort Bovisand: 19th-c. fort with Twin 6pdr emplacements on roof at SX489508and CASLs on headland; Devil's Point 12pdr Bty. at SX460534; Drakes Island: 6in and Twin 6 positions at SX470528; Hawkins Bty: 9.2in gun pits at SX441516; Lentney Bty: 6in emplacements at SX493495; Renney Bty: 9.2in positions at SX495489; Watch House Bty: 6in positions at SX493511; Western King Bty: Twin 6pdr emplacement minus tower at SX462534

Portishead (Somerset) aprons of two 6in gun pits and mg post at ST464776

Portland (Dorset) Breakwater forts: postwar Twin 6 emplacements; East Weare batteries: 9.2in and 6in gun pits at SY697735; Blacknor Bty: 9.2in gun pits and BOP at SY679716

Portsdown (Hants) Two 4in gunhouses west of Fort Purbrook at SU675064

Purfleet (Essex) First World War submarine-spotting tower/blockhouse at TQ793538

Rattray Head (Aberdeen) Six pillboxes and AT blocks around coastguard cottages

Rushmere (Suffolk) Two First World War and one Second World War pillboxes at TM490870

Rye Harbour (E. Sussex) Two local design mg posts at TQ948181

St Ishmael's (Pembs) Two 6in houses, CASLs, engine room etc at SM834063

St Mawes (Cornwall) 12pdr battery and other remains in Castle at SW840328

Sandend (Moray) 28a gunhouse, pillboxes and AT blocks at NJ55–66

Scremerston (Northumberland) gunhouse for 4in gun at NU032481

Sea Palling (Norfolk) circular First World War pillbox at TG422270

Sennen Cove (Cornwall) D-shaped pillbox and section post at SW34–26

Sheerness (Kent) Centre Bastion Bty: two First World War 4.7in gun towers, one with Second World War XDO post, the other with Second World War OP and BOP on third tower; Ravelin Bty: 9.2in gun pits; No.1 Bastion Bty: two 6in gunhouses at TQ91-75

Sheppey (Kent) Fletcher Bty: 9.2in gun pits, BOP and First World War pillbox at TR003727

Sinclair Bay (Highland) pillboxes on shore near Keiss at ND35-61

Southend (Essex) AT-blocks at TQ895847 and OP on short pier

Southsea (Hants) gun pits in use in the First and Second World Wars at Castle at SZ645980

Spey Bay (Moray) continuous line of pillboxes and AT blocks between Lossiemouth and Kingston, and Innes Links 6in battery

Spurn Head (E. Yorks) First and Second World War batteries, blockhouses, AT obstacles, jetty, BOPs, DEL/CASLs, engine rooms, etc. some in walled, defended enclosure

Stranraer (Wigton) Finnart Bay 5in Battery, two gunhouses, CASLs, at NX051724

Stratton (Suffolk) shelter for rail-mounted howitzer at TM251394

Sunk Island (E. Yorks) 6in gun towers at TA250176 and PWSS at TA252178

Swanage (Dorset) two 4in gunhouses and one other at Peveril Point at SZ040786

Tees Bay (Teesside) First World War fort, Second World War pillboxes, battery etc. on S Gare breakwater

Tentsmuir (Fife) Four miles AT blocks, pillboxes, beach lights, roadblock etc.

Tresilian Bay (Glam) Six pillboxes, some camouflaged with pebbles at SS94-67

Tynemouth (N. Tyne) Tyne Turret control at NZ237699 and batteries in Castle

Tywyn (Gwynedd) pillboxes along shore at around SN59 97

Upton (Dorset) First and Second World War 6in gun battery, two gunhouses and DEL at SY742814

Wallasey (Wirral) 19C Fort Perch Rock; two 6in positions and BOP at SJ 309947

Walton (Essex) ex-radar site and pillboxes around TM265235

Watchet (Somerset) loopholes overlooking harbour at ST071435

Wells-next-the-Sea (Norfolk) pair of double machine-gun posts at TF914441

West Aberthaw (Glam) AT blocks and disguised pillboxes at ST01-66

Weybourne (Norfolk) gunhouse at TG098433, Norcon at 093438 and others

Weymouth (Dorset) Nothe Fort: 19th-c. work with remounted 6in and 40mm guns and SL

Winterton (Norfolk) 6in battery and AT blocks, BOP in mill at TG497191-499198

CHAPTER 2: INLAND DEFENCE LINES

GHQ Line (Green)

Avening (Glos) type 24 pillbox at ST889971, one of several on this extension

Dinder Heights (Somerset) AT blocks, AT rails & type 24 pillboxes at ST57-45

Highbridge to **Meare** (Somerset) type 24 shellproof pillboxes every half-mile

Radstock (Somerset) AT rails sealing end of AT ditch at ST686544

Stoney Littleton (Somerset) AT blocks and pillboxes at ST73-56

GHQ Line (Blue)

Aldermaston Wharf (Berks) pillboxes and shelter etc at SU60/1-67/8

Enborne (Berks) two type-24 pillboxes and AT rails on bridge at SU439665

Honey Street (Wilts) AT blocks, AT rail sockets and pillboxes at SU10-61

Hungerford (Berks) twin type 28a, type 28a, type 24 and AT blocks at SU424671

Semington (Wilts) type 28a AT emplacements form bridgehead at ST89-60

Wootton Rivers (Wilts) twin type 28a AT blockhouse at SU194627

GHQ Line (Red)

Frilford (Oxon) two type 28a blockhouses and re-excavated AT ditch at SU432976

Newbarn Farm (Oxon) type 28a blockhouse and AT blocks at SU554946

Radcot Lock (Oxon) type 28a, type 24 pillboxes and breastworks etc. at SU287994

Sulham (Berks) strongest section of entire GHQ Line: twin type 28a blockhouses at SU640752, 643742, 638744 and 646737; pair of type 28a blockhouses at SU639747; type 24 pillboxes at SU646732 and 647731; type 28a modified for infantry use at SU638753; AT blocks at SU638745, 640743 and 641743; AT ditch and AT rails at SU642741

Theale (Berks) twin type 28a blockhouse at Beansheaf Farm at SU654715

GHQ Line South (Aldershot and Southern Commands, Lines A and B)

Bramshill (Berks) two prefabricated pillboxes at SU739626 and two type 25 Armco pillboxes at SU741612 and 742600

Burghfield Bridge (Berks) converted house with loopholes at SU680706

Chequers Bridge (Hants) type 24 pillboxes, Vickers mg pillboxes, AT blocks, AT ditch-between Coxmoor Wood, canal and Falkners Copse at SU78-50/1

Ewshott (Hants) concentration of mg and type 24 pillboxes at SU81-50; similar group of 4 Vickers mg posts and five type 24 pillboxes at Beacon Hill at SU82-50

Farnham (Surrey) cluster of Vickersand type 24 pillboxes at Hog Hatch at SU82-49; stretch from Farnham to Tilford via Waverley Abbey, contains nine field gun emplacements, similar number of type 24 and other pillboxes, AT pimples and blocks, lengths of AT ditch etc: at SU859473-879436

Hazeley (Berks) cluster of section posts, type 24 pillboxes etc at SU74-59

Shalford (Surrey) circular 6pdr blockhouse at TQ013475 and drum-shaped type 24 pillboxes built by Mowlem at TQ015475, 025476, 029477; roadblock in Shalford village at SU999475

Somerset Bridge (Surrey) field gun emplace-ment and type 24 pillbox at SU921441

Winchfield (Hants) three pillboxes and AT obstacles astride railway at SU749543

Winchfield Hurst (Hants) pillboxes and AT blocks on embankment at SU785548

GHQ Line South (Eastern Command)

Betchworth (Surrey) 12 pillboxes around church and bridge at TQ20/1-49

Blindley Heath (Surrey) cluster of pillboxes W of A22 road/bridge at TQ36-45

Box Hill (Surrey) type 28 and 24 pillboxes and two groups of AT cylinders at TQ17-50/1

Edenbridge (Kent) pillboxes covering rail/river crossing at TQ45-46

Chiddingstone Causeway (Kent) two double machine-gun posts at TQ522467

Smallfield (Surrey) front line of 12 type 24, Vickers, and 6pdr emplacements, with rear line of four type 22 pillboxes at TQ312438-328444

GHQ Line (Newhaven-Hoo)

Barcombe House (E. Sussex) cluster of pillboxes at rail/river crossing at TQ42/3-14

Buxted Park (E. Sussex) type 28a converted to l mg post at TQ490230and others

Groombridge (E. Sussex) cluster of type 28 and 24 pillboxes at TQ51-36/7

Hoo St Werburgh (Kent) type 28a (6pdr), and type 24 pillboxes at TQ78/9-71/2

Iford (E. Sussex) type 24 pillboxes at TQ424080, 424077, 420088 and 423082

Isfield Place (E. Sussex) type 28 for 6pdr gun, disguised type 24 pillboxes, and pillboxes built onto garden wall to simulate gazebos at TQ42/3-14

Lodge Hill (Kent) pair type 28a (6pdr), single 28a, type 25 Armco and standard type 24 (other 24s on Hoo to local design) at TQ75-73/4

Penshurst (Kent) junction of defence lines marked by heavy concentration of 13 type 28 (6pdr) and type 24 pillboxes and roadblock etc. at TQ52-43

Teston Bridge (Kent) type 28a and 24 pillboxes and others, both sides of river at TQ70-53

Twyford Bridge (Kent) nine type 28a (6pdr), type 24 and Vickers pillboxes at TQ69-49

GHQ Line East

Audley End (Essex) pair of type 24 pillboxes on bridge at TL521390, and pillbox and AT blocks at TL522381/523382

Benwick (Cambs) type 28a (6pdr) and type 24 and 350/40 pillboxes at TL34/5-90/1

Dog-in-the-Doublet (Cambs) cluster of pillboxes and spigot mortar at TL27 99

Hanningfield (Essex) cluster of six camouflaged pillboxes at TL75-00

Hartford End (Essex) type 28a (6pdr), six type 24, six rectangular l mg pillboxes and two spigot mortars; rear line of 10 type 22 pillboxes at TL67/69-17/18

Newborough (Cambs) type 24 thin-walled pillboxes at TL215062 and 218057

Newport (Essex) two type 28 (2pdr), three type 24 pillboxes and AT pimples at TL54-33

Parsonage (Essex) type 28a (6pdr), three type 24, and three Vickers at TL62-23

Pitsea (Essex) 9 type 28a (2pdr), 22 and rectangular l mg pillboxes at TR74/5-87/8

Pymore (Cambs) type 28a (6pdr) and 2 rectangular l mg pillboxes at TL498848

Sandon (Essex) Three type 28a (6pdr), and four rectangular l mg pillboxes at TL74-03/04

Tilty (Essex) type 28a (2pdr), two type 24, and pillbox inside barn at TL59/60-26

Wendens Ambo (Essex) excavated spigot mortar pit at TL515365

Whittlesey (Cambs) type 350/40 pillboxes at TL281975 and 290995

GHQ Line (Northern Command)

Aldwark Bridge (N. Yorks) roadblock at SE467622

Cromwell Bridge (Notts) spigot mortar and home guard store at SK808610

Naburn Bridge (N. Yorks) Loopholed barriers and home guard store at SE49 46

Torksey (Lincs) AT rail slots on (disused) railway bridge at SK836792

Eastern Command Line

Bures (Essex) CRE type small pillbox with central LAA mount at TL904346 and CRE type large pillbox with central LAA mount at TL904348; also CRE type small pillbox with solid roof at TL905340

Cavenham (Suffolk) CRE type small pillbox with central LAA mount at TL755725

Cockfield (Suffolk) oddly-shaped type 28a converted to lmg post at TL904545

Colchester (Essex) AT blocks at TL997256 and CRE small pillbox at TM006260

Icklingham (Suffolk) CRE type 28a pillbox (6pdr) at TL772725

Lackford (Suffolk) CRE type shellproof pillbox with solid roof at TL787708

Lavenham (Suffolk) tri-lobed pillbox with central LAA mount at TL915517

Long Melford (Suffolk) CRE large pillbox with central LAA mount at TL856445

Nordelph (Norfolk) bridgehead on Pophams Eau; one type 28a and one type 28, both for 2pdr AT guns, four type 24 pillboxes, and two explosives stores for demolition charges for the bridge at TF55-00/01

Santon Downham (Suffolk) two raised spigot mortar pits at TL825873

Ten Mile Bank (Norfolk) a 28a and three type 24 pillboxes and spigot mortar at TL60-96/7

Three Holes (Norfolk) type 28a (2pdr) at TF507003 and type 28 (2pdr) at 497002

Wakes Colne (Essex) type 28 (6pdr), CRE type shellproof and bulletproof solid-roofed pillboxes, two spigot mortars and AT blocks at TL89-28 under viaduct

West Row (Suffolk) type 28 (6pdr), 2 type 24, type 22 and spigot mortars at TL67-74

Fife Line

Collessie (Fife) double lines of AT pimples at NO283143-286139

Ladybank (Fife) type 24 pillbox and AT blocks astride railway at NO311104

Markinch (Fife) double machine-gun emplacement, type 24 pillbox, roadblock, loopholes in cemetery wall, AT walls at NO29/30-01/03

Cardigan-Pembrey Line (Rhos Llangeler)

Blaenantgwyn (Carms) type 24 pillboxes and 100-plus AT blocks at SN35-34

Cynwyl Elfed (Carms) loopholes in village buildings at SN373274 and 373277

Pembrey (Carms) type 22 and two type 23 pillboxes, AT rails in pairs and singles, AT blocks set diagonally and joined by rails at SN40-04

Taunton Stop Line

Axminster (Devon) 6pdr, type 24, and Vickers pillboxes and roadblock at SY29-97/8

Boshill Cross (Devon) 6pdr emplacement, four type 24 and two Vickers at SY26-92

Bridgwater (Somerset) two 2-storey pillboxes and AT blocks at ST308369

Durston (Somerset) two Vickers and one type 24 pillbox at SY304277

Ilton (Somerset) type 28a (6pdr), a 2-storey and two type 24 pillboxes at SY34-17

Wrantage (Somerset) 6pdr position, Vickers and type 24 pillboxes at SY30/31-22

Arun-Ouse-Rother Line (Sussex)

Amberley field gun shelters for 25pdr guns at TQ025131 and 018142

Bodiam Castle type 28a (6pdr) at TQ785255

Coldwaltham field gun shelters for 25pdr guns at TQ026162 and 034159

Ford field gun shelters for 25pdr guns at TQ003042 and 008041

Handcross type 28a (6pdr) and AT blocks straddling road at TQ245292

Pulborough field gun shelters for 25pdr guns at TQ040188 and 046188

Ryelands Farm type 28a (6pdr) and two type 24 pillboxes at TQ32-28

Slaugham two-storey pillbox at TQ249281

London Defence Lines

Barkingside Station AT blocks at TQ448895

Barnes and **Kew railway bridges** pillboxes and spigot mortars in walled pits

Batchworth two sets AT blocks, type 22, and two type 27 pillboxes at TQ074/80-94

Cheshunt type 27, and two type 22 pillboxes and two sets of AT blocks at TL331/3-046/9

Cuffley Three rows of sockets for AT rails, and AT blocks on Carbone Hill at TL293039; three pairs of AT blocks with slots for RSJs, and two pillboxes at TL299/304-041/3

Dagenham East *c.*200 AT cylinders, roadblock & AA tower at TQ503/5-852

Epping type 27 pillboxes at TL434028, 435026, 436016, 434013 and 436021

Epping Forest traces of AT ditch at TL431006 and 432001

Fairlop Station AT blocks at TQ450908

Hainault Station AT blocks at TQ450926

Iver pillboxes at Grand Union Canal crossing of River Colne at TQ04/5-80

Nazeing AT block and 14 AT rails (hairpins) at TL382053; crossing point of AT ditch marked by six AT blocks at TL404051

Newbury Park Station AT blocks (c100-plus) at TQ449888

Northaw pillbox and eight AT blocks on the Ridgeway at TL277038

Perry Hill three type 27 pillboxes at TL395055, 398052 and 398055

Potters Bar 25 large AT blocks up both sides of rail embankment at TL249024

Putney Bridge Station pillbox and defended signal-box on (high level) platform

Turnford tall pillbox and AT blocks on level-crossing at Slipe Lane at TL368052

Tamworth-Ashbourne Line

Burton–upon–Trent (Staffs) four small pillboxes on railway bridge at SK245210 and type 24 at 250223; two type 24 pillboxes at crossing of Trent Mersey Canal, A38 and River Dove at SK 268269 and 268268

Doveridge (Derbys) Two type 24 pillboxes at Dove Bridge at SK113335 and 111339

Elford (Staffs) type 24 pillboxes at SK189098 and 193090

Ellastone (Derbys) disguised gunhouse and type 24 pillbox on plinth at SK12-42

Fauld (Staffs) Two type 24 pillboxes astride Gypsum Mine tramway at SK180295

Hilton (Derbys) Two rectangular pillboxes (pitch roofs) at ex-railway bridge at SK243287

Hopwas Bridge (Staffs) type 24 pillboxes at SK179053 and 181050

Mayfield (Derbys) non-standard pillbox at SK159460

Tamworth (Staffs) type 24 pillboxes at SK183046, 189046, 198037, and 204036;

Tame-Trent confluence type 23, and 2 type 24 pillboxes at SK187/93-149/53

Yoxall Bridge type 24 pillbox at SK132176

Other stop lines (examples)

Ant Line (Norfolk) First World War circular pillboxes at TG296313, 272334, 307298 and 308295; and one D-shaped at

TG300307; 11 First World War and 11 Second World War in all

Avon Line (Hants) L-shaped section post at SU145137; defended barn and two type 26 pillboxes at SU164173

Avon Line (Worcs) 6pdr emplacement at SO952449, spigot mortar at 951452; prefabricated pillbox at SO922424 and spigot mortar at 922422

Gloucester and Sharpness Canal pillboxes at SO746085, 757095, 783061

Hobhole Drain (Lincs) type 28a (6pdr) at TF354566, 351583 and 344583; local design type 23 pillboxes at TF367439, 367416 and 366449; and type 22 pillboxes at TF374525, 379548, 382569, 360401 and 365400; blockhouse at TF361401

Kent Corps Line type 28a (6pdr) at TR225547; mounting for 6pdr at TR246511 type 24 pillboxes at TR235539 and 200550; AT blocks at TR250502; NB that line followed the Dover–Canterbury Railway, so pillboxes are built into viaducts

Leeds-Liverpool Canal (Lancs) 2-storey pillboxes at SD404118, 384014 and 429125; loopholed barns at SD415124, 432124, 442121, 367083, 366068;

Northumberland Lines lozenge-shaped pillboxes at NZ100994, NZ139984, NU065010, NT978000, NU986284, NT989285

Oxford Canal prefabricated pillboxes at SP458602, 460595, 461565, and 522758; AT blocks at SP459594, 457604, 503771, 488773; two thin-walled type 24 pillboxes SP495290/1 and two more similar at SP482/4-157

River Line (Essex/Suffolk) type 22 pillboxes at TL722296, 680414 and 675513

Severn Line 6pdr emplacements at SO825634 and 807713

Stockton-Sunderland Line lozenge-shaped pillboxes at NZ412345 and 409371; type 23 pillboxes at NZ403233, 408217, 403236, 404237

Teme Stop Line loopholes at SO504721; pillbox at SO715658

Trent Line two spigot mortars at Swarkestone Br at SK368285 and 371286; type 22 pillbox at Shardlow at SK441304; AT

blocks on bridge carrying Melbourne military railway over Trent at SK389274

Wyre Line (Lancs) gunhouse (2pdr AT and LAA) at SD477378 and gunhouse for field gun at SD485475; AT rails and AT ditch at SD473375

CHAPTER 3: THE DEFENCE OF VULNERABLE POINTS

Abergavenny (Gwent) cluster of semi-sunken strongpoints at SO310152

Alnwick (Northumberland) loopholes at NU195122 and two concrete sandbag pillboxes at NU202136 and 202137 and fragments of a third

Alton (Staffs) pillbox built into railway station at SK071427

Baildon (W. Yorks) loopholes and AT obstacles at SE130398

Beachley Point (Gwent) Two square pillboxes at ST547/9-903

Bigsweir Bridge (Glos) Two arrow-shaped section posts at SO543052 and 538057, and two rectangular pillboxes at SO543054 and 543053

Bognor Regis (W. Sussex) section post of unusual design at SU923015

Bollington (Cheshire) loopholes in parapet of canal aqueduct at SJ930774

Bonar Bridge (Highland) type 28a gunhouse at NH618913

Boston Docks (Lincs) two type 23 pillboxes at TF327433 and 329436

Bridge of Dye (Aberdeen) Two camouflaged pillboxes at NO652861

Builth Wells (Powys) sunken mg post with three table-mountings at SO031511

Cambridge (Cambs) type 28a (2pdr) at TL470592; rectangular lmg pillboxes at 469592 and 475603; type 24 pillboxes at 434570, 435598, 413617, 465616; others at 456566, 469523 and 491595

Cambridgeshire SL Sites with pillboxes at TL503462, TL368909, TF294058, TL574614

Carlisle (Cumbria) pillbox built into wall at NY403571

Charlbury (Oxon) loopholes in walls both sides of road at SP354195/6

Chattenden (Kent) two 11-sided, domed pillboxes at TQ757728

Christchurch (Hants) pillbox and 40 AT blocks at railway station at SZ154934

Cripps Corner (E. Sussex) pillbox and coffin-type AT blocks at TQ777204

Dover Castle (Kent) square spigot mortar pedestal at TR329419

Earith (Cambs) two spigot mortars and Allan-Williams turret at TL39-74

Egmere (Norfolk) Three pillboxes, two spigot mortars and explosives store at TF906/9-374

Elgin (Moray) Two rectangular pillboxes either side of railway at NJ113687

Enfield Lock (G. London) tall type 24 pillbox at former ROF at TQ373990

Everton (Hants) two section posts at SZ298939

Eye (Suffolk) spigot mortar pits with bomb lockers at TG151736 and 148735

Friston (Suffolk) four local design pillboxes guarding road junction at TM41-59

Glascoed (Gwent) tall type 24 pillboxes at ROF at SO332023 and 334023

Guist (Norfolk) domed spigot mortar pedestal at TF999137

Havant (Hants) Three section posts at SU733092, 738080 and 733089

Ipswich (Suffolk) type 28a (2pdr) at TM176464; 40 AT blocks at 197445; type 22 pillboxes at 124437, 161469, 161423 and 164470; spigot mortars at 127464 and 144446; 2 mg posts on foreshore at 195402; 9 AT blocks at 160469; two pillboxes at airfield at TM197410 & 193412

Kings Lynn (Norfolk) AT rail slots at TF625197 and spigots at 626205 and 629199

Kirkleatham (Redcar) anti-invasion HQ; pillboxes and defended lodges NZ59-21

Kirkwall (Orkney) hexagonal pillbox built of concrete sandbags at HY430118

Ladybank Depot (Fife) three canopied pillboxes at NO301104 and 300103

Leeds (W. Yorks) two strongpoints on wall of Kirkstall Forge at SE247/8-368/9

Leicestershire SL Sites with pillboxes at SK767206, 788058, 840151,790355, 775305

Lincoln AT rail sockets at SK981725 and AT wall at SK972272

Lincolnshire Sites with pillboxes at TL365212, TF300266, TF473721, SK911304

Llyn Ogwen (Gwynedd) pillboxes and spigot mortars at SH64/5-60

Lower Horsebridge (E. Sussex) local design machine-gun post at TQ574112

Mildenhall (Suffolk) hexagonal spigot mortar pedestal at TL714747

Narborough (Norfolk) 36 AT rails (hairpins) at river crossing at TF764144

Northampton two sewer-pipe pillboxes at SP765596

Northamptonshire SL Sites with pillboxes at SK824896, SP898851, SP821802, SP949860, SK840852 and SK904953

North Weald (Essex) Two Allan-Williams turrets at 19C redoubt at TL50-03

Norton Fitzwarren former army camp defended by pillboxes at ST20-25

Nottinghamshire SL sites with pillboxes at SK523302, 718308, 668311, 504403, 738455

Old Bewick (Northumberland) Two lozenge-shaped pillboxes at NU074/5-215

Oundle (Northants) Two HG explosives and inflammables stores behind drill hall at TL034883 plus spigot mortar at TL036881

Pen-y-Gwyrd (Gwynedd) Four rock-faced pillboxes at SH65/6-55/6

Poole (Dorset) Creekmoor ROF pillboxes and defended gatehouse at SY00-94

Porthcurnow (Cornwall) pillboxes protecting cable terminal at SW38-22

Rudyards Reservoir (Staffs) pillbox disguised as cottage at SJ956579

Shooters Hill (G. London) 13-sided spigot mortar pedestal at TQ429766

Stapleford (Notts) River Erewash crossing, Ruck pillbox (rare outside the northern counties)

Steeton (W. Yorks) Two-storey pillbox and police-posts at ex-ROF at SE030/3-447

Stradsett (Norfolk) Two type 22 pillboxes, two spigot mortars and shelter at TF66-05

Summerfield (Worcs) assorted pillboxes and police-posts at ROF at SO83-73

Witney (Oxon) Two Norcon pillboxes at SP362097 and loopholes at 355103

Wrexham (Denbigh)10 and assorted pillboxes and guard-posts at ROF at SJ 38/9-48/9

CHAPTER 4: AIRFIELD AND RADAR SITE
DEFENCE

Airfields

Acklington (Northumberland) pillbox with
upper level at NU238005

Alton Barnes (Wilts) Three pentagonal
pillboxes at SU102623, 103624 and 104623

Angle (Pembs) BHQ and windmill stump with
loopholes at SM867019

Atcham (Shrops) pillboxes and seagull trenches
at SJ57-09/10

Barton-le-Clay (Beds) Three pairs of pillboxes
and shelters at TL06/7-31

Bicester (Oxon) Two FC Construction
pillboxes and seagull trenches at SP597239;
other pillboxes and defended shelters by
hangars and control tower at SP59-24

Bodorgan (Anglesey) pillbox with instrument
mountings and LAA pit at SH391687

Bodney (Norfolk) BHQ, pillbox with open
LAA position on roof, and thickened
hexagonal pillbox at TL84-99

Bramcote (Warks) pillboxes with corner
loopholes at SP405874 and 417875

Brooklands (Surrey) hexagonal pillbox with
corner embrasures at TQ070630, three-
storey Bofors tower at TQ072629

Carew Cheriton (Pembs) seagull trench at
SN058032, BHQ at SN054021, hexagonal
pillboxes with open annexes at 055022,
054021 and 063025

Cark (Lancs) BHQ, 2 FC Construction, type
22 and other pillboxes at SD37-74

Catfoss (E. Yorks) BHQ and rare ?type
391/41 pentagonal pillbox at TA134477

Crail (Fife) hexagonal pillboxes at NO635093,
626081, 622080, 614092 with thickened
walls; other pillboxes, rooftop guard-posts
and steel turrets

Cranfield (Beds) Two hexagonal pillboxes with
open annexes at SP93/4-41

Culmhead (Somerset) loopholed dispersal and
assorted pillboxes at ST20-14

Debden (Essex) Six thickened hexagonal
pillboxes, and one octagonal, at TL56/7-
34/5

Detling (Kent) hexagonal type 27 pillboxes at
TQ812590, 809589 and 813591

Drem (Lothian) type 27 pillbox at NT505810
and loopholed dispersal at NT502804

Duxford (Cambs) hexagonal shellproof
pillboxes at TL455465 and 455459; two
shellproof rectangular mg posts at
TL459473 and 46347

East Wretham (Norfolk) strongpoint with
two double mg posts, two hexagonal
pillboxes and sunken magazine at TL91-89

Evanton (Highland) type 27 pillbox and
hexagonal pillbox at NH628666/8

Exeter (Devon) pillboxes recorded at SX99-93,
SY00/1-93/4

Feltwell (Norfolk) BHQ and two square
pillboxes at TL702887; two further
square pillboxes at TL702904 and 706896;
type 22 pillbox at TL704879

Filton (Glos) single-storey Bofors tower at
ST604812

Forres (Moray) Two hexagonal pillboxes with
2 exits at NJ016567 and 018571

Goxhill (Lincs) BHQ at TA108207 and two
pseudo BHQs at 113223 and 121221

Grafton Underwood (Northants) BHQ and
FC Construction pillbox at SP92-81/2

Great Sampford (Essex) thickened hexagonal
pillboxesTL609348 and 615360

Hampstead Norreys (Berks) three hexagonal
pillboxes at SU54-76/78

Hethel (Norfolk) strongpoint with mg pits,
trenches and magazine at TG153017

High Ercall (Shrops) pillbox attached to
hangar at SJ604187; two rectangular
pillboxes disguised as cottages at SJ598180
and 599189

Hinton-in-the-Hedges (Northants) two FC
Construction pillboxes, three seagull
trenches and BHQ at SP550372; pillbox
with DF tower on top at SP543374

Honington (Suffolk) FC Construction, types
22 and 23 pillboxes and double mg posts
with Turnbull mounts at TL88/9-76

Hornchurch (Essex) Two Tett Turrets at
TQ535842 and four type 22 pillboxes at
53-84

Hucknall (Notts) tower BHQ at SK519475;
pillboxes at 526464 and 528464

Hunsdon (Herts) BHQ and five thickened
hexagonal pillboxes at TL41/3-13/4

Ibsley (Hants) BHQ with two cupolas at
approx SU155090

Kemble (Glos/Wilts) Eight assorted seagull
trenches at ST94/6-95/7

Kingscliffe (Northants) BHQ and 2 FC Construction pillboxes at TL027973; two FC Construction pillboxes at 020/1-977/8; defended fighter-dispersals at 014978, 024973, 021979, 034975, 030976 & 020978; shelter/gunpost at 029976; sewer-pipe LAA mountings at 027973 and 033984

Lichfield (Staffs) large octagonal pillbox at SK150121 possibly served as BHQ; two hexagonal pillboxes at 135128 and 153117; rectangular pillbox at 153131; type 24 pillbox at 146136; two pentagonal pillboxes at 145137 and 146137

Llandow (Glam) Three hexagonal pillboxes and *ex situ* Pickett Hamilton fort at SS96-71

Llandwrog (Gwynedd) seagull trench and disguised pillbox at SH436/7-565

Long Marston (Warwicks) 3 FC Construction pillboxes and BHQ at SP175/6-494/5

Luton (Beds) unique BHQ, L-shapedand hexagonal cupola at TL126222

Martlesham Heath (Suffolk) type 22 and 23 pillboxes and trenches at TM24/5-44/5

Methwold (Norfolk) BHQ and LAA gun pit at TL740930, two pillboxes at 737945

Montrose (Angus) type 27 pillbox at NO725602, other hexagonal pillboxes including one with a raised LAA mount at NO721600

North Luffenham (Rutland) BHQ at SK946043, type 22 pillbox at SK941055, and defence post built into corner of small arms range at SK934046

North Weald (Essex) 2 FC Construction, five thickened hexagonal, one locally designed and three type 22 pillboxes at TL48/9-03/5; resited Pickett Hamilton

Oakington (Cambs) FC Construction pillboxes at TL402667, 416661, 414651, 415668, 416654, 416662, 416659; type 22 pillboxes at TL410670, 404664, 405662 and 418650; shellproof hexagonal at 412674, 404659 and 414672

Oulton (Norfolk) octagonal pillbox at TG151278 and mg post at TG142276

Ouston (Northumberland) circular pillboxes with porches at NZ077687/8

Penrhos seagull trench, pillboxes and loopholed shelters at SH33-33

Perranporth (Cornwall) perimeter with dispersals and defences largely intact

Peterhead (Aberdeen) BHQ at 073463; modified FC Construction pillboxes at NK079476, 073473, 073476, 074477, 074469 and 0733476

Polebrook (Northants) BHQ at TL099872; pillboxes with high and low loopholes at 093862 and 091872 and with normal loophole configuration at 097862

Portsmouth (Hants) Pickett-Hamilton fort resited at Southsea D-Day Museum

Rednal (Shrops) cluster of rectangular pillboxes at SJ37-27; also seagull trenches

Rochford (Essex) FC Construction and type 22 pillboxes at TQ86/7-88/9

St Athan (Glam) assorted pillboxes at SS99-69 and ST00/01-67/9

Sawbridgeworth (Herts) Four thickened hexagonal pillboxes each with either only two or three loopholes at TL458178, 459186, 454184 and 462184;

Selsey (W. Sussex) Four rectangular pillboxes and two L-shaped mg posts at SZ83/4-95

Shoreham (E. Sussex) Eight assorted pillboxes, some with LAA annexes at TQ20-05; field gun emplacement at TQ205058 and AT rail sockets on bridge at 207060

Silloth (Cumbria) spiral mg post at NY144568, hexagonal pillbox with loopholed corridors each side and hexagonal and rectangular pillboxes at NY11-53/4

Snailwell (Suffolk) three skirted pillboxes at TL646659, 659658 and 661659

Southrop (Glos) several Norcon-type pillboxes at SP175035

Spitalgate (Lincs) BHQ, Allen-Williams turret and hexagonal pillboxes at SK93/5-35

Stapleford Tawney (Essex) thin and thickened hexagonal pillboxes at TQ49-97

Thornaby-on-Tees (Teesside) pillbox with roof-top LAA position at NZ465157

Thorpe Abbotts (Norfolk) BHQ at TG 190812, Pickett Hamilton by museum

Tollerton (Notts) octagonal pillboxes at SK618358, 614364, 617365, 618366, 621367, 622368, 624356 and 623359; hexagonal ones at 619362, 619359, 616358, 615364, 617365 and 623366; pillbox inside hangar at 616360

Waterbeach (Cambs) BHQ with hexagonal cupola atop shelter at TL491667

Wellingore (Lincs) BHQ, Seven type 22 pillboxes and loopholed dispersals at SK99-54

Westhampnett (W. Sussex) two two-storey circular pillboxes at SU87-07

West Malling (Kent) four-storey Bofors tower at TQ670558

Weston-super-Mare (Somerset) Two type 24, four hexagonal shellproof pillboxes, and four rectangular mg posts at ST34/35-59/61

West Raynham (Norfolk) BHQ and circular, type 22, and other pillboxes at TF83/5-22/5

Woodford (Cheshire) open pillboxes with slab-roofs at SJ900807, 915817, 915822, 892832; pillbox at 892822; & blockhouse at 892818

Radar Sites

Bawdsey (Suffolk) assorted, mainly hexagonal pillboxes, some thickened to half-height, and/or revetted with sandbags; strongpoints built into cliff; mountings for Oerlikon LAA guns and sockets for Stork mountings; AT blocks and AT walls; explosives stores; at least 16 different constructions at TM33/4-37/8

Bempton (E. Yorks) Two square pillboxes with roof-top LAA positions at TA19-73

Canewdon (Essex) 4 type 22 pillboxes, one with Oerlikon mount at TR90/1-93/4

Drone Hill (Borders) type 27 pillboxes at NT848670, 849665, 847666, 845666, 846664, 848664 and 850663

Dunkirk (Kent) one-storey Bofors tower, LAA gun pit, type 22 pillbox at TR07-59

High Street (Suffolk) six L-shaped pillboxes at TM40/41-71

Ottercops Moss (Northumberland) Nine assorted pillboxes at NY94/95-88/90

Schoolhill (Aberdeen) rectangular pillboxes disguised as houses with pitched roofs at NO987983 and 908984; also others around site

Stoke Holy Cross (Norfolk) three hexagonal pillboxes, one of common design, two unique to site, one of which has Oerlikon LAA mount on roof at TG248/53-024

Swingate (Kent) at least one type 22 pillbox remains at TR335434

Ventnor (IoW) hexagonal pillbox at SZ566785

Wartling (E. Sussex) three square pillboxes, two of them with circular, open LAA annexes, with oval loopholes and mg mounts; also Armco pillbox; at TQ65-07

West Beckham (Norfolk) square pillboxes on top of radar blocks at TG140390

CHAPTER 5: AIRFIELDS

Dates and/or Drawing Numbers are given as available. Drawing numbers were issued in sequence by the Air Ministry with a date. Modifications were often added. Only the main drawing numbers are generally given here. The abbreviation 'tb' denotes 'temporary brick'.

Hangars and aeroplane sheds

Airship hangars Cardington (Beds) including one from Pulham (Norfolk)

Balloon sheds Rollestone Camp (Wilts) two different types

Aeroplane sheds 1910 Larkhill (Wilts), Filton (Glos), Farnborough (Hants), Montrose (Angus), Netheravon (Wilts)

GS coupled sheds 1916 Filton (triple) (Glos), Duxford (Cambs), Hucknall (Notts), Old Sarum (Wilts), all pairs of doubles, Hendon (G. London)

GS hangars c.1915/16 Tadcaster (N. Yorks), Yatesbury (3) (Wilts), Harling Road (Norfolk), Montrose (Angus)

Aircraft repair sheds 164/17 Old Sarum (Wilts), Bracebridge Heath (Lincs), Lympne (Kent)

Coupled Handley Page sheds 1397/18 Netheravon (Wilts)

Coupled GS shed (gabled roof) 2010/18 Henlow (Beds)

Seaplane shed 1914 Calshot (Hants)

RNAS Dutch barn-style shed (First World War) Baldock (Herts) *ex situ*, now garden centre

Admiralty seaplane shed Type F, 1916 Calshot (triple) (Hants), Mount Batten (Devon), Cranwell (Lincs) on original sites; others removed to Evanton (Highland), Stormy Down (Glam), Sywell (Northants)

Admiralty seaplane shed Type G, 1916 Calshot (Hants)

Hangar (Second World War) with bowstring roof as formerly at Helperby (the Brafferdrome); an example can be seen resited at Whittlesey (Cambs) at TL259973

A-type 19a/24 Bicester and Upper Heyford (6) (Oxon), Catfoss (E. Yorks), Martlesham Heath and Mildenhall (Suffolk), North Weald (Essex), Silloth (Cumbria) and Northolt (G. London)

Hinaidi 1136/27 Madley (Herefordshire)

B-type 454/33 Pembroke Dock (2) (Pembs)

Interwar hangars designed primarily for civilian use may be seen at: Waltham (Lincs), Netherthorpe (S. Yorks), Shoreham (W. Sussex), Speke (L'pool), Cambridge, Denham (Bucks), White Waltham (Berks)

Prototype C, not further developed, one example at North Coates (Lincs)

C-type 2029/34, 3264/35, etc. Bassingbourn (Cambs), Hemswell and Manby (Lincs), Cottesmore (Rutland), Kirkbride and Silloth (Cumbria)

C-type protected 1978/37, 9181/38 etc. Kinloss and Lossiemouth (Moray), Newton (Notts), Horsham-St-Faith (Norfolk), Leuchars (Fife), Tern Hill (Shrops), Wroughton (Wilts)

C-type unprotected Wick (Caithness) referred to as C2, and Protected as C1

C-type aircraft repair shed 6116/36 Manby (Lincs), Little Rissington (Glos), Shawbury and Tern Hill (Shrops)

D-type storage shed 2312-13/36 Silloth and Kirkbride (Cumbria), Kemble (Glos), Wroughton (Wilts), St Athan (Glam)

E-type storage shed 7305/37 Kemble and Little Rissington (Glos)

Lamella storage shed 6953/36 Kemble (Glos), Shawbury (Shrops)

J-type operational maintenance hangar 5836/39 Dumfries, Goxhill (Lincs) Polebrook and Chipping Warden (Northants), Syerston (Notts)

K-type storage hangar 3084/39 High Ercall (Shrops)

L-type storage shed 5163-5/39 Lichfield (Staffs), Kinloss and Lossiemouth (Moray), Llandow (Glamorgan)

Bellman 8349/37 Booker (Bucks) high and low versions; Baginton (Warks), Evanton (Highland), Drem (Lothian)

Callender-Hamilton 17346/40 East Fortune (Lothian), Castle Kennedy (Wigton), Barrow-in-Furness (Cumbria)

T1 hangar 7541/41 Calveley (Cheshire), Westhampnett (W. Sussex)

T2 hangar 8254/40 etc. Bottesford (Leics), Findo Gask (Perth), Tilstock (Shrops), Breighton (N. Yorks), Biggin Hill (Kent)

T3 hangar 3505/42 Topcliffe (N. Yorks)

Teesside S hangar 12819/40 Arbroath (Angus)

RNAS Pentad hangar 3304/43 Culham (Oxon), Hinstock (Shrops), Evanton (Highland)

RNAS Fromson Massillon hangar 3752/43 Culham (Oxon)

RNAS Mainhill S sheds Hinstock (Shrops), Henstridge (Dorset)

RNAS main hangar type A Burscough and Inskip (Lancs)

RNAS main hangar type B 195/53 Culham (Oxon)

RNAS electrical repair shop Crail (Fife), Arbroath (Angus)

RNAS aircraft repair shops Crail (Fife), Arbroath (Angus)

RNAS Second World War Dutch barn-style Crail (Fife), Worthy Down (Hants)

Blister hangar 12497/41 (timber) Hucknall (Notts)

Over blister hangar 12512/41 Little Walden (Essex)

Extra over blister hangar 12532/41 Caistor (Lincs)

Enlarged blister hangar 9392/42 Enstone (Oxon)

MAP type A1/2 hangars 454/43 Horsey Toll (Cambs), Hamble (Hants), Perth

MAP type B1 hangars 11776/41 Seighford (Staffs), Spilsby and Waltham (Lincs), Witchford and Wratting Common (Cambs), Tempsford (Beds)

MAP type B2 hangars Kemble (Glos), Wroughton (Wilts) pair of B2s at each for storage of gliders

MAP type R hangars Sywell (Northants), Bourn (Cambs), ?Luton (Beds)

Robins type B hangar 2204/41 High Post (Wilts), Finmere (Bucks), Abbots Bromley

(Staffs), Horsey Toll (Cambs), Marwell Hall (Hants)

Super Robins type A 2243/41 Lossiemouth (Moray)

Super Robins type B 6910/43 Woodley (Berks)

Boulton Paul VR2 Hangars Stormy Down (Glam), Evanton (Highland). Other MAP hangars may be seen at Cranage (Cheshire), Langar and Tollerton (Notts), Yatesbury (Wilts), Weston-super-Mare (Somerset), Cambridge (Cambs). Also of note: Saunders Roe *Columbine* hangar at East Cowes (IoW), hangar groups at Beaumaris (Anglesey), Thurleigh (Beds), Shoreham (W. Sussex)

Gaydon hangar Gaydon (Warwicks), Coningsby (Lincs), Wittering (Cambs)

Quick Reaction Alert hangar 1972 Binbrook (Lincs)

USAF Luria hangar Greenham Common (Berks)

USAF hangar 1958 Greenham Common (Berks), Bruntingthorpe (Leics)

Hardened aircraft shelters Honington (Suffolk), Alconbury (Cambs), Upper Heyford (Oxon), Marham (Norfolk)

Nimrod hangar Waddington (Lincs)

Watch offices and control towers

Watch offices 1918 Duxford (bdg 89) (Cambs), Tydd St Mary (Lincs)

Fort type (brick) 1959-60 Bicester (Oxon), Bircham Newton (Norfolk), Cosford (Shrops)

Fort type (concrete) 207/36 Watton (Norfolk)

Fort type modified 4698/43 etc. Bassingbourn (Cambs), Hemswell (Lincs), West Raynham (Norfolk), Cranfield (Beds), Leconfield (E. Yorks)

Flying training school 5740/36 Little Rissington (Glos), Hullavington (Wilts), Shawbury and Tern Hill (Shrops)

Watch office 756/36 (one only) Manby (Lincs)

Villa type (brick) 5845/39 Swinderby (Lincs), Waterbeach (Cambs), North Luffenham (Rutland), Middleton St George (Co. Durham)

Villa type (concrete) 2328/39 Newton (Notts), Topcliffe (N. Yorks), Wyton

(Cambs), Horsham St Faith (Norfolk) and Wick (Caithness) in timber

Watch office (tb) 518/40 Bottesford and Wymeswold (Leics), Rednal (Shrops), Barrow-in-Furness (Cumbria), Holme-on-Spalding-Moor (E. Yorks), Honeybourne (Worcs), Shipdham (Norfolk), Carlisle (Cumbria), and East Fortune (Lothian) EL464 without Metereological Section. Other interwar one-off design: Weston-super-Mare (Somerset)

Fighter satellite watch office 17658/40 Cark (Lancs), Ludham (Norfolk)

MAP satellite landing ground office Rudbaxton (Pembs), Wath Head (Cumbria), Chepstow (Gwent), Winterseugh (Dumfries)

Night fighter station watch office 12096/41 etc. Tangmere (W. Sussex), Coleby Grange and Hibaldstow (Lincs), Rattlesden (Suffolk), Woolfox Lodge (Rutland), Twinwood Farm (Beds), Kingscliffe (Northants), Bradwell Bay (Essex), Cark (Lancs), Elvington (N. Yorks)

Bomber satellite watch office types A/B 7345/41, 13079/41, 15898/40 etc. Langar (Notts), Long Marston and Edge Hill (Warwicks), Seighford (Staffs) Waltham and Ingham (Lincs), Attlebridge (Norfolk)

Bomber satellite and OTU watch office 13726/41 Turweston and Finmere (Bucks), Thorpe Abbotts and Seething (Norfolk), Long Newnton and Windrush (Glos), Little Staughton and Gransden Lodge (Cambs)

Watch office for all commands 12779/41 and 343/43 Llandwrog (Gwynedd), Haverfordwest (Pembs), Debach, Lavenham, Framlingham, and Rougham (Suffolk), Catfoss (E. Yorks), Bodney, Snetterton and North Creake (Norfolk), Sandtoft, Strubby and Sturgate (Lincs), Wigtown three-storey versions at Findo Gask (Perth), and Dumfries

Watch office and chief instructor's office 641/42 Shellingford (Oxon)

Office for air transport auxiliary Kirkbride (Cumbria)

RNAS tower early version Crail (Fife)

RNAS tower later, 1942, version Burscough and Inskip (Lancs), Henstridge (Dorset),

Hinstock (Shrops), Lee-on-Solent (Hants). Other wartime one-off designs at Carew Cheriton (Pembs), Wroughton (Wilts),Wigsley (Notts) three-storey, Henlow (Beds)

Very heavy bomber station control tower 294/45 West Raynham and Sculthorpe (Norfolk), Lakenheath (Suffolk)

Control tower (revised) 5223a/51 Biggin Hill (Kent), North Weald (Essex), Greenham Common (Berks)

Flying training school tower *c.*1951 Booker (Bucks)

SECO control tower WA15/213/53 Kirkbride (Cumbria)

V Bomber station control tower 1955 Gaydon (Warks), Wittering (Cambs) NB similarity of Thurleigh (Beds) four-storey build of 1957

Local control building (side-by-side) 7378a/55 Swinderby (Lincs)

Control tower vertical split 2548c/55 Manby and Scampton (Lincs), Benson and Abingdon (Oxon)

NB: several Second World War towers are still in service with VCR added etc; also apparent new designs at Odiham and Middle Wallop (Hants)

Airfield technical site buildings

HQ offices 245/17 Henlow (Beds)

RFC/RAF HQ Trenchard House, Farnborough (Hants) Bdg G1, now a museum

Station offices 1446/24 Martlesham Heath (Suffolk)

Station offices 1892/25 Tangmere (W. Sussex), Mildenhall (Suffolk)

Station offices 352/30 Duxford (Cambs)

Station offices 971/30 Thornaby-on-Tees (N. Yorks)

Depot HQ 2322-3/34 Henlow (Beds)

Station HQ 190/36 Manby (Lincs), Old Sarum (Wilts)

Station HQ 1723/36 Little Rissington (Glos), Waddington (Lincs), Bircham Newton (Norfolk)

Station HQ 2878/37 Kemble (Glos), Kirkbride (Cumbria), High Ercall (Shrops)

Operations block 1161/24 Duxford (Cambs), North Weald (Essex)

Operations block (protected) Old Sarum (Wilts)

Operations block 7040/38 Bircham Newton (Norfolk)

Squadron CO's office (tb) 7895/41 Little Staughton (Cambs)

Squadron office (tb) 12405/40 Tempsford (Beds)

Squadron & flight office (tb) 18364/40 Little Staughton (Cambs)

Flight offices & CO's office (tb) 4785/42 North Creake (Norfolk)

Operations blocks 4891/42, 228/43 etc. Harrington (Northants), Seething (Norfolk), Steeple Morden (Cambs), Bottesford (Leics)

Guardhouse First World War EF467 East Fortune (Lothian)

Guardhouse 166/23 Bircham Newton (Norfolk), Sealand (Flint), Henlow (Beds)

Guardhouse 959/25 Bicester and Upper Heyford (Oxon)

Guardhouse 1621/27 Hucknall (Notts)

Guardhouse 1288/32 Duxford (Cambs),

Guardhouse 2880/37 Lichfield (Staffs), Kemble (Glos)

Wardens' post 2881/37 Silloth (Cumbria), Lichfield (Staffs), Dumfries

Guardhouse 469, 494-7/38 Newton (Notts), Horsham-St-Faith (Norfolk)

Picket Post (tb) 14294/40 and **68/42** Faldingworth and Folkingham (Lincs)

Naval Guardhouse Evanton (Highland)

Guardhouse (tb) 18366/40 Little Staughton (Cambs), Strubby (Lincs), Downham Market (Norfolk)

Guardhouse radar site (brick) Drone Hill (Borders), Ottercops Moss (Northumberland), Canewdon (Essex), Stenigot (Lincs)

Guardhouse radar site (tb) Bawdsey (Suffolk)

Guardhouse, bloodhound site Rattlesden (Suffolk), Warboys (Cambs)

PBX (telephone exchange) 13727/41 Castle Camps (Cambs)

PBX (telephone exchange) 5648/41 Kingscliffe (Northants)

Speech broadcast building 10786/41 or 5648/41 Bruntingthorpe (Leics)

Station armoury and photographic block 4829/35, 7616/37 etc. Swinderby,

Hemswell and Binbrook (Lincs), Newton (Notts)

Station armoury (tb) 18365/40 Little Staughton (Cambs)

Station armoury (Nissen) 12777/41 North Creake (Norfolk)

Photographic block (tb) 15532/40 Holme-on-Spalding Moor (E. Yorks), Wymeswold (Leics)

Small arms ammunition store (tb) 16075/41 Peterhead (Aberdeen)

Station armoury 1950 Duxford (Cambs)

MT sheds First World War EF470 East Fortune (Lothian)

MT sheds 289/17 Orfordness (Suffolk)

MT sheds 8047/27 Hucknall (Notts)

MT sheds (concrete) 660/36 Watton (Norfolk), Binbrook (Lincs)

MT sheds (brick) 778/38 Horsham-St-Faith (Norfolk), Cranfield (Beds)

Firefighting & MT shed 3681/38 Tangmere (W. Sussex), Duxford (Cambs), Mildenhall (Suffolk), Newton (Notts), Watton (Norfolk)

MT sheds (tb) 5851/42 Debach and Rougham (Suffolk), Spanhoe (Northants)

Workshops 288/17 Duxford (Cambs)

Stores and workshops First World War-1920s Martlesham Heath (Suffolk)

Main workshops (brick) 2049/34 Cranfield (Beds), Little Rissington (Glos)

Main workshops (concrete) 4923/35 Binbrook (Lincs), Watton (Norfolk)

Main workshops (tb) 5245/41 Llandwrog (Gwynedd), Haverfordwest (Pembs)

Main workshops (Nissen/Romney) 5851 or 5540/42 North Creake (Norfolk), Little Staughton (Cambs), Shepherds Grove (Suffolk)

Main stores and barrack stores 285 and 284/17 Duxford (Cambs)

Main stores (brick) 2048/34, 2056/34 Cranfield (Beds), Wroughton (Wilts)

Main stores (concrete) 4287/35 & 7064/37 Newton (Notts), Watton (Norfolk)

Main stores (tb) 1256/40 Holme-on-Spalding-Moor (E. Yorks),

Fabric store (tb) 12773/41 Wing (Bucks), Goxhill (Lincs) Snetterton (Norfolk)

Main stores (Nissen/Romney/Iris) 5852/42 and 2883/43 North Creake and

Fersfield (Norfolk), Little Staughton (Cambs), Shepherds Grove (Suffolk)

Inflammables store 987/26 or 329/26 Duxford (Cambs)

Inflammables store 7242/38 Bircham N'ton and West Raynham (Norfolk)

Pyrotechnics store (tb) 5488/42 Goxhill (Lincs)

Station sickbay 1963/34 Manby (Lincs)

Station sickbay 7503-4/37 Hemswell, Binbrook and Swinderby (Lincs), Bircham Newton (Norfolk), Newton (Notts)

Decontamination centre (unwounded) 6224/37 West Raynham (Norfolk), Felixstowe (Suffolk)

Decontamination centre Type E 7074/39 Wroughton (Wilts)

Decontamination centre Type J 16696/39 Ringway (G. Manchester)

Decontamination centre 2425/40 Swinderby (Lincs)

Ambulance garage & mortuary 5703/36 Bircham Newton (Norfolk)

Ambulance garage & mortuary 5887/36 Duxford (Cambs)

Petrol tanker shed (brick) 2773/34 Duxford (Cambs)

Petrol tanker shed (concrete) 4157/36 Binbrook and Hemswell (Lincs), Watton and West Raynham (Norfolk)

Night flying equipment store 3235/39 West Raynham (Norfolk)

Night flying equipment store (tb) 17831/40 or 12411/41 East Fortune (Lothian), Little Staughton (Cambs), Elvington (N. Yorks), Swannington (Nfk)

Fire tender house (tb) 12563/40 Foulsham (Norfolk), Debach (Suffolk)

Fire tender house (Nissen) 12410/41 Little Staughton (Cambs)

Floodlight trailer/tractor shed (tb) 1296/40 Little Staughton (Cambs)

Dinghy shed (tb) 2901/43 North Creake (Norfolk), Little Staughton (Cambs)

Parachute store 2355/25 Thornaby-on-Tees (N. Yorks)

Parachute store 1971/34 Manby (Lincs)

Parachute store 175/36 Newton (Notts), Binbrook and Hemswell (Lincs)

Parachute store (protected) 6351/37 Middleton-St-George (Co. Durham)

Parachute store (tb) 17865/39 Peterhead (Aberdeen)

Parachute store (tb) 11137/41 Raydon (Essex), Gamston (Notts)

Parachute store (tb) 10825/42 Shepherds Grove (Suffolk)

Naval parachute store Crail (Fife)

Instructional and synthetic training buildings

Gunnery instruction huts 293/17 Duxford (Cambs)

Gun turret instruction 12167/39 Watton and West Raynham (Norfolk) both single, Bicester (Oxon) and Bassingbourn (Cambs) both double

Turret trainers 11023/40 Holme-on-Spalding-Moor (E. Yorks) single, Silverstone (Northants) double, Llandwrog (Gwynedd) triple

Free gunnery blister hanger 7316/42 Great Massingham (Norfolk)

Fisher gunnery trainer 10839/42 Bruntingthorpe (Leics), East Fortune (Lothian)

Link trainer 12386/38 Newton (Notts), Wyton (Cambs)

Link trainer (tb) 4188/42 triple at Little Staughton (Cambs), Haverfordwest (Pembs), double at Kimbolton (Cambs)

Crew procedure centre/airmanship hall (tb) Haverfordwest (Pembs)

Navigation hut 1852/18 Duxford (Cambs)

Navigation lecture rooms First World War, EF468 East Fortune (Lothian)

Navigation trainer (brick) 2075/43 Oakington (Cambs) and (tb) Swinderby and Strubby (Lincs)

Ship recognition trainer First World War, EF471 East Fortune (Lothian)

AML bombing teacher 47/40 Holme-on-Spalding-Moor (E. Yorks)

AML bombing teacher 1739/41 Silverstone (Northants) triple

AML bombing teacher 6301/42 Melton Mowbray (Leics) single, Peplow (Shrops) double

AML bombing teacher 816/43 Metheringham (Lincs)

Combined turret trainer/bombing teacher 936-7/43 Woolfox Lodge (Rutland), Darley Moor (Derbys)

Naval AML bombing teacher, airmanship hall & torpedo attack trainer Crail (Fife)

Dome AA trainer Mildenhall (Suffolk), Wyton (Cambs), Langham (Norfolk), Shoreham (W. Sussex), Pembrey (Carms)

Dome trainer for Rapier SAM (ADT3) West Raynham (Norfolk)

Domestic buildings

Cinema (tb) 1840/18, church and **gymnasium 670/36** Henlow (Beds)

Chapels Oakington and Waterbeach (Cambs), West Raynham (Norfolk)

Squash courts 2078/18 Bircham Newton (Norfolk)

Squash courts 1842/35 Duxford (Cambs)

Squash courts (tb) 16589/40 Syerston (Notts) low annexe, Tuddenham (Norfolk) high annexe

Gymnasium (*c.*1937 no number) Shawbury and Tern Hill (Shrops), Manby (Lincs)

Naval gymnasium/cinema Crail (Fife)

Gymnasium and **cinema** and **church (tb) 14604/40** and **8891/42** and **15424/41** Methwold and North Creake (Norfolk), Langar (Notts) all three; Ashbourne (Derbys), Benson (Oxon), Desborough (Northants) gym and church; Northcoates (Lincs) just church; Beccles (Suffolk) just gym

NAAFI shop Mildenhall (Suffolk), Wyton (Cambs)

Pump house/power house 694/23 Bircham Newton (Norfolk)

Booster house 1010/23 Bircham Newton (Norfolk)

Works service building 1134/27 Bicester (Oxon), Duxford (Cambs)

Water towers First World War Howden (E. Yorks), Tadcaster (N. Yorks)

Water tower 1178/25 Bicester (Oxon), Mildenhall (Suffolk)

Water tower and works services 5992/36 Binbrook and Hemswell (Lincs)

Water tower 1033-7/37 High Ercall (Shrops)

Water tower and works services 7957/38 Kirkbride and Silloth (Cumbria)

Braithwaite tanks 19-20/41 (paired) Middleton St George (Co. Durham), Oakington and Waterbeach (Cambs), Swinderby (Lincs)

Braithwaite tank 19–20/41 (solo) Glatton
(Cambs), Andrewsfield (Essex)

Water tower USAF post-Second World War
Mildenhall (Suffolk) double

Standby set house 607/36 Upwood (Cambs)

Standby set house 1059/38 Kirkbride
(Cumbria)

Standby set house 13241/41 North Creake
(Norfolk)

Standby set house 16302/41 Kelstern
(Lincs), Trimley (Radar) (Suffolk)

Standby set house 11274/42 Little
Staughton (Cambs)

Standby set house 8760/42 Glatton (Cambs)
Tuddenham (Suffolk)

Naval standby set houses Crail (Fife),
Evanton (Highland)

Barrack block (brick) First World War
Calshot (Hants)

Barrack block (tb) First World War
Orfordness (Suffolk), Duxford (Cambs)

Barrack block type A 641/22 Martlesham
Heath (Suffolk)

Barrack block type D 507/23 Tangmere (W.
Sussex)

Barrack block 1424/26 Sealand (Flint)

Barrack block type C 1100/28 Thornaby-
on-Tees (N. Yorks)

Barrack block type B 447–50/32 Tangmere
(W. Sussex), Duxford (Cambs)

Barrack block 62/32 Henlow (Beds)

Barrack block type R 2277/34 Cranfield
(Beds)

Barrack block (three storey) type J 74/35
Manby (Lincs)

**Barrack block (three storey) type B
177/35** Manby (Lincs)

Barrack block type Q 444/36 West
Raynham (Norfolk), Scampton (Lincs)

Barrack block 2357/36 Bircham Newton
(Norfolk)

Barrack block type 8/84 1132/38 Cranfield
(Beds), W. Raynham (Norfolk)

Barrack block type 8/56L 11587/38
Bircham Newton (Norfolk)

Institute 1331–5/29 (for 1217 inc. 128
corporals) Henlow (Beds)

Institute and sergeants' mess 915–21/30
Thornaby-on-Tees (N. Yorks)

Dining room and institute 852/32 Duxford
(Cambs)

**Dining room and institute (adjacent)
3013/35** Manby (Lincs)

Airmen's mess and NAAFI 1483/36
Bircham Newton (Norfolk)

Dining room and institute 1482–4/36 West
Raynham (Norfolk)

Institute and airmen's mess 8055–60/38
Watton (Norfolk), Hemswell (Lincs)

Single sergeants' quarters 4526/36 Bircham
Newton (Norfolk)

Single sergeants' quarters 8378/39 West
Raynham (Norfolk)

Sergeants' mess 191/24 Duxford (Cambs),
Martlesham Heath (Suffolk), North Weald
(Essex)

Sergeants' mess (three storey) 1015/35
Henlow (Beds)

Sergeants' mess 3699/35 Manby (Lincs)

Sergeants' mess 3484/36 Cranfield (Beds),
Bircham Newton (Norfolk)

Sergeants' mess 7858/38 Wyton (Cambs),
Cranfield (Beds)

Sergeants' mess Little Rissington (Glos)

Officers' mess 1912 Farnborough (Hants)

Officers' mess 1913 Upavon (Wilts)

Officers' mess 1914 Netheravon (Wilts)

Officers' mess 1916 Hendon (G. London)

Officers' mess 1917 Hendon (G. London)
now Aerodrome Hotel

Officers' mess First World War Yatesbury
(Wilts)

Officers' mess First World War Calshot
(Hants) now a hotel

Officers' mess/quarters 1921 Empire Pilots'
School Farnborough (Hants)

Officers' mess 1524/25 North Weald (Essex)

Officers' mess 1374–80/29 etc. Henlow
(Beds)

Officers' mess 7035/30 Peterborough
(Cambs), Warley (Essex), Deepcut and
Bordon (Hants)

**Officers' mess 2290–92/34 or 2948/34 or
570/37** Swanton Morley (Norfolk),
Newton and Syerston (Notts) Upwood and
Duxford (Cambs); only minor variations
such as flat roof at Oakington (Cambs), or
four or five windows flanking entry

Officers' mess (three storey) 3935/35
Manby (Lincs), Little Rissington (Glos)

Officers' mess (three storey) Ringway (G.
Manchester)

Officers' mess (tb) Ashbourne (Derbys), Downham Market (Norfolk)

Officers' mess 1960 Henlow (Beds)

Rocket site buildings

Bloodhound SAM sites with Missile Servicing Building, Arming Sheds, Launch Control Posts, refuelling Building etc.: Woolfox Lodge (Rutland), Rattlesden (Suffolk), Warboys (Cambs)

Missile servicing area for Mark II West Raynham (Norfolk)

THOR IRBM sites with buildings, other than only blast walls, remaining: North Luffenham (Rutland), Melton Mowbray (Leics), Harrington (Northants), North Pickenham and Feltwell (Norfolk). NB: clusters of BCF huts at Melton Mowbray, Tuddenham (Suffolk), and Breighton (E. Yorks) built for THOR personnel accommodation

Cruise missile storage at Molesworth (Cambs), and Greenham Common (Berks)

CHAPTER 6: BUILDINGS FOR THE ARMY AND THE NAVY

Ayr Chalmers Road Drill Hall built 1950s for Scottish Yeomanry TA

Barrow-in-Furness (Cumbria) BAe Trident submarine building *c*.1985

Bovington (Dorset) built First World War and 1920s, now RAC depot and tank museum

Bulford Camp (Wilts) built 1920s/30s, still in use

Chelsea Barracks rebuilt 1962, still in use

Church Gresley (Derbys) Drill Hall, 1913, for Notts and Derby Regt. TF

Colchester (Essex) pre-First World War experimental barracks, and post-Second World War barracks

Connahs Quay (Flint) TA Centre built 1980s

Cumbernauld (Lothian) TA Centre built 1970s

Devonport Keyham Naval barracks completed by 1907, still in use; Frigate complex, Fleet maintenance base and submarine refit complex all built 1971-80

Edgware (G. London) Drill Hall opened 1938 for RE (TA) searchlight unit

Edinburgh 89 East Claremont St Drill Hall, 1912 for HQ and 9 Battalion. Royal Scots TF

Faslane (Argyll) nuclear submarine base, built 1960s, still in use

Greenock Fort Matilda rebuilt 1940s for RN, Royal Marines and Coastguard

Hounslow (G. London) 1911 for Middlesex Regiment TF at 210 Hanworth Road

Knightsbridge Barracks rebuilt 1972 for Household Cavalry

Larkhill Camp (Wilts) completed 1930s, RA base, still in use

Llanelli (Carms) Murray Street, Drill Hall, 1910, for 4 Battalion. Welch Regiment TA

Llanion Barracks Pembroke Dock, 1904, now housing and commercial uses; NB 1950s AA operations room for Pembroke GDA in underground bunker

Newhaven (E. Sussex) tunnels under Guinness Holiday Home, via Museum

Portsmouth (Hants) naval barracks, dockyard

Queensferry (Flint) Drill Hall, 1936, for Royal Welch Fusiliers TA

Redford Barracks Edinburgh built 1909-15; Dreghorn Bks later; in use

Rosyth (Fife) dockyard opened 1909-14; nuclear submarine facilities from 1970s

St Just (Cornwall) Drill Hall built *c*.1936 to Junkers design

Skegness (Lincs) Butlins Camp served as HMS *Royal Arthur* during Second World War

Tidworth Camp (Wilts) built to new designs by 1908

Truro (Cornwall) Drill Hall built *c*.1936 in International Modern style

Trusthorpe (Lincs) Holiday Camp served as army camp during Second World War

Tynemouth (Northumberland) Drill Hall, 1928, for Tyne Electrical Engineers (TA)

CHAPTER 7: AIR DEFENCE

Acomb (N. Yorks) Shelley House, semi-sunken ROC HQ building, 1961

Anstruther (Fife) GCI Radar site of 1950s, then RSG at NO568089

Bempton (E. Yorks) Second World War CHL and 1950s GCI Radar sites at TA19-73/4

Blakelaw (Northumberland) Second World War Filter-room, 13 Fighter Group RAF at NZ214669

Blyth (Northumberland) Gloucester Lodge HAA Battery at NZ321785

Brislington (Glos) 1950s Regional War Room at ST623700

Cambridge ARP Warden's Post at TL468572; RSG at TL455566

Capel (Kent) Abbots Cliff Sound Mirror at TR270386

Cheshunt (Herts) AA tower at TL367019 and magazine at TL371027

Clipston (Northants) ROC underground and Second World War brick posts at SP703825

Cold Overton (Rutland) ROC underground post at SK806097

Cosheston (Pembs) bombing decoy block-house at SN001046

Dersingham (Norfolk) ROC underground post at TF696318

Dover (Kent) Farthingloe HAA Battery at TR297399

Drone Hill (Borders) CH Radar site NT84-66

Dumfries bombing decoy blockhouse at NY005789

Duxford (Cambs) assorted air-raid shelters in Museum

Elvaston (Derbys) Second World War HAA site and postwar AA Operations Room at SK413323

Erith (Kent) HAA Battery on Crayford Marshes at TQ530773

Farlington (Hants) bombing decoy block-houses at SU680044 and 684041

Fiskerton (Lincs) ROC Group HQ 1950s at TF046725

Folkestone (Kent) underground ROC post at TR240367

Freshwater West (Pembs) HAA battery at Gravel Bay at SM883008

Fulwell (Northumberland) First World War sound mirror at NZ389596

Gautby (Lincs) bombing decoy blockhouse at TF164718

Gosforth (Northumberland) Tyneside AA Operations Room at NZ245704

Grantham (Lincs) HAA site at SK944360

Gravesend (Kent) New Tavern Fort has a 3.7' HAA gun from one of the offshore forts at TQ653742

Great Badow (Essex) radar tower from Canewdon, re-erected at TL727039

Greatstone (Kent) slab, bowl, and strip sound mirrors at TR075213

Greyfriars (Suffolk) Radar site opened 1944, blast walls stand at TM477690

Hack Green (Cheshire) 1950s ROTOR station then RSG at SJ645479

Halnaker Mill (W. Sussex) four DF tower bases at SU921098

Hamble (Hants) LAA emplacement with Bofors mounted at SU482059

Hartley Crag (Northumberland) CD/CHL Radar site at NZ343762

Hope Cave (Devon) ROTOR station, then RSG for South-West at SX67-39

Horsham (W. Sussex) ROC above-ground Group HQ at TQ173303

Hythe (Kent) sound mirror at TR139346

Ickleton (Cambs) ROC underground and brick visual post on stilts at TL475415

Ipswich (Suffolk) ARP Warden's Post at TM168455

Iver (Bucks) AA tower at Admiralty Compass Laboratory at TQ044806

Iwade (Kent) HAA Battery at TQ899689

Kelvedon Hatch (Essex) 1950s ROTOR station then RSG at TQ56-99

Killingworth (N. Tyne) AA magazine and equipment store at NZ289707

Kilnsea (E. Yorks) First World War sound mirror at TA411167

Langtoft (Lincs) Second World War happidrome and 1950s GCI site at TF154130

Loch Ewe (Highland) HAA batteries at Firemore, Tournaig Farm and Mellon Charles

Loch Ryan (Wigton) HAA Battery at NX089631

Lodge Hill (Kent) First World War AA battery at TQ758740

Mablethorpe (Lincs) ARP Reporting Centre at TF510848

Manorbier (Pembs) AA Practice Camp at SS08-97

Manston (Kent) one-man steel shelter outside Museum

Marsden (S. Tyne) Lizard Lane HAA Battery at NZ401637

Maxey (Cambs) bombing decoy blockhouse at TF144083

Mistley (Essex) 1950s AA Operations Room, then Civil Defence at TM12-31

Nazeing (Essex) bombing decoy site at TL41-05

Newark (Notts) single-storey Bofors tower, Kelham Road depot at SK794544

New Buckenham (Norfolk) ROC underground and ORLIT B posts at TM093907

Newhaven Fort (E. Sussex) reconstructed ROC surface post, 1960s

Norwich (Norfolk) ROC semi-sunken Group HQ at TG236112

Orfordness (Suffolk) experimental RDF tower 'Black Beacon' at TM445488

Ottercops Moss (Northumberland) CH Radar site at NY94-89

Plymouth (Devon) Down Thomas HAA site at SX508491; Bere Alston HAA site at SX453660; Hooe Hill Z Battery at SX504517

Porlock (Somerset) ROC Second World War two-storey brick visual spotting post at SS886475

Portishead (Somerset) single-storey Bofors tower at ST474766

Purfleet (Essex) First World War blockhouse with roof-top AA gun at TQ538793; Second World War AA magazines at TQ549789;

Quidenham (Norfolk) LAA position with ammunition rollers at TM009915

Rame Peninsula (Cornwall) traces of HAA batteries at St John's Down at SX404530 and at Maker Heights at SX436515

Rose Valley (Moray) bombing decoy blockhouse at NJ111662

Rugby (Warks) LAA holdfast for Bofors gun at SP495768

Rushden (Northants) Consol Shelter *ex situ* at SP956672

Saffron Walden (Essex) 50-person surface air-raid shelter at TL537385

Schoolhill (Aberdeen) CH Radar site NO90-98

Scremerston (Northumberland) CD/CHL Radar site at NU008501

Skipsea (E. Yorks) ROC underground, and brick visual spotting posts at TA176548

Southend (Essex) Butlers Farm HAA site; four 3ft 7in emplacements at TQ898889

Stenigot (Lincs) complete CH Radar site with mast at TF257825

Stone Creek (E. Yorks) HAA Battery at TA239188

Strumble Head (Pembs) CHL Radar site at SM887395

Sutton Bassett (Northants) ROC u'ground and Second World War brick posts at SP777906

Swansea (Glam) AA Operations Room at The Grange at SS612886

Swingate (Kent) CH Radar site with three masts at TR335428

Synah Common Hayling Is (Hants) Second World War HAA Battery at SZ699994

Traquair (Peebles) ROC underground and ORLIT A posts at NT328343

Trimley Heath (Suffolk) 5.25in HAA Battery, built 1945 at TM277360

Ulceby Cross (Lincs) GEE installation at TF405726

Waltham Abbey (Essex) single-storey Bofors tower at TL370022; and First World War AA bty. on summit of hill at TL386024

Warmington (Northants) bombing decoy blockhouse at TL082919

Watnall (Notts) Second World War Filterroom, 12 Fighter Group RAF at SK506454

Weybourne (Norfolk) 5.25in HAA mountings at TG098439 and practice camp

Wibtoft (Warwicks) bombing decoy blockhouse at SP467865

Willenhall (W. Midlands) Second World War decontamination centre at SO965984

Woking (Surrey) type 55402 command post of HAA battery at TQ021566

Wormegay (Norfolk) bombing decoy blockhouse at TF653126

CHAPTER 8: LOGISTICAL SUPPORT

Aberporth (Cards.) rocket test range at SN243518

Ardeer (Ayr) Nobel explosives factory at NS28-40

Ashchurch (Glos) MoD Depot at SO93-33

Avonmouth (Glos) explosives factory at ST520797

Barnham (Norfolk) PAD, postwar atomic weapons store at TL85-79

Bicester (Oxon) Ordnance Depot at SP58-20

Bishopton (Renfrew) explosives factory opened 1937 at NS44-69

Bourn (Cambs) MAP canteen, offices etc. at TL349595

Bridgend & Brackla (Glam) ROFs Second World War at SS92-79 and 916810

Bridgwater (Somerset) Puriton ROF at ST332424 opened 1939

Bulford (Wilts) First World War practice trench system on Beacon Hill at SU19-42

Burghfield (Berks) ROF opened 1942 at approx SU68-68

Caerwent (Gwent) RN Propellant Factory at ST477907

Cardington (Beds) Airship Works Administration Building 1917 at TL075471

Caxton (Cambs) Mobilisation Depot at TL305570

Chorley (Lancs) ROF opened 1938 at SD563208

Croyde Bay (Devon) mock-up of Atlantic Wall defences for training at SS435396

Dalbeattie (Dumfries) Nobel explosives factory at NX848632

Drigg (Cumbria) range quadrant towers of gunnery ranges at SD04-98; ROF site at SD055990

Druridge Bay (Northumberland) quadrant tower of bombing range at NZ274977

Ellesmere (Shrops) Mobilisation Depot at SJ40-30

Elstow (Beds) former ROF No. 16 at TL045441

Erith (G. London) First World War Thames Ammunition Works at TQ53-77

Fakenham (Norfolk) Mobilisation Depot at TF930305

Faldingworth (Lincs) PAD, postwar atomic weapons store at TF02-84/5

Finchale (Co. Durham) ammunition storage at NZ283471

Glascoed (Gwent) ROF opened 1940 at SO34/5-01

Goswick (Northumberland) quadrant towers of bombing range at NU067449 and 051481

Grimsthorpe (Lincs) quadrant tower of bombing range at TF031205

Hankley Common (Surrey) mock-up of Atlantic Wall for training at SU88-41

Hatfield & Stevenage (Herts) post-Second World War de Havilland aircraft and rocket factories with airfield and test facilities at TL209096 and 235230

Haughley Junction (Suffolk) emergency grain silo 1954 at TM042624

Hirwaun (Glam) site of Second World War ROF at SN94-06

Holton Heath (Dorset) naval cordite factory at SY946906

Hooton (Wirral) gatehouse and guard-posts of ROF 10 at SJ34-77

Kirkby (Merseyside) site of ROF at SJ432998

London Colney (G. London) Second World War tank assembly sheds at TL176031

Long Marston (Worcs) former RE Depot at SP15/7-46/7

Marchwood (Hants) magazines at SU396112

Metheringham (Lincs) protected railway control blockhouse at TF076615

Middlewick (Essex) Colchester Garrison rifle range at TM00-22

Ranskill (Notts) traces of ROF at SK678862

Ruddington (Notts) traces of ROF at SK575620

St Boswells (Borders) Nobel/MAP incendiary bomb factory Second World War at NT585295

Shoeburyness (Essex) gunnery range TQ93-84

South Witham (Lincs) bomb storage in Morkery Wood at SK95-18

Norton Fitzwarren (Somerset) former REME Command Depot at ST20-25

Old Dalby (Leics) REME Depot at SK68-23/4

Orfordness (Suffolk) Bomb Ballistic Building at TM445491, Pagodas at 433482

Oundle (Northants) Mobilisation Depot at TL043857

Preston Capes (Northants) quadrant tower of bombing range at SP592550

Priddy's Hard (Hants) former RN Armaments Depot at SU619012

Putney (G. London) protected signal-box at Putney Bridge Station at TQ244759

Queensferry (Flint) First World War explosives factory at SJ328680

Setchey (Norfolk) Mobilisation Depot at TF634146

Spadeadam (Cumbria) missile-testing facility at NY62-74

Steeton (W. Yorks) ROF at SE032448

Stirling (Central) mock-up of Atlantic Wall for training purposes at NN838037

Summerfield (Worcs) explosives factory at SO835735

Swynnerton (Staffs) ROF open 1940s–1950s at SJ350338

Tentsmuir (Fife) quadrant towers of bombing range at NO501260 and 504267

Tern Hill (Shrops) Mobilisation Depot at SJ64-31

Tetbury (Glos) Mobilisation Depot at ST89-93

Thorpe Arch (W. Yorks) ROF at SE450465

Topcliffe (N. Yorks) Mobilisation Depot at SE40-79

Upnor Castle (Kent) RN Armaments Depot at TQ758732

Weedon (Northants) former Ordnance Depot at SP62-59

Weymouth (Dorset) RE Bridging Camp at SY65-77

Whaplode (Lincs) Land Army Hostel at TF318121

Woolwich (G. London) Royal Arsenal at TQ440793

Wrexham (Denbigh) ROF at SJ37/8-48/9

APPENDIX 1

PILLBOX TYPES

INTRODUCTION

The development of the twentieth-century pillbox can be traced back to the free-standing caponier standing in the ditch of a Renaissance town as envisaged by, amongst others, Albrecht Durer in his designs for fortifications, via the blockhouses of the Boer War, and Napoleon's *tours modèles*. A number of Edwardian and late-Victorian coast defence works were provided with concrete block-houses loopholed for musketry. Examples, differing in both shape and size, survive at Renney and Lord Howard's Batteries, Plymouth; at Spurn Point, East Yorkshire; at South Gare, Teesside; and at Warden Point Battery on the Isle of Wight.

PILLBOXES IN THE FIRST WORLD WAR

A number of designs emerged from the Home and Western Fronts. German types were often rectangular with a very thick front face containing a single embrasure for a machine-gun. These either faced the front, or were designed to provide enfilade fire. There were other designs including some with multiple loopholes. British designs were, at least initially as ad hoc as the German ones, each being built as a one-off to meet a particular need, in a particular set of circumstances. The building of the GHQ Line behind the Front in 1917/18, however, necessitated the use of standard models. The Moir pillbox was designed by the Royal Engineers and supplied in kit form to be shipped from Richborough Military Port in Kent, for assembly on site. It is circular, and built of interlocking concrete blocks. A steel dome-shaped roof is supported on iron pillars, providing an all-round field of fire for the machine-gun on its mounting, suspended from the roof. Another common design is an hexagonal pillbox with two embrasures for Vickers machine-guns in alternate faces. Moir pillboxes can still be seen at Ypres and elsewhere, and the hexagonal design near Hazebrouck. At home, there were two common types of pillbox. Many examples of the circular design, constructed of concrete blocks, having four or five loopholes, sometimes set at different heights, and with or without an overhanging roof, can be seen in East Anglia. This was the design, likened to the pharmacist's packaging, from which all such structures were generalised. The other common type was hexagonal with five loopholes *(151)*. Both types had low, steel doors, and, often, steel shutters over the loopholes.

INTERWAR PILLBOX DESIGNS

In the late 1930s, the British army was involved in the construction of two schemes of defence based on pillboxes. From 1938, dozens of pillboxes were built on Malta as anti-beach-landing defences.

151 Rushmere, Suffolk; hexagonal First World War pillbox at TM491870 NB steel doors, and distinctive loophole shape; this is one of a pair, plus another added during the Second World War

They are all different but embody a number of common principles. Some are cubes with two floors and a higher observation turret, probably quite intentionally resembling scaled-down versions of the Knights' Towers which dot the Maltese coastline. Others are low and camouflaged by an outer layer of rocks. Their shapes are determined by their situation, as many are sited on rocky ledges. Different combinations of rifle and machine-gun embrasures give individual strongpoints a wide range both of armament and of manning level. The second theatre in which defences were constructed was the Franco-Belgian border where, due to Belgian sensitivities, the Maginot Line stopped short. Anti-tank ditches and French blockhouses defined the actual line, but, from autumn 1939, defence in depth was provided by British fixed defences which consisted of pillboxes.

PILLBOXES IN THE SECOND WORLD WAR

These pillboxes along the Franco-Belgian frontier, are of a small range of types. A rectangular pillbox contains two Vickers machine-guns mounted on tables side-by-side. A shellproof pillbox, in the shape of a regular hexagon has five loopholes. A third type is a rectangle with half-hexagonal ends, one of whose long faces generally has three loopholes, with a further two or three in the end faces. Many of these pillboxes are grouped in mutually-supporting threes and fours behind the AT ditch. It is pertinent to note here, that there appear to be only a few connections between these pillboxes, and the range designed by the War Office's Fortifications and Works Department 3, for use at home in 1940. The interior dimensions of the shellproof hexagonal pillbox above are identical to those of the FW3 Type 22 bulletproof pillbox, and there are some examples in Fife of a machine-gun pillbox similar to that above. Otherwise there appears to be little link. Given that II Corps built pillboxes to RE designs in France, in 1939-40, it appears odd that the same troops then built pillboxes in East Anglia in 1940-41, to an entirely different set of designs provided by FW3. However there is a strong resemblance between the hexagonal shellproof pillbox in France, and a shellproof hexagonal pillbox which is common on the Eastern Command Line, and may represent the locally-designed

CRE1113. This originated in the RE office at Eastern Command's Colchester HQ which may have included RE personnel from II Corps who had served in France, and been evacuated from Dunkirk. The officer responsible for building BEF pillboxes around the Cysoing area, south of Lille, especially the double machine-gun post with modifications which enabled the section corporal a better view of approaching targets, was captured and spent the War in German PoW camps. The BEF designs can be seen all along the frontier from Lille to Montmedy, following the line of the N43 road.

This following schedule attempts to list the most commonly-found pillbox types in Britain, variations on these types, and some of the one-off derivatives, or totally unrelated examples. For unique specimens the ngr is given, and where the only known examples are found at a single location, this is given.

KEY TO PILLBOX TYPES

NB: pillboxes are here described with base as 1, then clockwise numbering of other faces; the base is usually the side containing the entrance.

1 Bullet-proof (wall thickness 12-24in/30-61cm) regular hexagons

1a   Type FW3/22 *(152)*: length of side: external 7ft 6in (2m); internal 6ft (1.8m)
         variations/details: porch/blast wall; anti-ricochet wall; loophole design; number of
         loopholes especially in entry face; shuttering material; skirt; open annexe; provision for
         specific weapons: mg, AA lmg, or AT rifle; shutters, doors etc; raft, platform or height
         difference; camouflage
1b   pillbox with second storey or open roof platform (airfield types)

152 Castle Donnington, Leicestershire; type FW3/22 pillbox with low entry, and two pistol-loops, at SK445264; Appendix I: 1a

1c	pillbox with 6 loopholes and low entrance (airfield type)
1d	pillbox with 2 loopholes in some sides eg 3 & 6, or 5 & 6; at Polebrook (Northants) airfield
1e	pillbox with corner loopholes; at Brooklands (Surrey) airfield, TQ070630
1f	Eastern Command Line pillbox ?Type CRE1094: with or without open central pit for mounting LAA lmg; with tunnel entrance and 6 loopholes; exterior wall-length 9ft (2.7m)
1g	pillbox as Type 22, shorter sides: 5ft (1.5m) externally, would fit inside a Type FW3/22 pillbox; at West Raynham (Norfolk) airfield, TF836251
1h	pillbox as Type 22, longer sides: 10ft (3m) externally; at Llandow (Glamorgan) airfield

2 Bullet-proof (wall thickness 12-24in/30-61cm) irregular hexagons

2a	truncated Type 22 with shorter faces 2 & 6 without loopholes; as in Northumberland and elsewhere
2b	Type FW3/24: length of side: external 1 13' 6' (4.1m), 2-6 7' 6' (2.3m); internal 1 10' (3m), 2-6 5' (1.5m); normally five loopholes for lmgs, and a pistol-loop each side of entry; as on GHQ Line, and Tame/Trent/Dove Line, and elsewhere
	variations/details: height (ROF version); shuttering materials; porch; shutters; low loopholes for AT rifles; low entry with sixth lmg loophole over; second storey
2c	Outer London Line version as Type 24, but low entry, low L-shaped blast wall, and sixth loophole over
2d	pillboxes with proportions of Type 24 but larger dimensions; as in Suffolk, and elsewhere
2e	lozenge-shaped pillbox, two long and four short sides, lengths of sides 12ft (3.7m) and 6ft (1.8m); different loophole configurations; as in Northumbria
2e(i)	as 2e but rifle loops in long walls and lmg loops in short ones; as general in Holderness
2e(ii)	as 2e but larger; lengths of sides 19ft (5.8m) and 9ft (2.7m); one lmg loophole and nine for rifles
2e(iii)	as 2e but all sides 8ft (2.4m) externally; one lmg loophole in each face; as on Southern Region Railway sites, particularly Thames bridges
2e(iv)	as 2e but fewer loopholes; as in South Wales
2f	mg post based on lozenge-shape with embrasures in 3 and 5 which are 8ft (2.4m) long, as are 2 and 6; 4 is 6ft (1.8m); an integral porch extension,13ft (4m) long, with two entrances, forms side 1; as on Yorkshire coast; often referred to as 'eared' pillbox
2g	pillbox with lengths of sides: 1 10ft (3m), 2 and 6 12ft (3.7m), 3-5 5ft (1.5m); 5 rifle loopholes and mount for 20mm Oerlikon on roof; at Stoke Holy Cross (Norfolk) radar site
2h	pillbox with 3 long 12ft (3.7m) sides, and 3 short 4ft 6in (1.4m) sides; two loopholes in each long side; loophole or entry in each short; LAA on roof; as on radar sites e.g. Stenigot (Lincolnshire), and Ventnor (Isle of Wight)
2j	pillbox with lengths of sides: 1 8ft 6in (2.6m), 2 & 6 9ft 3in (2.8m), 3-5 3ft 9in (1.1m); rifle loops in front three faces only; as on Suffolk coast
2k	pillbox with 1 side 16ft (4.9m) and 5 sides 6ft 6in (2m); lmg loopholes in five faces, rifle loops in four angles, and 2 rifle loops in base; as at Barrow-in-Furness *(153)*
2m	as 2a with 90° base angles and rectangular open annexes; loopholes in sides 2-6; as at ROFs
2m(i)	as 2m but smaller; as on Cornish coast *(154)*

153 Barrow-in-Furness, Cumbria; a type of pillbox confined to this important dockyard town, this particular example being at SD221694; Appendix I: 2k

154 Sennen Cove, Cornwall; a pillbox at SW34-26; it is D-shaped with an open rear annexe; Appendix I: 2m(i)

155 Weybourne, Norfolk; a beach-defence pillbox at TG097440; the irregular loophole pattern allows machine-guns to be given fixed firing lines to enfilade the beach; Appendix I: 3b(ii)

3 Shell-proof (wall thickness 24-55in/61-140cm) regular hexagons

3a	Type FW3/22(s): same interior dimensions as 1a; wall thickness 42' (107cm); exterior wall length 10' (3m); five lmg loops in sides 2-6, and one pistol loop beside entry; Y-shaped anti-ricochet wall; as on GHQ Line Red
3a(i)	as 3a but rear wall 12ft (30cm), shortening sides 2 & 6 to 7ft (2.1m); and extending base to 12ft 6in (3.8m); as on GHQ Line Red and Blue
3a(ii)	as 3a but wall thickness up to 48in (1.2m) increasing external wall length to 10ft (3m); (airfield type)
3a(iii)	as 3a(ii) but with external wall-length 11ft (3.4m)
3a(iv)	as 3a but thickened to 55in (1.4m)
3b	Eastern Command Line pillbox ?Type CRE1113: wall thickness 42in (107cm); length of side 7ft 6in (2.3m) internally, and 11ft 6in (3.5m) externally; six lmg loopholes; low, roofed entry; straight anti-ricochet wall diagonally from 1 to 4
3b(i)	as 3b but with open central pit for LAA mounting; as on Eastern Command Line
3b(ii)	as 3b but different combinations of loopholes for rifles and lmgs; as on Essex coast and elsewhere *(155)*
3b(iii)	as 3b but loopholes for lmgs in five faces; blastwall in front of entry; as on Eastern Command Line
3c	pillbox increased from a wall thickness of 15in (38cm) to 49-53in (1.2-1.3m) with side lengths 12ft 10in externally and 7ft 6in internally; (airfield type)
3d	as 3b(i) but external wall length of 13ft 6in (4.1m); (airfield type)
3d(i)	as 3d but external wall-length of 15ft (4.6m); airfield type

4 Shell-proof (wall-thickness 24-42in/61-107cm) irregular hexagons

4a Type FW3/24(s) pillbox: wall-thickness 42in (107cm); wall-lengths: 1 16ft (4.9m), 2 & 6 10ft (3m), 3-5 9ft (2.7m); five lmg loopholes in faces 2-6; pistol loop each side of entry; Y-shaped anti-ricochet wall; chamfered roof on all sides except base; as on GHQ Line in Essex

 variations/details: porches (open, covered, L-shaped), blastwalls; raft, plinth, second-storey, raised or sunken doorways; shuttering materials; camouflage; design of loophole; base angles either obtuse or right-angles; different dimensions as follows:

4a(i) 1 20ft 9in (6.3m), 2 & 6 11ft 9in (3.6m), 3-5 8ft 6in (2.6m) as on GHQ Line Sussex

4a(ii) 1 18ft (5.9m), 2 & 6 11ft 3in (3.4m), 3-5 9ft 3in (2.8m), as on GHQ Line Green

4a(iii) 1 17ft 6in (5.3m), 2 & 6 9ft 9in (3m), 3 & 5 9ft (2.7m), 4 8ft 6in (2.6m) GHQ Line Kent

4a(iv) 1 17ft 3in (5.2m), 2-6 10ft 6in (3.2m) as on GHQ Line Sussex

4a(v) 1 17ft (5.2m), 2 & 6 13ft (4m), 3 & 5 9ft (2.7m), 4 10ft (3m), E Cmd. Line Norfolk

4a(vi) 1 21ft (6.4m), 2 & 6 12ft (3.7m), 3-5 8ft 6in (2.6m), as on Kent coast

4a(vii) 1 16ft 6in (5m), 2 & 6 10ft 8in (3.3m), 3-5 9ft (2.7m), as on GHQ Line Green

4a(viii) 1 16ft 6in (5m), 2 & 6 10ft 6in (3.2m), 3 & 5 9ft 6in (2.9m), 4 8ft (2.4m), as on GHQ Line Cambridgeshire

4a(ix) 1 16ft (4.9m), 2 & 6 10ft (3m), 3 & 5 9ft 6in (2.9m), 4 8ft 6in (2.6m), Eastern Command Line Suffolk

4a(x) 1 17ft (5.2m), 2 & 6 11ft (3.4m), 3 & 5 9ft 6in (2.9m), 4 9in (2.7m), as on Eastern Command Line Cambridgeshire

4a(xi) 1 19ft (5.8m), 2 & 6 15ft (4.6m), 3 & 5 10ft (3m), 4 8ft (2.4m) as on Fife Line

4b as 4a but base wall-thickness reduced to 12-15in (30-38cm), giving wall lengths: 1 19ft (5.8m), 2 & 6 6ft 6in (2m), 3 & 5 11ft (3.4m), 4 9ft 9in (3m), as on GHQ Line Sussex

4b(i) 1 16ft (4.9m), 2-6 8ft (2.4m); 4 loopholes; as on Norwich defences

4b(ii) 1 18ft (5.5m), 2 & 6 7ft (2.1m), 3-5 9ft (2.7m); 3 loopholes; as on Sussex River Ouse Line

4c front-half only: 1 25ft 6in (7.8m), 3 & 5 12ft (3.7m), 4 8ft 6in (2.6m) GHQ Line

4d Type 350/40 as 4a but minor differences; dimensions as follows: 1 17ft 6in (5.3m), 2 & 6 11ft 3in (3.4m), 3-5 9ft 6in (2.9m) as on GHQ Line Norfolk and Cambridgeshire

4e pillbox with mg embrasure in each of five faces, and two in base above low entrance; all embrasures with deep stepping; Y-shaped anti-ricochet wall; at Duxford (Cambridgeshire) airfield

4f mg post with embrasures with Turnbull mounts in 3 & 5; sunken entry with L-shaped blast wall; external dimensions: 1 27ft (8.2m), 2 & 6 8ft (2.4m), 3 & 5 12ft (3.7m), 4 6ft (1.8m); as on GHQ Line Kent

4g mg post with embrasures backed by table mountings in 3 & 5; entry with blast wall; external dimensions: 1 24ft (7.3m), 2 & 6 7ft 6in (2.3m), 3 & 5 11ft (3.4m), 4 10ft (3m); at Blythburgh and elsewhere on Suffolk coast

5 Shellproof (wall thickness 24-54in (61-137cm)) squares and rectangles

5a post for Vickers mg; FW3 plan 1936, modified c1940; TL62 in Somerset, also described in 1940 document as FW3/27; externally 13ft 6in x 14ft 6in (4.1 x 4.4m); chamfered front corners; side entry with blast wall; deep-stepped embrasure in front wall backed by table mounting for mg; one or two loops in other sides; wall-thickness 42in (107cm)

 variations/details: raised on raft or sunken; integral blast wall; additional loopholes in sides or blast wall; sunken entry; second mg embrasure; anti-ricochet wall, often loopholed to cover entry

5a(i)   two units joined at 45°, as on north Norfolk coast

5b   pillbox for 3 lmgs; once described as FW3/27a; external measurements: 15ft 6in x 14ft (4.7 x 4.3m); entry with loopholed blast wall; wall-thickness 42in (107cm); as on GHQ Line in Eastern Command

variations/details: integral porch/entry; extension to, or absence of blast wall; number of rifle:lmg loopholes; thinner rear walls

5b(i)   as 5b but 15ft 6in x 12ft 6in (4.7 x 3.8m); as on GHQ Line

5b(ii)   as 5b but 14ft 3in x 14ft (4.3 x 4.2m); as on GHQ Line

5c   mg post for 3 mgs; 3 deep, stepped embrasures with Turnbull mounts; wall-thickness: 54in (137cm); external dimensions: 17ft 9in x 15ft 6in (5.4 x 4.7m); at Duxford (Cambridgeshire) airfield

5d   mg post for two Lewis guns; wall thickness 42in (107cm) in two forward faces, and 18in (45cm) on reverse; crosswall; as on North Norfolk coast

5d(i)   L-shaped mg post with single stepped embrasure; wall-thickness 24in (61cm); as on North Norfolk and Northumberland coasts

5e   post for two mgs mounted on continuous shelf, using adjacent, stepped embrasures; external dimensions 23ft x 17ft (7 x 5.2m), wall-thickness 48in (1.2m); one lmg loophole to side; sunken entry down steps, with blast wall; as on Fife Line

5f   mg post with external dimensions 19ft 6in x 14ft (5.9 x 4.3m), wall thickness 36in (91cm); sunken, roofed entry with blast wall; wide, shallow embrasures, one next to entry, one in each end wall, two in other long side; chamfered concrete roof; as on East Sussex coast

5g   mg post with external dimensions 23ft x 15ft 6in (7 x 4.7m), wall thickness 30in (76cm); 6 wide embrasures backed by table mountings; loophole in each forward corner; entry in end wall; as at Rye Harbour (East Sussex)

5g(i)   as 5g but embrasures reduced in height to narrow slits; same location

5g(ii)   as 5g but all but one embrasure blocked; as at Camber (East Sussex)

5h   pillbox for 5 lmgs; external dimensions 23ft x 15ft 6in (7 x 4.7m), wall thickness 42in (107cm); entry and lmg loophole in one long side, one in each end wall, two in other long side; at Hayling Island (Hampshire) SU720038

5j   pillbox to Drawing No.390 August 1941; external dimensions 30ft x 14ft 9in (9 x 4.5m), wall thickness 42in (107cm); two internal cross-walls and bunks; two loopholes with Turnbull mounts; two barrel-baths built in; 3 alternative layouts provided, all with same provision; designed for airfield defence; no examples identified

5k   pillbox with external dimensions 21ft x 16ft (6.4 x 4.9m), wall-thickness 42in (107cm); 7 assorted widely splayed loopholes for a mixture of rifles and lmgs; two slightly different examples at Ludham (Norfolk) airfield

5m   pillbox with 3 forward-facing loopholes in 42in (107cm) thick wall; other sides 15in (38cm); externally 16ft 6in x 8ft (5 x 2.4m); at SU739590 on GHQ Line

5n   square pillbox with lmg loopholes in two sides, widely splayed loophole with central pillar in third side, and entry in fourth; 16ft x 16ft (4.9 x 4.9m) externally; wall thickness 48in (122cm); at TR314407 Dover (Kent)

6 Bullet-proof (wall-thickness 12-24in/30-61cm) squares and rectangles

6a   Type FW3/23 pillbox *(156)*; square, roofed chamber with 3 loopholes, entry down steps from open annexe with LAA mounting; external dimensions 14ft x 9ft (4.3 x 2.7m) overall, wall thickness 15in (38cm); annexe entered by doorway, or over solid wall via rungs in outside wall

variations/details: two loops per side; blast wall; raised on plinth

6a(i)   two chambers with open bay in between; all found in Lincolnshire

156 Boston, Lincolnshire; type FW3/23 pillbox at TF327433; NB the post in the annexe, for a light anti-aircraft machine-gun; Appendix I: 6a

6a(ii)	as 6a(i) but roofed; extra loopholes; with or without roofed porch
6a(iii)	as 6a(i) but mg embrasure in one or more sides
6a(iv)	as 6a(i) but central, open bay projects; at Newton (Notts) airfield
6b	pillbox with external dimensions 15ft 6in-19ft x 8ft-9ft (4.7-5.8 x 2.4-2.7m), wall thickness 15in (38cm); various combinations of rifle and mg embrasures backed by integral shelves/platforms in two compartments, divided by cross-wall or entrance passage; porch entries; as found throughout the North-East
6c	pillbox with external dimensions 15ft 3in-15ft 9in x 10ft 3in-10ft 9in (4.6-4.8 x 3.1-3.3m), wall thickness 12-15in (30-38cm); various combinations of rifle and mg loops backed by shelves; divided into two compartments by lengthways wall; as in northern Northumberland
6d	pillbox with external dimensions 11ft-14ft x 9ft (3.4-4.3 x 2.7m), wall thickness 12-15in (30-38cm); covered square chamber with 3 loopholes for lmgs, and open square, rectangular or L-shaped entry annexe, reached by built-in rungs; as on Tywyn beach, Gwynedd
6e	mg post with external dimensions 11ft 9in x 9ft (3.6 x 2.7m), wall thickness 15in (38cm); mg embrasure in either side or front wall, backed by table-mount; two lmg loops in two other walls, entry with blast wall in fourth; at Weston-super-Mare (Somerset) airfield
6f	mg post with external dimensions 14ft x 9ft (4.3 x 2.7m), wall thickness 15in (38cm); two mg embrasures with table mountings in short walls enfilade beach, along lines of AT blocks; as on Moray coast
6g	Four Compartment Defence Post No. 2843; external dimensions 14ft 3in (4.3m) square, wall thickness 24in (61cm); divided into compartments, lmg loop in each, by cross-walls; no example identified; for Scottish Command
6h	pillbox with sloping roof; one loophole in each side; doorway; solid anti-ricochet wall; examples of two sizes: one is 13ft 6in x 10ft (4.1 x 3m), the other 10ft 6in x 7ft 3in (3.2 x 2.2m), wall thickness 18in (46cm) in both; some are raised on plinths; as on River Dove, Derbyshire

157 Felixstowe, Suffolk; this style of pillbox is confined to the Suffolk coast; this example stands at TM317364; Appendix I: 6j

6j   pillbox built by 558 Field Coy. RE on Suffolk coast *(157)*; shuttered in concrete blocks with prefabricated loopholes; external dimensions are 12ft 6in x 12ft 6in (3.8 x 3.8m), wall thickness 15in (38cm); usually two loopholes in each of 3 sides with one in the entrance side, all with shelves; no anti-ricochet wall

         variations/details: L-shaped blast wall protecting entry, sometimes with loophole, sometimes half-height and chamfered to give wider field of fire; open annexe with LAA mounting added to one side; integral porch; three loops in one side

6k   Type FW3/26 pillbox with four rifle loops and a doorway; it measures 10ft x 10ft (3 x 3m) externally, with wall thickness 15-18in (38-46cm)

         variations/details: smaller or larger dimensions, 8ft-12ft (2.4-3.6m); brick or wood shuttering; low-level or full-height doors; only 3 loopholes;

6k(i)   pillbox 9ft (2.7m) square with two loopholes with Lewis gun mountings, another with three similar; two have circular, open annexes for LAA mounts, a third has an L-shaped blast wall; at Wartling (East Sussex) radar site

6m   pillbox with external dimensions 15ft 6in x 11ft 6in (4.7 x 3.5m), wall thickness 18in (46cm); loophole with Turnbull mount in each side; straight anti-ricochet wall lengthways; false pitched roof as camouflage; at High Ercall (Shropshire) airfield

6m(i)   as 6m but 12ft x 8ft (3.6 x 2.4m), and only 3 loops; as in Staffordshire

6m(ii)   as 6m but 10ft 6in x 6ft 3in (3.2 x 1.9m), and 2 loops in sides; at Schoolhill (Aberdeenshire) radar site

6n   open pillboxes with walls 4ft (1.2m) high, and overhanging slab roof supported on corner pillars; external dimensions 8ft x 8ft (2.4 x 2.4m); wall thickness 12-15in (30-38cm); as in Cheshire and Lancashire coast

6n(i)   as 6n but 13ft x 10ft (4 x 3m) externally; as in Cheshire

6n(ii)   as 6n but one curved corner; as in Cheshire

6n(iii)   similar to 6n but solid corner pillars and interval supports in sides; the most common (10 out of 20) roof-slab size is 17ft (5.2m) square; most are square but some are rectangular; wall thickness 12in (30cm), as in Dover

6p   pillbox 13ft (4m) square, wall thickness 15in (38cm), with loopholes in four sides and three corners; entry adjacent to fourth corner; L-shaped brick-built LAA position on roof, reached by rungs fixed into wall; at Bempton (E. Yorks) radar site

6q   pillbox 11ft x 9ft (3.6 x 2.7m) externally, wall thickness 15in (38cm), with loopholes in four sides and at four corners; sunken entry at one corner

     6q(i)   as 6q but two loops in two long sides; at Bramcote (Warks) airfield

6r   two rectangular pillboxes joined as pairs; each one measures 28ft x 12ft (8.5 x 3.7m), wall thickness 24in (61cm), and is divided by a cross-wall into two compartments each with a loophole; the two are joined by a passageway, the whole sharing a roof-slab 28ft (8.5m) square; also a single nearby

     6r(i)   as 6r but units not equal length; porches link; also singles; as at ROFs

6s   RUCK pillbox consists of loopholed concrete Stanton-shelter sections bolted together on a rectangular base; externally 12ft x 6ft (3.7 x 1.8m); many built in North-East England, one stands in Nottingham

6t   ?STENT prefabricated pillbox consists of hollow concrete sections bolted together and filled with rubble and poured concrete; 13ft x 13ft (4m x 4m), wall thickness 24in (61cm); loophole in each side with one next to door

     variations/details: double version; L-shaped blast wall; mg table backs one loophole; used throughout England

6u   L-shaped mg post 14ft (4.3m) square with 5ft x 4ft (1.5 x 1.2m) corner taken out; mg embrasure backed by table mounting in front wall; loophole and entry in rear; wall thickness 24in (61cm); 9in (23cm) thick concrete slab roof; at Selsey (West Sussex) airfield

     6u(i)   L-shaped pillbox; main chamber 11ft 6in x 12ft (3.5 x 3.7m), wall thickness 18in (46cm), with one lmg loophole and two rifle loops in each of three sides; integral, full-height annexe attached to fourth wall, 5ft x 7ft (1.5 x 2.1m), wall thickness 15in (38cm), with three rifle loops and an entry below one of them; at High Street (Suffolk) radar site

6v   pillbox measuring 18ft 6in x 9ft 6in (5.6 x 2.9m), wall thickness 15in (38cm); three loopholes in each long side; loophole and doorway in each end wall; low blast wall outside each entry forming rectangular mortar-pit or LAA position; as in Lincolnshire coast and Teesside

6w   pillbox designed for Royal Marines; 13ft 6in (4.1m) square; four loopholes in each of three sides, entry in fourth; cruciform anti-ricochet wall; Hampshire

6x   pillbox designed for Royal Navy; 9ft x 9ft 6in (2.7 x 2.9m) with a loophole in each side; attached is an annexe 19ft x 7ft (5.8 x 2.1m) containing a LAA mount, and low entry below loophole; as at naval bases

6y   guard-post used by RN and ROFs; 6ft x 7ft (1.8 x 2.1m) with three or four loops; low entry with half-height blast wall, often roofed below loophole level

     6y(i)   as 6y but integral blast wall to full-height forming porch

     6y(ii)   as 6y but with one face half-hexagonal

     6y(iii)   as 6y but 10ft (3m) square, with open platform on top for LAA mount, reached by ladder attached to side;

6z   mine-watchers' post, used by RN; 8ft 6in x 8ft (2.6 x 2.4m) externally, wall thickness 18in (45cm); two wide openings across front corners; loophole and entry in rear wall; some have additional central loophole in front wall; used across Britain

7 Trapezoidal pillboxes (all one-offs)

7a   shellproof pillbox with two lmg loops in each of three sides, and entry with blast wall in fourth; three sides 12ft 6in (3.8m) and one 16ft (4.9m); wall thickness 42in (128cm); on GHQ Line at SU862465

7b   bulletproof pillbox with two rifle loops in each of three sides, and entry in rear wall; three sides of 12ft (3.7m), and one of 24ft (7.3m); built into bank at side of road, with short spur-walls; at Alford (Aberdeenshire) NJ528063

7c   bulletproof pillbox with two rifle loops in front face, and one in each of others; entry in back wall; front face 12ft 6in (3.8m), two sides 8ft 3in (2.5m), and rear face 20ft 9in (6.3m); at Mendham (Suffolk) TM269829

7d   bulletproof pillbox similar to 6n(iii) with diagonally set corner pillars; the front face has one wide embrasure, there are two in each side, and another, plus pistol-loop and entry in back wall; front face 9ft (2.7m), sides 11ft 6in (3.5m) and back 15ft 9in (4.8m); wall thickness 24in (61cm) and roof-slab measures 22ft x 17ft (6.7 x 5.2m); at Dover (Kent) TR306406

8 Pentagonal pillboxes

8a   Drawing No. 391, August 1941; regular pentagon with 16ft (4.9m) sides; two versions each with only two loopholes fitted with Turnbull mounts; 3-way anti-ricochet wall, bunks, barrel baths; low entry; wall thickness 42in (107cm); designed for airfield defence; only one example known, at Catfoss (East Yorkshire) TA134477

8b   double mg post with two wide, stepped embrasures, backed by table mountings in front faces, and entry covered by blast wall in back wall; cross-wall divides interior into two compartments; front walls 14ft (4.3m), sides 10ft (3m), base 16ft (4.9m); wall thickness 45in (114cm); chamfered corners; at East Wretham (Norfolk) airfield

     8b(i)   as 8b but three embrasures with table-mountings and Turnbull mounts, and two rifle loops; entry with blast wall in rear wall; wall thickness 21in (53cm); higher structure than 8b; at Honington (Norfolk) airfield

8c   pillbox with four lmg loops, rear wall with entry protected by full-length blast wall with two rifle loops; 2 front walls 9ft (2.7m), 2 side walls 7ft (2.1m), back wall 18ft (5.5m); wall thickness 48in (122cm); on GHQ Line TQ523260

8d   pillbox with four loopholes with Turnbull mounts; two entrances in base angles, curved base wall 8ft (2.4m) long; other four walls 10ft (3m); magazine built on interior of base with extended anti-ricochet wall; wall thickness 24in (61cm); at Alton Barnes (Wilts) airfield

8e   pillbox with three or four rifle loops and entry in side wall; base wall 11ft 3in (3.4m), 2 side walls 8ft (2.4m), and 2 front walls 6ft 6in (2m); wall thickness 15in (38cm); at Lichfield (Staffordshire) airfield but on Canal defence line

9 Octagonal pillboxes

9a   Type FW3/27; regular octagon with 11ft (4.4m) sides; lmg loopholes in each of seven sides, with loopholed porch on eighth; open, central platform for observation or LAA mounting; wall thickness 30in (76cm); as on Outer London Defence Line

     9a(i)   as 9a but 10ft (3m) side, and enclosed porch; wall thickness 18in (46cm); exterior locker; as on radar sites and airfields in Scotland

     9a(ii)   as 9a but 7ft (2.1m) side; LAA holdfast on roof; wall thickness 18in (46cm); at Windrush (Glos) airfield SP182119

     9a(iii)   as 9a(ii) but with no central platform; one face curved; seven loopholes, one with solid semi-circular mg table-mounting; at Oulton Street (Norfolk) airfield TG151278

     9a(iv)   as 9a(iii) but loophole over low entrance, eight straight sides of 7ft 6in (2.3m), and no mg table; at Horsham St Faith (Norfolk) airfield TG228130

9b   pillbox designed for use on sea walls; two long sides 18ft 6in (5.6m), and six sides of 6ft (1.8m); 10 loopholes for rifles; cruciform anti-ricochet walls; entry half-way along one long side; wall thickness 15in (38cm); Essex coast

9b(i)   as 9b but split in half by cross-wall; separate entrance on opposite long sides for each discrete compartment;

9b(ii)   as 9b(i) but two halves at different levels

9c   pillbox with two long sides 21ft (6.4m) and six sides of 10ft (3m); there are loopholes with Turnbull mounts in all sides with an extra one in one long side; the other long side has a tunnel entrance with roof over; cross-walls divide the interior into three compartments; at Lichfield (Staffs) airfield SK150121

9d   pillbox with four long sides 20ft 6in (6.2m) and four short ones 7ft (2.1m); two entrances on one long side protected by pentice; wide, stepped loops with Turnbull mounts in limited number of faces, long or short: minimum two, maximum five; wall thickness 30in (76cm); at Newton and Tollerton (Nottinghamshire) airfields

9e   irregular octagon with sides (starting with the entrance) 4ft 6in (1.4m), 16ft (4.9m), 8ft (2.4m), 8ft (2.4m), 8ft (2.4m), 14ft (4.3m), 8ft (2.4m) and 12ft (3.7m); there are two lmg loopholes in each long side, and one in each of three short sides; in addition, three sides have low-level loops for AT rifles; wall thickness 36in (91cm); at Deal (Kent), TR370554

9f   pillbox with two long sides of 16ft (4.9m) and 14ft (4.3m), and six short sides of 8ft (2.4m); one short side has the entrance, and there are two deeply stepped embrasures, fitted with Turnbull mounts, in each long side, and one in each of three short ones; a cross-wall divides the interior into two compartments; at Debden (Essex) airfield, TL573344

9g   pillbox with 12 assorted loopholes; two long sides 12ft 9in (3.9m) each with three loopholes, 2 end walls 7ft (2.1m) each with a mg loop, 4 angled walls 3ft 6in (1.1m) each with one rifle loophole; protected sunken entry with loophole above; long anti-ricochet wall; at Allerton, Liverpool SJ414855

10 Gunhouses

10a   Type FW3/28a Twin; designed for 2-pounder AT gun; there are embrasures in two adjacent faces, but only one may be used at a time; externally 26ft 3in x 27ft (7.9 x 8.1m); alongside each AT position is a lmg position; other lmg loops and entrance in other two sides; wall thickness 42in (107cm); as on GHQ Line Red and Blue

10b   Type FW3/28a; designed for 2-pounder AT gun; chamber for AT gun, and loopholes for four or more lmgs; externally 27ft x 19ft (8.2 x 5.8m); wall thickness 42in (107cm); as on GHQ Line

10b(i)   as 10b but fitted for 6-pounder Hotchkiss QF gun, with narrower embrasure and pedestal with fixing bolts (9 or 12); as on GHQ Line
variations/details: loophole configuration, often two lmg loops in one short side; blast walls with and without loopholes; absence of cross-wall; substitution of spigot mortar for 6-pounder; conversion to infantry pillbox by blocking gun embrasure and inserting loopholes instead

10b(ii)   ?CRE1116 designed by CRE, Colchester, for use on Eastern Command Line; apparently indistinguishable from 10b(i)

10c   Type FW3/28; designed for 2-pounder AT gun; single chamber with gun embrasure and usually two lmg loopholes; externally 20ft x 19ft (6.1 x 5.8m), wall thickness 42in (107cm); as on GHQ Line

10c(i)   as 10c but fitted for 6-pounder Hotchkiss QF gun, with narrower embrasure and pedestal with fixing bolts; as on GHQ Line and Eastern Command Line
variations/details: side entry; conversion to infantry pillbox; blast wall

10d   gunhouse for 6-pounder Hotchkiss QF; TL55 in Somerset; also appears in Suffolk, and on Worcestershire Avon Line; circular, hexagonal or D-shaped pit with overhead cover; canopy semi-cicular, half-hexagonal, hexagonal or rectangular; gun mounted on steel or

158 Pulborough, West Sussex; an open-backed, concrete, field gun emplacement, around 20 examples of which were built in Sussex; this one is at TQ040188; Appendix I: 10e

concrete pedestal with fixing bolts; in some examples a central pillar supports the canopy at the front of the pit

10d(i)   as 10d but no canopy, just a circular or hexagonal pit; as on the GHQ Line, and at Corton (Suffolk) TM551955

NB also examples of just the concrete pedestal in isolation, presumably once supported by fieldworks; as in Kent and elsewhere

10e   shelter for field gun *(158)*; roofed, open-backed, half-hexagonal concrete shelter with embrasure in front wall; externally front wall 13ft (4m), 2 sides 15ft 6in (4.7m), and back 25ft (7.6m); wall thickness 45in (114cm); possibly for French/US 75mm gun, said to have been for 25-pounder gun; used in W. Sussex

10f   gunhouse for field gun; large stepped embrasure in front face, and wide rear entrance to admit gun; 3 front walls 12ft (3.7m), 2 sides 13ft (4m), and back wall 29ft (8.8m) with 8ft (2.4m) opening; on the GHQ Line, a number of these gunhouses in Aldershot Command have different appearances, but are basically alike; wall thickness 48in (122cm)

10f(i)   as 10f but horseshoe-shaped; open front 10ft (3m) across, 2 straight sides 13ft (4m), and curved back wall with entry, *c.*40ft (12.2m); roof carried across front on steel girder; bench built into interior walls; wall thickness 36in (91cm); one example in Dover (Kent) at TR318430

10f(ii)   gunhouse for field gun with open front 9ft (2.7m), 2 faces 8ft (2.4m), 2 sides 11ft (3.4m), and back wall 22ft (6.7m), with entry down steps and blast wall; only access for gun through front; concrete pillars support gabled roof as camouflage; wall thickness 24in (61cm); at Ellastone (Derbys) SK120424

10g   gunhouse for 75mm gun; central chamber 10ft x 13ft (3 x 4m); to each side, magazine and crew-room, each 8ft (2.4m) square, entered down three steps; canopy over gun position; wall thickness 15in-18in (38-46cm); used on south coast

10h   gunhouse for 2-pounder AT gun; main chamber 19ft x 17ft (5.8 x 5.2m); open front under canopy, two lmg loops in side walls; wall thickness 42in (107cm); access for gun through rear wall; attached to rear, open annexe 10ft x 19ft (3 x 5.8m) with LAA mount on higher platform; wall thickness 15in (38cm); at Inskip (Lancashire) SD477378

10j   open-fronted rectangular gunhouse for field gun 12ft x 13ft (3.7 x 4m), wall thickness 18in (46cm); two rifle loops in each side, one loop and entry in rear wall; overhanging concrete slab roof; at Garstang (Lancs) SD485475

10k   rectangular gunhouse for field gun with embrasure in front, and open-backed; externally 18ft x 21ft (5.5 x 6.4m); half-hexagonal projection on one side; wall thickness 54in (137cm); at Weybourne (Norfolk) TG098433

10m   circular gunhouse built by Mowlem for 6-pounder Hotchkiss QF gun on GHQ Line in Surrey; cf. 11a; external diameter 18ft (5.5m); embrasure with pedestal and fixing bolts, with lmg loophole alongside; wide entry opposite; at East Shalford (Surrey) TQ012475

10n   rectangular gunhouse for 6-pounder Hotchkiss QF gun; chamber *c*.12ft x 16ft (3.7 x 4.9m) entered in rear corner down steps with overhead cover and raised to prevent flooding; pedestal with fixing bolts; only two out of 19 such emplacements remain in Northumberland at Bamburgh NU178355, and at Lynemouth NZ314895

10p   gunhouse for field gun; entered down sloping ramp at right-angles to chamber for gun; chamber measuring 24ft (7.3m) long, and 10ft (3m) wide where the ramp turns, tapers to 7ft (2.1m) wide internally at the embrasure; one recess on each side wall; outside Newhaven Fort (East Sussex) TQ450002

11 Circular and rounded pillboxes

11a   shellproof pillbox built by Mowlem on the GHQ Line in Surrey; this is based on the FW3/24 but built using curved shuttering; this gives a circular pillbox with 19ft (5.8m) diameter but with a squared-off base of 14ft (4.3m) with entry and two rifle loops; there are five lmg loops in the curved part; wall thickness 42in (107cm); cf. 10m

11b   D-shaped pillbox with base 15ft (4.6m) and curved face on a diameter of 15ft (4.6m); wall thickness 15in (38cm); four loops in the face backed by continuous shelf, entry down steps at one end of base; at Dover (Kent)

11c   circular stone-built pillboxes with uneven stones set on end around top; low entry with blastwall; two or three loopholes set irregularly and at different heights; one example has open firing platform attached; diameter 16ft (4.9m), wall thickness 24in (61cm); at Holyhead (Anglesey)

11d   circular open pillbox with thick roof-slab supported on 4 pillars; 10ft (3m) in diameter, wall thickness 15in (38cm), roof-slab 24in (61cm) thick; near River Severn crossing (Gwent) at ST504873

11e   circular pillbox with 6 loopholes at one level, and 5 of different design alternating at a higher level; curved half-height entrance tunnel extending a third of the circumference of the pillbox; diameter 10ft 9in (3.3m), 15in (38cm) wall thickness; at West Raynham (Norfolk) airfield

11e(i)   similar to 11e but lower with only one set of loopholes, and smaller entrance; at Bettws Newydd (Gwent) SO353058

11f   Type FW3/25 pillbox designed by ARMCO *(159)*; circular pillbox, diameter 8ft 6in (2.6m), wall thickness 15in (38cm); small, raised entry hatch, and two or three loopholes; usually shuttered in corrugated iron, which is often then left in place; used all over Britain

11g   NORCON pillbox to drawing no. CP/6/40/11; concrete pipe, diameter 6ft (1.8m), wall thickness 4in (10cm); five loopholes and low entry; standard design has no roof, but there are examples which have roofs, domed or flat; one flat roof having an entrance hatch, cf. 12a; designed to be sited over a hollow, with earth heaped up to loop height; used all over Britain

159 Lodge Hill, Kent; type FW3/25 ARMCO pillbox, still retaining its corrugated iron shuttering, on the Hoo peninsula at TQ755740, quite near the surviving First World War anti-aircraft battery; Appendix I: 11f

11g(i)	Yarnold Sangar in use *c.*1970-present; built of interlocking concrete blocks, roofed, and with outer, curved half-height blast wall; 3 loopholes
11h	CROFT PD541 pillbox; similar to 11g but six loopholes, no entrance, and 6ft 8in (2m) diameter; built by Leicester company for Scottish Command
11j	prefabricated concrete pillbox similar to 11g and 11h; diameter 9ft (2.7m), wall thickness 6in (15cm); six loopholes, steel door; domed concrete roof with removable central cupola; three lifting rings set in roof; an example at Southrop (Glos) uses two complete pillboxes set into the front corners of a brick rectangular pillbox; used in Berkshire, Oxon, Glos airfields
11k	prefabricated concrete pillbox on base diameter 7ft 3in (2.2m), widening to 10ft 3in (3.1m), wall thickness 15in (38cm); no roof; low entrance and four wide firing/observation slits; two at Northampton Power Station SP766597
11m	circular pillbox diameter 10ft (3m), wall thickness 18in (46cm); 5 wide firing slits with continuous bench below; rectangular annexe reached down steps, containing entrance; thick concrete roof slab 30in (76cm); comma-shaped pit in floor; at Ouston (Northumberland) airfield
11n	FC Construction pillbox, also known as Mushroom, Oakington, Fairlop and with Drawing Numbers 9882/41, T/5291, TG/14; circular open pit with wall 3ft (91cm) high, and domed concrete roof cantilevered off central pillar, which incorporated anti-ricochet walls, either cruciform, or butterfly shape; rail holding two mg mounts ran around inside of wall giving 360° field of fire; diameter 13ft (4m), wall thickness 12in (30cm); for airfield defence
11n(i)	some examples at Oakington (Cambs) show signs of blocking part of the space between roof and wall, to reduce vulnerability but also general effectiveness

11n(ii) Drawing No. 303/41 has the gap totally blocked and two stepped loopholes substituted, thus completely nullifying the advantages of the all-round panoramic view; at Peterhead (Aberdeenshire) airfield

11n(iii) domed pillbox added to end of Stanton shelter; as at Penrhos (Gwynedd) airfield, SH331338 and 338333

11p design for mg and AT rifle posts by G. Lockwood, Cumberland County Surveyor, 1941; both feature a central column with a circular passage; loops are provided for the different weapons at a variety of heights; only one example appears to survive; this is a mg post faced with concrete sandbags at Silloth (Cumberland) NY144568

11q circular, two-storey pillbox with loopholes at both levels; diameter *c*.15ft (4.6m); at Westhampnett (West Sussex) airfield

12 Turrets

12a Pickett-Hamilton Fort, designed for airfield defence in 1940; a sunken concrete sleeve, contained a cylindrical pillbox with three loopholes, which, in its dormant position, had its roof flush with ground level; when raised, by pneumatic, hydraulic or manual means, it stood 2ft (61cm) above ground, and fire could be brought to bear; when lowered, all that shows is a 10ft (3m) diameter concrete circle with a hatch in it; about 500 were installed, usually in threes, on airfields throughout Britain, but experienced widespread operating difficulties

12a(i) smaller sunken non-retractable version with roof-hatch used by USAF after the war on East Anglian airfields

12a(ii) alternative, manually operated version at Middle Wallop airfield

12b Tett Turret designed and built by Burbidge Ltd, *c*.1941; this was a sunken concrete tube with a revolving, loopholed steel turret on top; of the tiny number of survivals, only the concrete collar remains; generally felt to have few advantages over a slit trench

12c Allan-Williams Turret designed *c*.1940; a buried steel tube, 3ft (91cm) high and 4ft (1.2m) in diameter, is topped by a rotating steel dome with two shuttered mg mountings, one for LAA; it is entered through a hatch and short tunnel; used throughout Britain

12c(i) similar to 12c, found at Crail (Fife) airfield

13 Airfield battle headquarters (BHQ)

13a Drawing number 3329/41; surface structure, felt to be too vulnerable, and converted to PBX, and replaced by 13b; as at Kingscliffe (Northants), TL029978

13b Drawing number 11008/41; sunken rectangular box with PBX annexe, and access hatches above ground at each end; a square observation room with all-round visibility is capped by a thick concrete cupola
variations/details: two cupolas as at Ibsley (Hants); raised on mound as at Swinderby (Lincs); extra floor under cupola as at Little Staughton (Cambs); heightened tower with standard cupola as at Goxhill (Lincs); earth-covering and modified entrance as at Thorpe Abbotts (Norfolk); interconnecting PBX and external shelter as at Spitalgate (Lincs)

13c Drawing number 11747/41 appears on Air Ministry plans eg Docking (Norfolk); no surviving example of this BHQ yet traced;

13d BHQ consisting of L-shaped brick shelter-type structure with two entrances and small, hexagonal concrete cupola with 6 observation slits, on outer corner; at Luton (Bedfordshire) airfield, TL126222

13e BHQ consisting of large Stanton shelter with cupola, cf. 13d; at Waterbeach (Cambs) airfield, TL491667

13f Drawing number RH18; BHQ consisting of underground structures as in 13b, with the usual two access points, but hexagonal cupola with sides 5ft 7in (1.7m), low external entrance, six narrow, vertical observation slits, and an access-hatch in the floor; at Redhill (Surrey) airfield

14 Section posts, Seagull trenches and concrete trenches

14a L-shaped section post; two intersecting chambers 24ft x 9ft 6in (7.3 x 2.9m), with five loopholes in each outer, long wall, and one in one end wall; entrance in re-entrant angle; wall thickness 24in (61cm); as on north Norfolk coast and Hampshire Avon Stop Line;

14a(i) as 14a but shorter chambers with only three loopholes in each side, and one in each end wall; at Havant (Hants) SU738080

14b section post 28ft 6in x 8ft (8.7 x 2.4m) externally; wall thickness 24in (61cm); projecting, half-hexagonal mg position and four rifle loops on front wall; one loophole in each end wall, and two more on rear wall, along with steps down to sunken entry with steel door; at Everton (Hants) SZ298939

14c boomerang-shaped section post; outer wall, in two lengths of 18ft (5.5m) and end walls 6ft (1.8m); four loopholes in each length of outer wall, three in each inner, and one in each end, making a total of 16; entrance with blast wall at each end of inner wall; shelf along outer wall; at Cayton Bay (N. Yorks) TA075841

14c(i) similar to 14c but short, straight section between long sides; loopholes only on outer and end walls, 13 in all; at Hart Warren (Teesside) NZ494363

14c(ii) section post in five segments, with five loops on the outside, one in each end wall, one on the inside, and one across an outer corner, 9 in all; at Sennen Cove (Cornwall) SW334262

14d arrow-head-shaped section post; front part with two wide embrasures to the front and two rifle loops to the sides; wall thickness 42in (107cm); front walls each 15ft (4.6m) long; behind, an extended chamber 13ft x 10ft (4 x 3m), with four loops in its rear wall, a side entrance with loopholed blast wall, and weapons tables; at Bersted (West Sussex) SU923015

14e boomerang-shaped concrete trench with two loops in each 12ft (3.7m) forward face; end walls 8ft (2.4m), one containing entrance; wall thickness of front walls 36in (91cm); at Hazeley (Hants) on GHQ Line at SU740591

14e(i) similar examples at Bigsweir Bridge on River Wye Line

14f straight-sided concrete trenches; 16ft 9in x 6ft 6in (5.1 x 2m), with four loops in the front wall, one in each end, and a projecting entrance; and a similar one with three loops in a 13ft 6in (4.1m) front wall; at Havant (Hants)

14g straight-sided concrete trench 14ft x 8ft (4.3 x 2.4m) with four loops in front wall, one in back, one in one end, and entrance in other end; wall thickness 15in (38cm); at Selsey (W. Sussex) airfield

14h straight length of Seagull trench 23ft 6in x 6ft (7.2 x 1.8m) with middle section 18ft 6in (5.6m) roofed giving three firing bays 4ft 3in wide on each side; entered down steps at each end; at Kemble (Glos) airfield, but typical

14h(i) as 14h but roofed to each end; as at Penrhos (Gwynedd) airfield

14j L-shaped Seagull trench, one arm 18ft 6in x 6ft (5.6 x 1.8m), and other 13ft 9in x 6in (4.2 x 1.8m), all but the end 3ft (91cm) being roofed; two 4ft (1.2m) wide firing bays in each outside face; entry down rungs set in each end wall; at Kemble (Glos) airfield but typical

14k V-shaped Seagull trench, each arm 13ft x 6ft (4 x 1.8m), all but the end 2ft 6in (76cm) being roofed; two 4ft (1.2m) wide firing bays in each outside face; entry via rungs set across corners of end walls; at Kemble (Glos) but typical

14k(i) as 14k but each arm 16ft 6in, roofed entire length, two ammunition recesses to rear, mg mount, and six firing bays of different widths; at several Northants, Oxon and Glos airfields

14m segmented Seagull trench, as 14k, but 10ft (3m) section with two firing bays inserted between the two arms; at Kemble (Glos) airfield, but typical

14n W-shaped Seagull trench, two V-shaped trenches joined; examples at several airfields in Shropshire, Cheshire and Gwynedd

14p defended air-raid shelter, 32ft x 9ft (9.8 x 2.7m), with 10 loopholes on front wall, and one in each end; entered down steps at each end; at Bicester (Oxon) airfield

15 Spigot mortar positions

15a hexagonal concrete pit *c.*13ft (4m) across with central pedestal; lockers for ammunition set into five sides of pit; sixth side open as access; as in St Albans (Hertfordshire) where excavated by Fred Nash in 1991, and in IWM photographs of Home Guard manoeuvres; at Bramford (Suffolk) TM127464

15b circular brick or concrete revetted pit *c.*11ft (3.4m) across with central pedestal; 4 ammunition recesses, and access trench; at Hertford TQ316130

15b(i) as 15b but above ground at Eye (Suffolk) TG148735 and 151736

15b(ii) as 15b but only two recesses; as at Minsmere (Suffolk) TM477682

15b(iii) as 15bii but octagonal pit; as at Wendens Ambo (Essex) TL515365

15b(iv) narrow rectangular pit with central pedestal and a locker at each end

15c surface concrete-walled rectangular enclosure with central pedestal; used on London railway bridges eg Kew TQ195775

15c(i) as 15c but hexagonal; as at Thetford (Norfolk) TF865834

15c(ii) as 15c but cruciform with half-hexagonal projection; as at Santon Downham (Suffolk) TL825873 and 826872

NB different shapes of pedestal:

• most common CIRCULAR but note steeply domed example at Guist (Norfolk) TF999137

• found throughout Norfolk and Suffolk HEXAGONAL

• uncommon SQUARE examples at Dover Castle (Kent) TR326420, and Pershore Bridge (Worcestershire) SO951452

• unique 13-sided pedestal at Shooters Hill, south-east London, TQ429766

16 Hybrids and unclassifiables, generally one-offs

16a combination FW3/22 and FW3/23 joined together end on; at Bawdsey (Suffolk) TM351392

16b square 6j with raised platform for LAA position built on one side; at Trimley St Martin (Suffolk) TM277374

16c front half of hexagonal pillbox, with open annexe to rear and double blast wall; at Hucknall (Nottinghamshire) airfield, SK526464

16d FW3/22 pillbox with loopholed corridors extending *c.*30 yards in two directions; at Silloth (Cumbria) airfield NY121534

16e complex of two 3b(ii) pillboxes *(160)* with mg embrasures in two forward-facing sides, joined together by a 9ft x 12ft rectangular chamber with mg embrasure, making five in all; three remaining faces in each pillbox has lmg loophole; at the back is an open, raised, hexagonal platform, based on the same dimensions as the pillboxes; at Southminster (Essex) TQ995983

16f pillbox 1f with central platform for LAA mounting; chamber measuring 9ft x 7ft (2.7 x 2.1m) with three loopholes, built onto three alternate sides; the other three sides are

160 Southminster, Essex; the unique double pillbox at TQ995983; Appendix I: 16e

	blank save for one containing entrance; on Eastern Command Line outside Lavenham at TL915517
16g	small octagonal pillbox with three loopholes in each long side, one in each of three short sides, and loopholed entrance chamber on fourth short side; 13ft x 9ft (4 x 2.7m) overall; at Kenmore (Tayside) NH783454

NB Types FW3/ 45 and 46, only appearing in the record in 1941, remain to be identified, as do South-Eastern Command's 124/41 & Scottish Command's 2717. The three Colchester types need to be confirmed more securely than their tentative identification above. There is still confusion over the designation 'FW3/27', referring to a rectangular Vickers mg post on the Taunton Stop Line, but generally accepted to have been the large octagonal pillbox used on the Outer London defences, and elsewhere. However, the lmg version of the Vickers mg post seems to have been referred to as a Type 27a in East Anglia. There is still work to be done in matching known types to drawing numbers, and in rediscovering both types/drawing numbers in the documentation, and examples in the field.

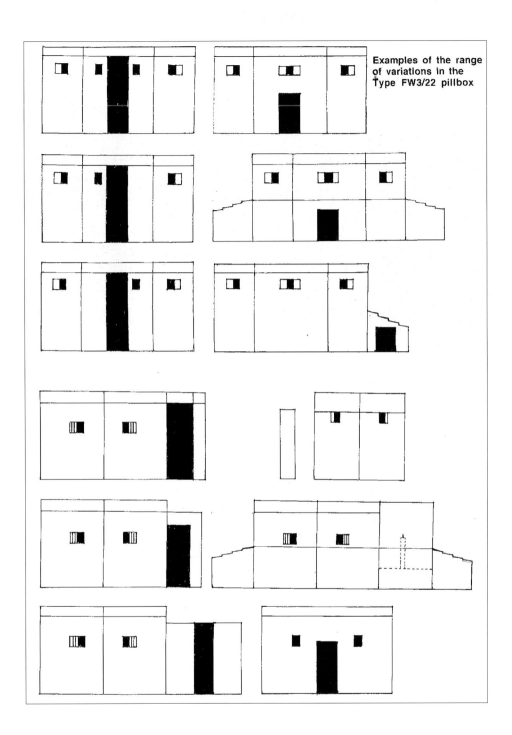

Examples of the range of variations in the Type FW3/22 pillbox

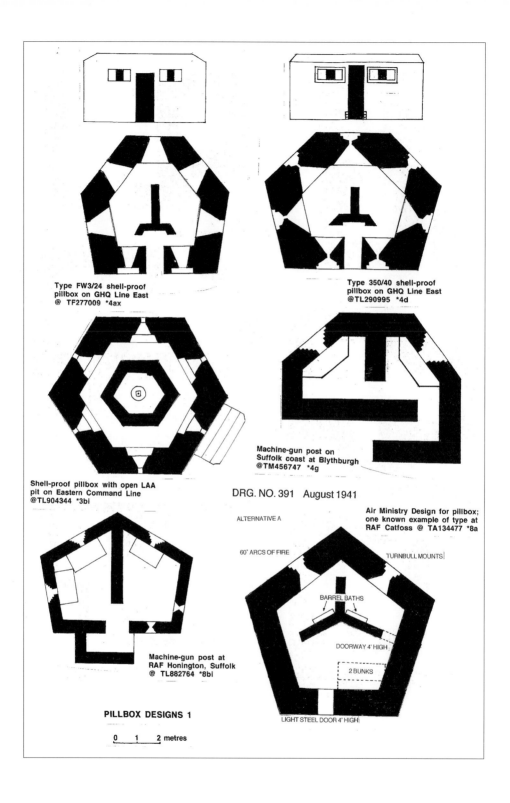

Type FW3/24 shell-proof
pillbox on GHQ Line East
@ TF277009 *4ax

Type 350/40 shell-proof
pillbox on GHQ Line East
@TL290995 *4d

Machine-gun post on
Suffolk coast at Blythburgh
@TM456747 *4g

Shell-proof pillbox with open LAA
pit on Eastern Command Line
@TL904344 *3bi

DRG. NO. 391   August 1941

ALTERNATIVE A

60° ARCS OF FIRE

Air Ministry Design for pillbox;
one known example of type at
RAF Catfoss @ TA134477 *8a

TURNBULL MOUNTS

BARREL BATHS

DOORWAY 4' HIGH

2 BUNKS

Machine-gun post at
RAF Honington, Suffolk
@ TL882764 *8bi

LIGHT STEEL DOOR 4' HIGH

PILLBOX DESIGNS 1

0   1   2 metres

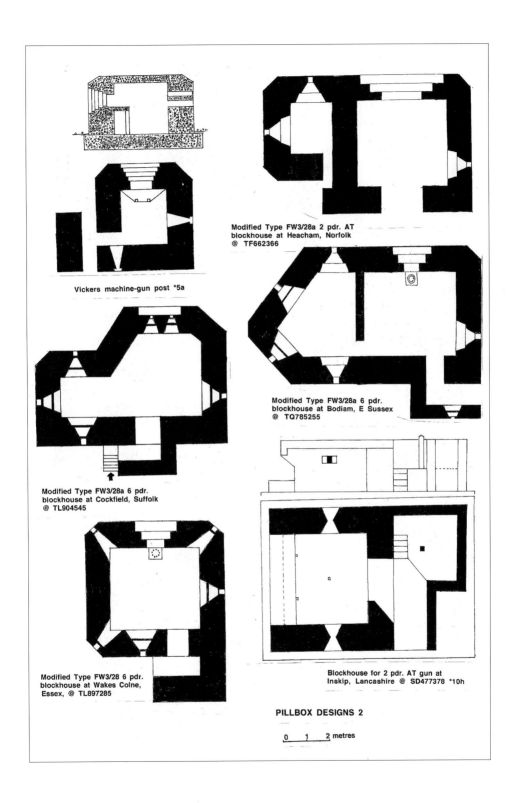

Vickers machine-gun post *5a

Modified Type FW3/28a 2 pdr. AT
blockhouse at Heacham, Norfolk
@ TF662366

Modified Type FW3/28a 6 pdr.
blockhouse at Bodiam, E Sussex
@ TQ785255

Modified Type FW3/28a 6 pdr.
blockhouse at Cockfield, Suffolk
@ TL904545

Modified Type FW3/28 6 pdr.
blockhouse at Wakes Colne,
Essex, @ TL897285

Blockhouse for 2 pdr. AT gun at
Inskip, Lancashire @ SD477378 *10h

PILLBOX DESIGNS 2

0   1   2 metres

267

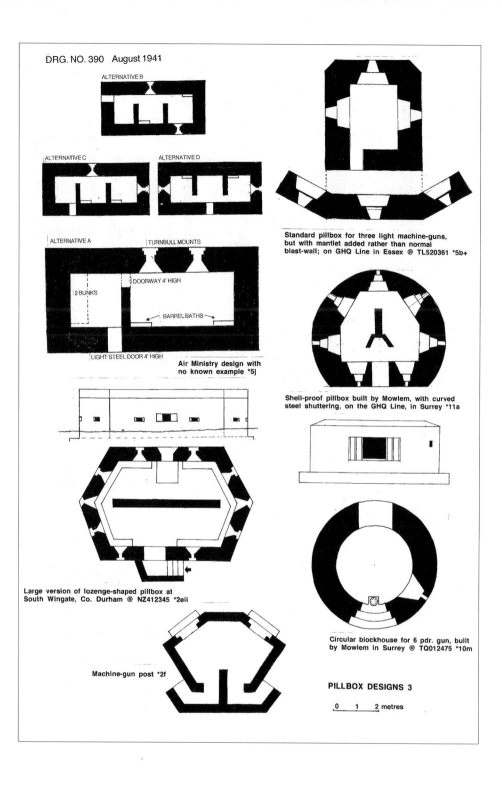

DRG. NO. 390   August 1941

ALTERNATIVE B

ALTERNATIVE C

ALTERNATIVE D

ALTERNATIVE A

TURNBULL MOUNTS

2 BUNKS

DOORWAY 4' HIGH

BARREL BATHS

LIGHT STEEL DOOR 4' HIGH

Air Ministry design with no known example *5j

Large version of lozenge-shaped pillbox at South Wingate, Co. Durham @ NZ412345 *2eii

Machine-gun post *2f

Standard pillbox for three light machine-guns, but with mantlet added rather than normal blast-wall; on GHQ Line in Essex @ TL520361 *5b+

Shell-proof pillbox built by Mowlem, with curved steel shuttering, on the GHQ Line, in Surrey *11a

Circular blockhouse for 6 pdr. gun, built by Mowlem in Surrey @ TQ012475 *10m

PILLBOX DESIGNS 3

0   1   2 metres

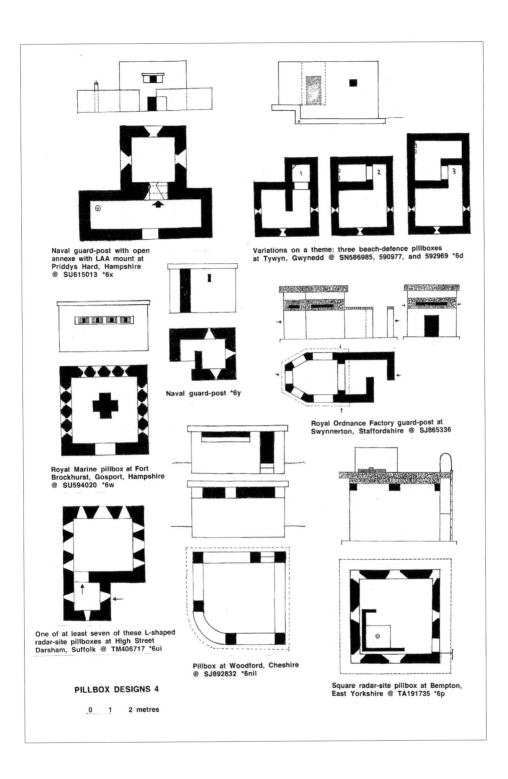

Naval guard-post with open annexe with LAA mount at Priddys Hard, Hampshire @ SU615013 *6x

Variations on a theme: three beach-defence pillboxes at Tywyn, Gwynedd @ SN586985, 590977, and 592969 *6d

Naval guard-post *6y

Royal Marine pillbox at Fort Brockhurst, Gosport, Hampshire @ SU594020 *6w

Royal Ordnance Factory guard-post at Swynnerton, Staffordshire @ SJ865336

One of at least seven of these L-shaped radar-site pillboxes at High Street Darsham, Suffolk @ TM406717 *6ui

Pillbox at Woodford, Cheshire @ SJ892832 *6nii

Square radar-site pillbox at Bempton, East Yorkshire @ TA191735 *6p

PILLBOX DESIGNS 4

0   1   2 metres

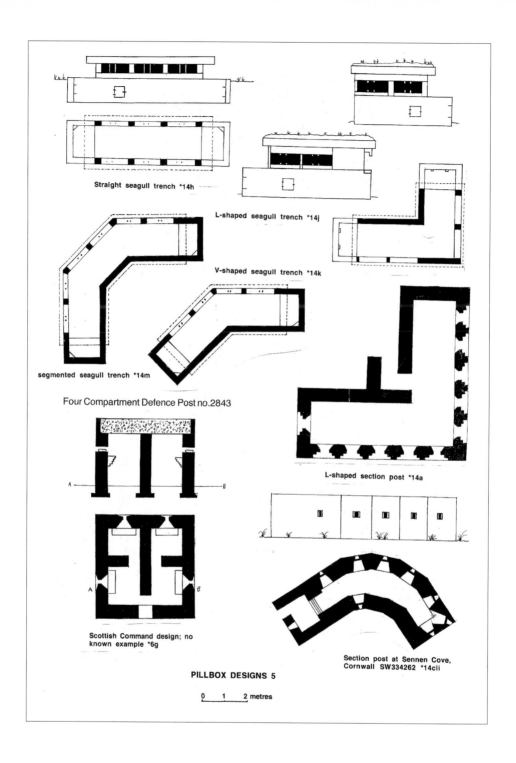

Straight seagull trench *14h

L-shaped seagull trench *14j

V-shaped seagull trench *14k

segmented seagull trench *14m

Four Compartment Defence Post no.2843

L-shaped section post *14a

Scottish Command design; no known example *6g

Section post at Sennen Cove, Cornwall SW334262 *14cii

PILLBOX DESIGNS 5

0   1   2 metres

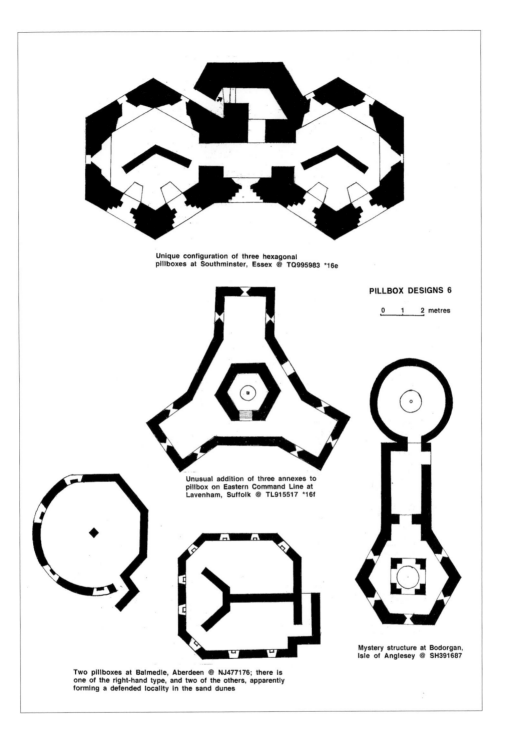

Unique configuration of three hexagonal
pillboxes at Southminster, Essex @ TQ995983 *16e

PILLBOX DESIGNS 6

0   1   2 metres

Unusual addition of three annexes to
pillbox on Eastern Command Line at
Lavenham, Suffolk @ TL915517 *16f

Mystery structure at Bodorgan,
Isle of Anglesey @ SH391687

Two pillboxes at Balmedie, Aberdeen @ NJ477176; there is
one of the right-hand type, and two of the others, apparently
forming a defended locality in the sand dunes

APPENDIX 2

A NOTE ON CAMOUFLAGE

DEFENCE WORKS

There is an argument that many of the emergency anti-invasion works of late 1940 were left visible as either a warning, or a bluff, to the enemy. Given that the best record of many of these works remains the German aerial reconnaissance photographs of that autumn, that view may hold or not. To extend Ironside's and Alanbrooke's analogy, if everything was apparently in the shop window and was brightly-illuminated, who knew what was under the counter? However, there were serious and successful attempts at camouflage *(161)*. If a pillbox loophole is visible now 200 yards away, across a field, on the edge of the wood, it was not always so. Dazzle-painting was first developed in the First World War by French painters conscripted into the trenches. Cdr. Rawlinson, who set up the mobile AA brigade which defended London against Zeppelin attack in 1915, had been involved in setting up the defence of Paris. He had seen the effects achieved by the set designer from the Paris Opera, and brought these techniques to England. Such systems were used widely in both World Wars, going a long way to breaking up silhouettes and hard lines. Features like loopholes would be contained in the darker-coloured stripes. Simple camouflage netting with strips of cloth, or even vegetation, was also useful. On the beach, pillboxes were covered in pebbles *(162)*. In some cases buildings were completely disguised. Just as the expertise of the film studios was exploited in the construction of decoy airfields in the Second World War, the experts were, once again, called up for camouflage duty. Oliver Messel, for instance, the stage designer, worked in Somerset and in East Anglia. He utilised all the tricks of his trade to produce convincing deceptions, including fake stone finishes. The most important principle in all of this is context. Buildings must fit in, so pillboxes as ice-cream kiosks are fine at the seaside, and as public conveniences in the town. One fake sports pavilion only worked because the necessary fake goalposts were put up as well. In the countryside, and on the coast, a different range of structures was fabricated. There were cow sheds, chicken houses, pigpens, hotels and boat-houses. Some of the AT emplacements on the enemy side of the GHQ Line in Berkshire, were disguised as thatched cottages, and even hay-ricks. Soon, the RE Companies were learning the techniques themselves. A plan for a pillbox in Cad Green (Somerset), for instance, presented as a very convincing bus-shelter, complete with bus timetable, is signed by F Silvester-White (Lt.), of 552 Coy. RE. A bit of chicken-wire, hessian and gauze could go a long way, matched with imagination and ingenuity. In one case, turning the pillbox into a gothic cottage was not enough. The RE officer directing operations even specified that a polygonum in a tub, or *Rosa ragosa* should be planted, and turf should be laid, to complete the effect of an established dwelling. Some of the plans for agricultural disguises include optional manure heaps.

161 Druridge Bay, Northumberland; a pillbox disguised as a cottage, at NZ283946

162 Minehead, Somerset; a pillbox at SS998456, with a covering of beach pebbles to disguise it; Appendix I: 4a

AIRFIELDS

The straight lines of airfields, and the grouping of 1930s airfield buildings made it difficult to do much about disguising them, but successful attempts were, nevertheless, made. Airfield buildings were painted in browns and greens, the aim being particularly to disrupt the straight edges. Airfield buildings, particularly aircraft factories near built-up areas were painted to resemble streets of houses. Bitumen-based surfaces were developed which toned down concrete runways, perimeter tracks and hard-standings. Ultimately the solution lay in a sustainable wood-chip composition. Where possible, trees, hedges and undergrowth were retained around airfield perimeters, and hedges were painted across the flying areas themselves. At Glatton (now Peterborough airport) a farm survived, uniquely, within the triangle of runways, and this must have gone some way to enhancing the station's agricultural credibility.

AIR DEFENCE

Motivated by the same desire to deprive the enemy of waymarks, which prompted the removal of signposts on the ground, attempts were made to disguise features which might aid bombers in reaching their targets. In Liverpool, for instance, the great glass roof of the palm-house at Sefton was painted grey and green to prevent reflections providing an orientation point. For the same reason, but on a larger scale, a way was found to float coaldust on the surfaces of the reservoirs between Macclesfield (Cheshire) and Leek (Staffordshire), thus depriving the enemy of a moonlit signpost to Manchester. Sometimes, of course, the solution to one problem created a greater one. The anti-tank ditch which was dug through the chalk Gog and Magog hills in late 1940, to carry the GHQ Line around Cambridge, provided a straight white-line for enemy bombers to follow direct to the city.

ABBREVIATIONS

AA — anti-aircraft
AAOR — Anti-Aircraft Operations Room
AAP — Aircraft Acceptance Park
AAP — Advanced Ammunition Park
ADT3 — Air Defence Tactical Training Theatre
AFV — Armoured Fighting Vehicle
AM — Air Ministry
AML — Air Ministry Laboratory, as in synthetic bombing teacher
AMTB — anti-Motor Torpedo Boat
ARG — Airfield Research Group
ARP — Air Raid Precautions
ARS — Aircraft Repair Shed/Section
ASU — Aircraft Storage Unit
AT — anti-tank
ATS — Auxiliary Territorial Service
ATS — Armament Training School
AW — Allan-Williams (Turret)

BAC — Bristol Aircraft Company
BCF — British Concrete Federation (hut type)
BHQ — Battle headquarters (airfield defence)
BL — breech loader (gun)
BMEWS — Ballistic Missile Early-Warning System
BOP — Battery Observation Post
BR — British Rail/Railways
BSA — British Small Arms

CAD — Central Ammunition Depot
CASL — Coast Artillery Searchlight (Second World War)

CB — Counter-bombardment (coast battery)
CD — Coast Defence
CH — Chain Home (CHEL: CH Extra Low, CH L: CHLow); radar types
CND — Campaign for Nuclear Disarmament
COSSAC — Chiefs of Staff Supreme Allied Command
CPRE — Council for the Preservation of Rural England
CRE — Commander Royal Engineers

DEL — Defence Electric Light (First World War CD searchlight)
DEMS — Defensively Equipped Merchant Ships
(D)FW3 — (Department) of Fortifications and Works (War Office)
DL — Defended Locality
DoB — Defence of Britain Project
DORA — Defence of the Realm Act

EFTS — Elementary Flying Training School
EH — English Heritage

FAD — Forward Ammunition Depot
FDL — Forward Defence Line (pre-GHQ Line, Second World War)
FIDO — Fog Investigation and Dispersal Organisation

GCHQ — Government Communications Headquarters

GCI	Ground Control Interception (radar for directing fighters to target)	OTU	Operational Training Unit (RAF)
GDA	Gun-Defended Area (anti-aircraft zone)	PAD	Permanent Ammunition Depot
GHQ Line	General Headquarters (defence) Line, (First World War in France, Second World War in Britain)	PBX	Private Branch (telephone) Exchange
		PF	position-finding cell (coast artillery)
GS	General Service (First World War Hangar)	PLUTO	Pipe Line Under The Ocean
		PoW	prisoner of war
		PWSS	Port War Signal Station
		QF	quick-firing (gun)
HG	Home Guard, previously LDV (qv)	QRA	Quick Reaction Alert
H/LAA	Heavy/Light Anti-Aircraft		
		RA	Royal Artillery
ICBM	Inter-Continental Ballistic Missile	RAE	Royal Aircraft Establishment
IRBM	Intermediate Range Ballistic Missile	RAF	Royal Air Force
		RAOC	Royal Army Ordnance Corps
IWM	Imperial War Museum	RASC	Royal Army Service Corps
		RCHME	Royal Commission on Historical Monuments England
KRDG	Kent Defence Research Group	RDF	radio direction-finding
LADA	London Air Defence Area	RE	Royal Engineers
LDV	Local Defence Volunteers, later Home Guard	REME	Royal Electrical and Mechanical Engineers
lmg	light machine-gun	RFC	Royal Flying Corps (to 31 March 1918)
LMS	London Midland & Scottish Railway		
LNER	London and North-Eastern Railway	RIM	receipt, inspection & maintenance (RAF process re SAMs, *q.v.*)
		RM	Royal Marines
		RML	rifled muzzle-loader (gun)
MAP	Ministry of Aircraft Production (Second World War)	RN	Royal Navy
		RNAS	Royal Naval Air Service (to 31 March 1918)
MoD	Ministry of Defence		
mg	machine-gun	RNSD	Royal Navy Supply Depot
MT	motor transport	ROC	Royal Observer Corps
MoWP	Ministry of War Production (Second World War)	ROF	Royal Ordnance Factory
		RSG	Regional Seat of Government
MU	(RAF) Maintenance Unit	RSJ	rolled steel joist
NCO	non-commissioned officer	SAA	small-arms ammunition
NFE	night-flying equipment	SAM	surface-to-air missile
NFF	National (shell) Filling Factory	SF	Starfish (decoy site)
NHS	National Health Service	SL	searchlight
		SLG	Satellite Landing Ground (used by MAP)
OB	Operational Base (auxiliary unit hide)		
		SMLE	Short-magazine Lee-Enfield (rifle)
OCTU	Officer Cadet Training Unit (Army)	SMR	Sites and Monuments Record
		SOC	Sector Operations Centre
OP	observation post	SOE	Special Operations Executive
OTC	Officer Training Corps		

TA	Territorial Army (from 1920)	VCR	Visual Control Room
TAC	Territorial Army Centre	VHF	very high-frequency
TF	Territorial Force (1908–18)	VP	Vulnerable Point
TL	Taunton (Somerset) Line		
		WRAF	Women's Royal Air Force
UKADGE	United Kingdom Air Defence Ground Environment	W/T	wireless-telegraphy
UKFC	United Kingdom Fortifications Club	XDO	Extended Defence Officer's post (minefield control)
UKWMO	United Kingdom Warning and Monitoring Organisation	ZAA	Anti-Aircraft Z battery, 3ft unrotated rocket projectiles
USAAF	United States Army Air Force (throughout Second World War)		
USAF	United States Air Force (post-Second World War)		

BIBLIOGRAPHY

General works, including studies of specific localities or topics which cover more than a single chapter, are listed first. Works relating to discrete topics are listed under the relevant chapter heading.

GENERAL WORKS

Bell, A. *Stranraer in World War Two*, Stranraer District Local History Trust, 1999
Bennett, D. *A Handbook of Kent's Defences 1540-1945*, KDRG, 1977
Bird, C. *Silent Sentinels: Norfolk's 20th century defences*, Larks Press, Dereham, 1999
Burridge, D. *20th Century Defences in Britain: Kent*, Brasseys, London, 1997
Burridge, D. *Defending the Gateway, Dover's 20C Fixed Defences*, Dover, 2001
Cadman, G. *20th Century Military Remains in Northants*, Northants SMR, updates
Cheshire County Council *Discovering Wartime Cheshire 1939-45*, Chester 1985
Cocroft, W., & Thomas, R. *Cold War*, EH, Swindon, 2003
Collier, B. *The Defence of the UK, (official history)*, HMSO, 1957, reprinted 1995
Dobinson, Colin. *Twentieth Century Fortifications in England: Vols XI/i and XI/ii, The Cold War: Text and Appendices*, CBA, York, 2000
Foot, W. *A Review of the Defence of Britain Project*, CBA, York, 2002
Fortress Study Group *Holderness Pilot Study*, unpublished, 1992
Gander, T. *Military Archaeology*, PSL, Cambridge, 1979
Gardiner, M. *Britain's Finest Hour*, Fortress 5, 1990
Gilman, P., & Nash, F. *Fortress Essex*: Essex County Council, Chelmsford, 1995
Hawkins, M. *Somerset at War 1939-1945*, Hawk, Wimborne, 1989
Hoare, A. *Standing Up To Hitler: Norfolk's Home Guard*, Wymondham, 1997
Jarvis, R. *Lowestoft at War 1939-45*, Heritage Workshop Centre, Lowestoft, 2002
Jeffrey, A. *This Time of Crisis: Glasgow, the Clyde, the West of Scotland & North-West Approaches*; *This Dangerous Menace: Dundee & the River Tay*; *This Present Emergency: Edinburgh, the River Forth & the South-East of Scotland* (all Second World War), Mainstream, 1992-1993
Kent, P. *East Anglian Fortifications in the Twentieth Century*, Fortress 3, 1989
Lane, M. *Defensive Installations on Wirral*, Loopholes 12, June 1995
Longstaff-Tyrrell, P. *Front-Line. Sussex*, Sutton, Stroud, 2000
Lowry, B (ed), et al. *20th Century Defences in Britain*, CBA, York, 1995
Lowry, B. *The Anti-Invasion Defences of Western Command 1940*, Fort 27, 1999
Lowry, B. *British Home Defences 1940-45*, Osprey 2004
Mace, M. *Sussex Wartime Relics & Memorials*, Hist. Mil. Press, Storrington, 1997
Mallory, K., & Ottar, A. *Architecture of Aggression*, Architectural Press, 1973
Osborne, M. *20th Century Defences in Britain: Lincolnshire*, Brasseys, 1996;
Osborne, M. *20th Century Defences in Britain: Cambridgeshire*, Concrete Pubs, 2001

Osborne, M. *20th Century Defences in Britain: The East Midlands*, Concrete Pubs, 2003

Pomeroy, C. *Military Dorset Today*, Silver Link, Wadenhoe, 1995

Pye, A., & Woodward, F. *Historic Defences of Plymouth*, Cornwall CC, 1996

Redfern, N. *Twentieth Century Fortifications in the UK: Vol. i Introduction & Sources; Vol. ii Site Gazetteers: Wales*, CBA, York, 1998

Redfern, N. *Twentieth Century Fortifications in the UK : Vols iv & v: Site Gazetteers: Scotland i & ii* CBA, York, 1998

Robertson, S., & Wilson, L. *Scotland's War*, Mainstream, Edinburgh, 1995

Ruddy, A.J. *British Anti-Invasion Defences 1940-1945*, Hist. Mil. Press, Storrington, 2004

Smith, V. *Front-Line Kent*, Kent County Council, Maidstone, 2001

Thomas, R. *Survey of 19th & 20th Century Military Buildings in Pembrokeshire*, 1994

Ward, A. *Resisting the Nazi Invader*, Constable, London, 1997

Wilson, J. *West Cumberland at War*, Distington, 1999

CHAPTER I: COAST DEFENCES

Andrews, E.A., & Pinsent, M.L. *The coastal defences of Portland & Weymouth*, Fort 9, 1981

Arnold, Col. B.E. *Conflict across the Strait*, Crabwell/Buckland, Dover, 1982

Brown, M., *et al. Beacon Hill Fort, Essex*, RCHM(E), Cambridge, 1997

Brown, M., *et al. Coast Artillery Fortifications: Isle of Grain, Kent*, RCHM(E), 1998

Burridge, D. *The Dover Turret: Admiralty Pier Fort*, Rochester, 1987

Cantwell, A. *Fort Victoria 1852-1969*, Isle of Wight County Council, Newport, 1985

Cantwell, A., & Sprack, P. *The Needles Defences:* Solent Paper 2, Ryde, 1986

Cantwell, A. & Moore, D. *Victorian Army & Submarine Mining*, Fort 18, 1993

Clark, N.H. *Twentieth century coastal defence of the Firth of Forth*, Fort 14, 1986

Clements, B. *The Medway Martellos*, Fort 29, 2001

Cobb, P. *Smaller Defences of Portsmouth*, Loopholes 5, September 1993

Cobb, P. *XDO Posts in British service 1939-45*, Loopholes 7, March 1994

Coleman, R. *Battery at Battery Gardens Brixham*, Brixham, 1989

Dobinson, C. *Twentieth Century Fortifications in England: Vol vi Coastal Artillery 1900-56: i Text, ii Appendices*, CBA, York, 2000

Dorman, J. *Guardians of the Humber 1856-1956*, Humberside Libraries, 1990

Dorman, J. *Later Defences of Falmouth*, Ravelin Special 4, KDRG, 1990

Dorman, J. *Orkney Coast Batteries 1914-1956*, 1996

Dorman, J. *A Visit to Cromarty & Loch Ewe*, Ravelin Special 7, KDRG, 1996

Hamilton-Baillie, J.R.E. *The Coast Defences of Orkney in two world wars*, Fort 9, 1981

Hogg, I.V. *Notes on the Identification of Coast Artillery Gun Emplacements*, Fort 8, 1980

Hogg, R. *The Tyne turrets: coastal defence in the First World War*, Fort 12, 1984

Kenney, J. *The Ravelin Bty, Sheerness, Kent*, RCHM(E), Cambridge, 1993

Linzey, R. *Fortress Falmouth Vol ii History & Gazetteer*, EH, 2000

Pattison, P. *Cliffe Fort Brennan Torpedo Slipways, Medway*, RCHM(E), 1993

Pearson, M. *Coast defence radar*, Fort 19, 1991

Pinsent, M. *Defences of the Bristol Channel in last two centuries*, Fort 11, 1983

Reed, J. *The Cross-Channel Guns*, After The Battle 29, Plaistow Press, 1980

Saunders, A., *et al. Guns Across the Severn*, RCA & HM (W), Aberystwyth, 2001

Smith, V. *Defending the Forth: 1880-1910*, Fort 13, 1985

Smith, V. *Defending London's River 1540-1945*, N Kent Books, Rochester 1985

Stevenson, I.V. *Some West Country Defences*, Fort 17, 1989

Taylor, S. *Bull Sand Fort*, RCHM(E), York, 1999

Tendring District Council *Beacon Hill, draft plan*, Harwich, 1989

CHAPTER 2: INLAND DEFENCE LINES

Alexander, C. *Ironside's Line*, Historic Military Press, Storrington, 1999

Dobinson, C. *Twentieth Century Fortifications in England: Vol. II Anti-Invasion Defences of World War 2*, CBA, York, 1996

Glover, D.G. *A Command Stop Line on Rhos Llangeler*, The Carmarthenshire Antiquary, xxvi 1990

Green, Maj. M., & Plant, J. *The Bristol Outer Defences on the Cotswold Plateau, parts 1 & 2*, Loopholes 4, May 1993, & 5, September 1993

Green, Maj. M. *Warwalks: Stop Line Green*, Reardon, Leckhampton, 1999

Greeves, I.D. *The Construction of the GHQ Stop-line: Eridge to Newhaven, June-November 1940*, Fortress 16, 1993

Hellis, J. *The Taunton Stop-Line*, Fortress 14, 1992

Kerr, A.G. *Tamworth to Burton-on-Trent Stop Line*, Loopholes 6, December 1993

Mace, M. *Defence Lines of W. Sussex 1939-45*, Hist. Mil. Press, Storrington, 1996

Rudd, A & Clarke, D. *Northumberland Stop Lines*, Loopholes 8 & 21, June 1994 & July 1998

Wills, H. *British Invasion Defences*, After The Battle 14, Plaistow Press, 1976

Wills, H. *Pillboxes: A Study of UK Defences 1940*, Leo Cooper/Secker, 1985

CHAPTER 3: VULNERABLE POINTS

Burridge, D. *Chatham anti-Invasion Plan*, Loopholes 19-20, June/Dec 1997

Hollowell, S. *Defending the Heart of England: Northampton 1940-44*, Northants Archaeology, 28, 1998-9

Hurt, F. *Lincoln during the War*, Lincoln, 1991

Lampe, D. *The Last Ditch*, Cassell, London, 1968

Locock, M. *Neath Valley Defences*, Loopholes 7, March 1994

Lowry, B., & Wilks, M. *The Mercian Maquis*, Logaston, 2002

Nash, F. *Spigot Mortar Pit at St Albans*, After The Battle 81, Plaistow Press, 1993

Sainsbury, T. *Pillboxes in North Northumberland*, Loopholes12, June 1995

Sanderson, I. *Home Guard & VPs (W. Yorks & Leeds)*, Loopholes 17 & 18, 1996

Schmidt, Maj. E. *Defences of Blandford Forum*, Blandford Museum, 1987

CHAPTER 4: AIRFIELD DEFENCE

Dobinson, C. *Twentieth Century Fortifications in England: Vol. X Airfield Defences in the Second World War*, CBA, York, 2000

Francis, P. *Airfield Defences at Middle Wallop*, A R Publishing, Ware, 1998

Lowry, B. *Two RAF Strongpoints in Shropshire*, Loopholes 20, December 1997

Lowry, B. *Airfield Defences*, Airfield Review 92, October 2001

Osborne, M. *The Magic Mushroom: FCC pillboxes*, Loopholes 20, 1997

Purcell, S. *Battle HQs, Airfield Defences etc*, Loopholes 5, 17, 22, 1993-9

Towler, R. *(Canadian) Pipe Mines*, Airfield Review 100, October 2003

CHAPTER 5: AIRFIELDS

Ashworth, C. *Military Airfields of the South-West, Action Stations 5* PSL, Sparkford, 1982
Ashworth, C. *Military Airfields of the Central South and South-East, Action Stations 9*, PSL, Sparkford, 1985
Berry, P. *Ayrshire Airfields*, Airfield Review 83, July 1999
Betts, A. *RAF Airfield Construction Service 1939-46*, AR Publishing, Ware, 1995
Blake, R., *et al. Airfields of Lincolnshire since 1912*, Midland, Earl Shilton, 1984
Bonser, R. *Aviation in Leicestershire & Rutland*, Midland, Earl Shilton, 2001
Bowyer, M. *Military Airfields of East Anglia, Action Stations 1*, PSL, Sparkford, 1979 & 1990; revised edition 2001
Bowyer, M. *Military Airfields of the Cotswolds & Central Midlands, Action Stations 6*, PSL, Sparkford, 1983 & 1990
Davies, K. *Lakeland Aviation & Airfields of the 20th Century*, Regional, 2001
Dobinson, C. *Twentieth Century Fortifications in England: Vols IX/i & IX/ii Airfield Themes: Text & Appendices*, CBA, York, 2000
Francis, P. *Control Towers*, Airfield Research Publishing, Ware, 1993
Francis, P. *British Military Airfield Architecture*, PSL, Sparkford, 1996
Gibson, M. *Aviation in Northamptonshire*, Northants Libraries, 1982
Halfpenny, B.B. *Military Airfields of Lincolnshire & the East Midlands, Action Stations 2*, PSL, Sparkford, 1981
Halfpenny, B.B. *Military Airfields of Yorkshire, Action Stations 4*, PSL, 1982
Halfpenny, B.B. *Military Airfields of Greater London, Action Stations 8*, PSL, Sparkford, 1984 & 1993
Hancock, T. *Bomber County Vols 1 & 2*, Lincolnshire Libraries, 1978 & 1985; new combined edition 2004
Higham, R. *Bases of Air Strategy*, Airlife, Shrewsbury, 1998
Innes, G.B. *British Airfield Buildings of the Second World War*, Midland, 1995
Innes, G.B. *British Airfield Buildings Vol 2 The Expansion & interwar Periods*, Midland, Earl Shilton, 2000
Quarrie, B., *et al. Supplement & Index, Action Stations 10*, PSL, Sparkford, 1987
Smith, D. *Military Airfields of Wales & the North-West, Action Stations 3*, PSL, Sparkford, 1981
Smith, D. *Military Airfields of Scotland, the North-East & Northern Ireland, Action Stations 7*, PSL, Sparkford, 1983, 1989, 1993
Smith, D. *Britain's Military Airfields 1939-45*, PSL, Sparkford, 1989
Temple, J., & Francis, P. *New Guidelines for Listing Military Airfield Buildings in England*, Report Commissioned by EH, 1973

NB the indispensable Airfield Review, journal of the Airfield Research Group; at least four issues each year containing comprehensive guides to individual airfields and particular building types, and also general up-to-date situation reports on the state of airfields, aircraft factories, and associated establishments in Britain.

CHAPTER 6 BUILDINGS FOR THE ARMY & THE NAVY

O'Connell, G. *Southwick, the D-Day Village that went to War*, WE, 1984
Dietz, P. *Garrison: 10 British Military Towns*, Brasseys, London, 1986
Douet, J. *British Barracks 1600-1914*, EH, HMSO, Norwich, 1998
Evans, D. *Building the Steam Navy, 1830-1906*, EH and Conway, 2004
Osborne, M. *Drill Halls in England*, report for EH of a survey, 2003
Ring, J. *We Come Unseen*, London, 2001

Save Britain's Heritage *Deserted Bastions*, SAVE, London, 1993
Warlow, Lt-Cdr B. *Shore Establishments of the Royal Navy*, Liskeard, 1992/2000

CHAPTER 7 AIR DEFENCE

Cadman, G. *Northants Bombing Decoys*, Northants Archaeology 28, 1998-9
Campbell, D. *War Plan UK*, Burnett Books, London, 1982
Catford, N. *The ROC Underground in Kent & Essex*, Ravelin 8, KDRG, 1999
Cocroft, W. *Cambridge RSG: Survey Report*, RCHM(E), Cambridge, 1997
Cocroft, W. *RAF Langtoft: Survey Report*, RCHM(E), Cambridge, 1998
Dobinson, C. *Twentieth Century Fortifications in England*
    Vol. I.i Anti-Aircraft Artillery 1914-46: Text
    Vols I.ii, I.iii. & I.iv AA Artillery 1914-46 Site Gazetteers WWI, HAA/ZAA, & LAA
    Vol. I.v AA Artillery 1914-46 Sources, CBA, York, 1996
    Supporting Paper AA/I: Searchlight Sites in WWII, CBA, York, 2000
    Vol. III Bombing Decoys of WWII, Vol IV Operation Diver, CBA, York, 1996
    Vols VII/i & VII/ii Acoustics & Radar: Text & Appendices, CBA, York, 2000
    Vol. VIII Civil Defence in WWII, CBA, York, 2000
Dobinson, C. *Fields of Deception*, Methuen/EH, London, 2000
Dobinson, C. *AA Command*, Methuen/EH, London, 2001
Dobinson, C. *Building Radar*, Methuen/EH, London, 2004
Fairhead, H. *Decoy Sites in Norfolk & Suffolk*, Flixton, nd
Hogg, I. *Anti-Aircraft Artillery*, Crowood, 2002
Jenkins, S.C. *Pendennis Castle, Cornwall*, Fort 25, 1997
Locock, M. *An Anti-Aircraft Battery at Newport, Gwent*, Fort 23, 1995
McCamley, N.J. *Cold War Secret Nuclear Bunkers*, Leo Cooper, Barnsley, 2002
Ministry of Information *Roof Over Britain*, HMSO, 1943
Parker, C. *The Royal Observer Corps in Lincolnshire*, Lincoln, nd
Pile, Gen. Sir F. *Ack-Ack*, Harrap, London, 1949
Price, A. *Blitz on Britain 1939-45*, Purnell, Abingdon, 1977
Rawlinson, A. *The Air Defence of London 1915-18*, A Melrose, London, 1923
Sockett, E.W. *Stockton-on-Tees 'Y' Station*, Fortress 8, 1991
Sockett, E.W. *Loftus under Zeppelin Attack 1914-1918*, Fortress 13, 1992
Spaven, M. *Fortress Scotland*, Pluto Press & Scottish CND, London, 1983
Wood, D. *Attack Warning Red*, Carmichael & Sweet, Portsmouth, 1976 & 1992

CHAPTER 8 LOGISTICAL SUPPORT

Cocroft, W. *Dangerous Energy*, EH, Swindon, 2000
Dobinson, C. *Twentieth Century Fortifications in England: Vol V: Operation Overlord*, CBA, York, 1996
Forder, N. *The National Aircraft Factories*, Airfield Review 99, July 2003
Haslam, E.B. *The History of RAF Cranwell*, HMSO London, 1982
Hughes, M. *The Archaeology of D-Day: the remains at Stone Point, Lepe*, Fortress 15, 1992
McCamley, N.J. *Secret Underground Cities*, Leo Cooper, Barnsley, 1988 & 2001
Pattison, P., *et al.* *Purfleet Gunpowder Magazines*, RCHM(E), Cambridge, 1994
Reed, J. *London's Wartime Headquarters*, After The Battle 37, Plaistow Press, 1982
Richardson, H. *English Hospitals 1660-1948*, EH, Swindon, 1998

APPENDIX I

Hamilton-Baillie, J. personal communications

Hughes, Q. *A Project for the Defence of Paris*, FORT 12, 1984

Oldham, P. *Pillboxes on the Western Front*, Leo Cooper, London, 1995

Oldham, P. *The Hindenburg Line*, Leo Cooper, London, 1997

Spiteri, S. *British Military Architecture in Malta*, Valletta, 1996

Tomlinson, R. *Masonry blockhouses of the Anglo-Boer War*, FORT 26, 1998

INDEX

References in italics denote figure numbers

If you are interested in purchasing
other books published by Tempus, or in case you have
difficulty finding any Tempus books in your local bookshop,
you can also place orders directly through our website

www.tempus-publishing.com